Selling your Story to Wall Street

Selling your Story to Wall Street

The Art & Science of Investor Relations

Michael A. Rosenbaum

McGRAW-HILL

New York San Francisco Washington, D.C. Auckland Bogotá
Caracas Lisbon London Madrid Mexico City Milan
Montreal New Delhi San Juan Singapore
Sydney Tokyo Toronto

McGraw-Hill

*A Division of The **McGraw·Hill** Companies*

ISBN 1-55738-507-6

Printed in the United States of America

BB

3 4 5 6 7 8 9 0

To Jill,
my best friend

CONTENTS

15 CHOOSE YOUR WEAPONS: SALES AND DISTRIBUTION   205

16 LISTS, LISTS, LISTS   217

17 FEEDBACK MECHANISMS   229

18 INVESTOR TARGETING   239

EXHIBITS

FOREWORD

This book is meant to be read. It is meant to have penciled notations in the margins and paper clips on key pages. If it is merely an accessory in the well-appointed Investor Relations office, it has not served its purpose.

When I was approached with the prospect of writing a book on investor relations, I recalled all the texts I had read in school and the scholarly tomes I have slogged through since. It was not a happy thought.

Authors, as a rule, seem to believe they must deliver the gospel from a lofty perch. In an effort to present universal truths, personality and opinion are banished. Ultimately, many texts end up unreadable—and far less useful in terms of daily application—simply because the pursuit of Universal Truth leads to overwritten generalities.

I am grateful to my editors for allowing me to depart from this hallowed tradition. *Selling Your Story to Wall Street* is a very personal volume. It focuses on the *how* as much as the *why,* and reflects my specific experiences in representing more than 100 public companies. While the lessons included here are applicable to other people and other companies, they flow from the perspective of my own intimate involvement in day-to-day battles for investor support.

Nothing related to investor relations practice should ever be sanitized or objective. Investor relations is a marketing discipline, and it must be approached with all the passion and personal fervor needed to drive a good marketing program. Research is important. Quality of presentation is important. In fact, all the tools and tactics applied to investor relations are important. But the essence of the practice is passion.

An investor relations executive is the company's ombudsman with sometimes hostile constituent groups. The IR executive is the champion of a cause, and the cause is the company. An effective practitioner falls in love with the company's story, with its opportunities and its potential. That doesn't mean the IR marketer is blind to reality, or that he allows hope to replace judgment. It does mean, however, that the company and its cause will be championed, not merely represented.

A good marketer invests some of her identity in the product being promoted. This personal investment, this commitment and belief, shine through in dealings both inside and outside the company. Passion for the company and its story unleashes enormous persuasive power.

The text that follows represents my attempt to transmit some of that passion and perspective. The recommended approaches aren't the *best* way to pursue the IR discipline. As with any complex assignment, hundreds of possibilities can be equally effective. Within the constraints of ethical conduct and personal integrity, one effective approach is as good as another.

The reader's task, then, is to assimilate those lessons that make the most personal sense, and incorporate other experiences and insights to create an approach that works. Investor relations is results-oriented, so the *best* approach is one that achieves goals consistently or, at least, predictably. Theory gives way to tactics and, in the daily heat of battle, instinct prevails.

I write from the perspective of a soapbox, not a pulpit, and it is my sincere hope that each reader will become a bit more effective as a result of the ideas shared here. Please keep a pencil or highlighter in hand when reading these pages and feel free to drop me a note on any points that spark passionate agreement or disagreement.

I can be reached at:

The Financial Relations Board, Inc.
875 North Michigan Avenue
Chicago, Illinois 60611

ACKNOWLEDGMENTS

As I began writing this dedication, I realized why all those Academy Award acceptance speeches run on as long as they do. It is simply impossible to credit all the people whose efforts and insights contribute to a particular work.

I am certainly indebted to Ted Pincus, chairman of The Financial Relations Board, who had the courage to take a chance on me and who still provides valuable guidance. Likewise, it is difficult to imagine a co-worker, past or present, whose insights aren't reflected somewhere in my own professional mindset.

In drafting this book, I have benefited from the wisdom of my partners, Jack Queeney and Donna Limper; Cindy Knoebel, director of investor relations at VF Corporation; Gerald Murray, editor of the *Investor Relations Newsletter;* William G. Gardner, treasurer and chief financial officer at Apogee Enterprises, Inc.; Robert Kuschke, assistant controller at Apogee; and Jeffrey R. Patt, associate at Katten Muchin & Zavis. These brave souls served as my peer review committee, reading every word and lending valuable commentary. Any deficiencies herein result from my failure to heed their advice.

From a personal perspective, this text would not exist without the contributions my wife, Jill, has made to my career and my life. Finally, I must give thanks to my parents, my lifelong source of guidance. My father sets a daily standard of courage and decency that I will never match, and my mother's insights into the human condition provide continual enlightenment.

Thanks.

1

MARKETING 101

Investor relations (IR) is a marketing discipline. Let's repeat that thought just once. Investor relations is a marketing discipline.

This definition is so obvious it hardly warrants note. But IR practice in the United States reflects a different reality. The great number of approaches taken suggests that many chief executives can't quite figure out what kind of animal this is.

In some ways, the confusion is understandable. IR is a marketing function that employs public relations tools to further the financial goals of the corporation. It is alternately assigned to the public relations department, to the treasurer, to advertising, marketing, corporate communications and, every so often, to the corporate secretary.

In rare instances, usually at the largest companies, investor relations merits its own department. But even then, the reporting line can get fuzzy. Some IR departments report to the vice president of corporate communications or the vice president of administration. The correct line, of course, is directly to the chief executive officer (CEO) and/or chief financial officer (CFO).

Ultimately, the reporting line will migrate more to the CEO and CFO, with increased direct involvement by the CEO. This trend reflects the growing importance of the investor constituency. Just as purchasing and sourcing became more critical during the supply-short/inflationary 1970s, and just as environmental policy continues to demand increasing attention from senior management, the demands of investors and the battle for capital are raising the profile of IR programs.

The sources of this trend are many, but a few major developments deserve mention.

1. Increasing competition from international firms, most notably the Japanese but including all corners of the globe, has led to increased focus on how to raise and apply capital most effectively and competitively. While most popular press articles focus on management and labor practices, these practices always exist within the constraints of existing plant, equipment and technology.

2. In the 1980s, Wall Street awoke to the opportunity to profit more quickly and certainly via the hostile takeover and leveraged buyout than had been possible with the patient holding of shares. Although the buyout frenzy included a relatively small percentage of all public companies, the perception of stability was lost for most firms and their managers.

3. More recently, major institutional investors, the megafunds with so many billions to manage they are as much prisoners to the market as they are investors, are seeking to use their holdings as a lever to change corporate governance practices. Some of these efforts are rather clumsy and self-serving, as reflected in requests for special proxy status and assertions that board seats are appropriate for institutions. Whatever the outcome, it is clear that this 500-pound gorilla is growing restive.

4. Top executive compensation grew unchecked during the 1980s as aggressive compensation consultants and docile boards combined to create a powerful inflationary spiral in at least one area of the economy. Worse, the same top executives pushed through various golden parachute arrange-

ments that guaranteed massive payouts and other benefits in the event of a takeover, but left the average employee unprotected.

5. Finally, in a classic case of bad timing, bonuses paid to chief executive officers and the exercise of generous stock options collided with a steady stream of headlines about corporate downsizing programs. In the minds of many, including Congress, it appeared that the best way for a CEO to make an extra million was by cutting $2 million in payroll costs. (This is the same Congress that exempts itself from most laws and protects its pensions and benefits with unchecked passion, but that's another book.)

In many ways, nothing is the same. A few highly publicized cases of board revolt—IBM and General Motors being two of the largest—sound a warning to complacent boards and chief executives that the old days are gone. The Securities and Exchange Commission (SEC) has required greater and more comparative disclosure of executive compensation practices in the proxy statement. Major institutional activists, lauded by business publications as if they were unbiased white knights rather than self-interested investors, have gained added clout with boards and officers. Compensation experts are promoting more performance-oriented plans for rewarding executives.

At the same time, nothing has changed, at least for most companies. Directors still serve at the pleasure of the chief executive, major shareholders continue to receive the same attention they did or didn't in the past, and compensation is linked only marginally to performance. (In fairness, performance is a much tougher issue to measure than most people assume, and the cause/effect component of the equation is the toughest of all.)

Oddly enough, these raging debates on corporate governance and institutional activism are matters of nuance for the investor relations practitioner. Each is one megatrend among many, one issue of hundreds to be addressed, and significant only as it applies to the practitioner's own organization. (See 1-1, *Spheres of Influence.*)

1-1   Spheres of Influence

While everything from the phase of the moon to the typeface on product packaging can affect the price of stock, the IR executive directs most effort in those arenas that can be controlled, or at least explained most directly, through the investor relations program.

Listed below are spheres of influence that surround any company, ranging from macroeconomic issues to local matters. Although the IR executive will track the larger issues, company-specific factors present the greatest opportunity for successful marketing.

Megaspheres

- Global economy
- National economy
- Government regulation
- Corporate governance trends
- Management fads
- Institutional activism
- Brokerage-firm research spending
- New types of investment products

In the Neighborhood

- Industry trends
- Investor sentiment toward industry
- Investor sentiment toward company's investment parameters
- Changing technologies
- Customer/vendor industry trends
- Events influencing direct competitors

Right at Home

- Sales and earnings trends
- Corporate structure and governance
- Selection of marketing tools and targets
- Effective implementation of strategies
- Competitive positioning

For a firm with relatively little institutional ownership, for example, the growing level of activism among major institutions might influence a decision to continue focusing on individual shareholders. But that decision might be influenced equally by the cost of servicing small accounts and the number of shares available for trading (float).

The megatrends issues engulf the country's largest corporations more than they do the smaller public companies. The Fortune 500 and other large firms have the highest profiles among investors, regulators, and the public at large. As a rule, they also have the highest compensation levels for top executives and tend to have the highest concentration of institutional ownership. Needless to say, they get the most press attention, too.

But the formidable size that makes them easy targets also makes them defensible fortresses. These companies have household names that make their shares salable to individuals and smaller funds with minimal backgrounding. Their larger float makes them attractive to institutions that trade in large blocks, and that transaction efficiency can more than compensate for other perceived weaknesses.

Just as each strength has its limits, each weakness represents opportunity. It is in this tug-of-war that markets are made and in this maelstrom that the IR professional pursues the marketing discipline.

In the best of cases, it's a complex challenge. While most marketers build a case for a package of corn flakes or a car or some other easily definable product, the IR practitioner has an intangible product: confidence in the corporation's potential to provide a profit to investors.

Clearly, the product is not the corporation itself. Although shares of stock represent ownership, the investor doesn't perceive his or her purchase as the equivalent of buying a second home. Unlike jewelry or paintings or other property that offers personal satisfaction even if values don't rise, the ownership of shares has practically no utility other than wealth creation.

Shares of the corporation are not the product either, although purchase of shares is the intended transaction. Except for the rare public offering, the corporation itself isn't involved directly in the sale of stock and gains no immediate benefit. In fact, each transaction adds to corporation costs through transfer fees.

Ultimately, the product is confidence, a belief in the investment potential of the corporation. This is another factor differentiating the IR role from more traditional marketing assignments. Rather than seeking to build support for a product or service, the IR professional seeks to build support for a concept.

As in all marketing, the first step is to define the product and its features. If the product is confidence, what features support confidence and thereby build demand for the stock? As we'll see later, these features can include both strengths and weaknesses. Marketing theses can range from "This company has built margins for five straight years, so six will be easy" to "This company has been beaten down so badly, it can't go anywhere but up from here."

Weaknesses are especially important because public companies must meet very specific disclosure requirements. In the investment community, it is just as likely that the dominant focus will be on the product's weaknesses (declining margins, environmental problems) as on its strengths (technology, management track record).

For each strength and weakness, relative valuations are required. Because hundreds of factors combine to create an investment story, it is essential to focus on those that are most responsible for the resulting valuation. Our firm refers to these critical factors as the "investment appeals," while others describe them as the "core message" or in similar terms.

Regardless, the IR professional will identify the factors with the highest leverage and emphasize them repeatedly. This culling process is especially critical because of two major limitations.

1. *The budget is limited.* Whether the budget is defined in dollars, staff or management time, each IR program is limited by available resources. No good IR person runs out of ideas to help market the company as an investment. Every good IR professional reaches the limits of budget.

2. *The audience is busy.* Except for a handful of analysts or other professionals who will get to know the company in detail, most people likely to invest will do so on the basis of

a few core ideas. Just as it's important to select the right core ideas, it's also critical that the savvy investor relations executive not overwhelm the more casual investor with a confusing array of detail and nuance.

Thus, the IR professional selects the right set of investment appeals for the majority of the firm's investors, bolstering that presentation with supporting data for the most intimately involved analysts and fund managers. Once those key messages have been selected and priorities assigned, the IR professional creates the proper mix of tools and techniques for implementing the program.

In most programs, the tools utilized are more heavily oriented toward public relations, which sometimes leads to the false conclusion that IR is a public relations discipline. Less common in IR programs are such marketing mainstays as advertising. But the mix varies from company to company and an active IR program will include some combination of all marketing tools: audience and competitive research, media relations, collateral materials, advertising, corporate events, and so on.

Thus, investor relations becomes a series of analyses and programming efforts that combine to build investor confidence in the public corporation. Because each company is unique, there are no step-by-step instructions for effective implementation. However, enough common themes repeat from company to company that consistent rules and practices will apply.

2

THE TRUTH,
THE WHOLE TRUTH . . .

Before delving into the hows and whys of investor relations strategies, let's devote some thought to a philosophy—mine, specifically—that I hope will be adopted by readers of this book.

Simple in concept and difficult in practice, the proper goal of investor relations professionals is credibility. Credibility is the single best way to enhance confidence in the company and the most important builder of the trust that leads to long-term support.

Yet credibility is honored as much in the breach as in practice among public companies. It's not so much that executives intend to mislead at any given time, as that sometimes these flesh-and-blood leaders are embarrassed by the results of their initiatives or the glow from good results tempers the desire to explain how transitory the numbers really are.

A LONELY CRUSADE

It's up to the investor relations executive to take the longer view, to fight for disclosures or details that protect credibility even when they cause some personal embarrassment to the CEO. And in many cases, the IR exec will be alone on the battlefield.

It has been my frequent and disappointing experience in representing hundreds of companies to see corporate counsel or SEC counsel come down on the side of nondisclosure when the question is in a nominally gray area. More often than not, asking the CEO to check with counsel will blow up the IR case.

While I don't have empirical evidence, I suspect that the reasons for nondisclosure relate to the learned tendency of attorneys to consider information to be dangerous. The more a company discloses, the more likely someone is to sue. The more the company sticks to the minimum requirements, the less likely that the CEO will be hanged later.

The defensive posture can be pursued to silly extremes. *One example: Annual report text on industry trends was slashed by counsel because discussion of industry growth could be interpreted as a promise that the company would attain the same growth rates.*

Another example: The controversial CEO of a public company also served on the board of a second firm. At the second firm's annual meeting, he mentioned to the audience a previously undisclosed intention to resign as CEO of the first company within a year. No amount of cajoling could convince in-house counsel or SEC attorneys that a disclosure event had occurred.

In the interest of equal time: Two SEC practitioners who reviewed this text argue that they are far more expansive on disclosure than these examples suggest. The issue that divides attorneys from IR practitioners is one of degree and timing, not intent, they argued. From a legal perspective, they are probably correct in this assertion, especially as it relates to "structured disclosure." Attorneys tend to define the issue differently, based on law rather than marketing. Still, this author has never encountered a situation in which SEC counsel was more aggressive than IR counsel regarding the need and level of detail required in disclosure. However, the author and colleagues have been more aggressive on this subject many times.

Investment bankers, likewise, tend to come down on the side of limited disclosure. Here, the limitation is to everyone but the investment banker. Depending on the length of time since the last public offering, the investment banker might believe that he or she can control market perceptions by controlling the flow of information into the network of investors that the investment banker placed in the stock.

A third extreme example: An investment banker demanded and received a change in the numbers a client company was preparing because investors in the initial public offering (IPO) had been told to expect a given level of earnings. The conservative assumptions originally made regarding accruals were scaled back and a more positive, aggressive earnings number resulted. It's legal, but bad practice.

Whatever the case, the IR executive must assume she is alone in pursuing the long-term credibility of the company. The chief executive will support the idea, in almost every case, and the counsel and investment banker will also think credibility is good overall. But the IR exec must be the one who can be counted on to turn this belief into consistent practice. (See 2-1, *Establishing Your Role as Chief Credibility Officer.*)

INFORMATION REDUCES RISK

For the IR practitioner, credibility must become a mantra. It directs a program toward full and forthright disclosure, to frequent and open communications with investors. It directs the company to be just as open when the numbers are poor as when they are strong. And it directs the company to present core messages consistently over an extended period of time.

Fortunately, this single-minded pursuit of credibility is good business. It is the essence of successful, long-term investor relations. And it is worth millions or billions of dollars in market capitalization on any given day.

An example: An analyst visited a client company and, in my debriefing session with him, expressed his primary concern. Once a high-growth company, the firm was involved in two cyclical industries that were in a long-term slump. The company was still profitable, but earnings weren't likely to recover for quite some time. Still, the analyst complained, the price never seemed to go

11

2-1   Establishing Your Role as Chief Credibility Officer

The credibility battle often puts the IR executive, the company's chief credibility officer (CCO), in seeming conflict with the chief executive, corporate counsel, investment banker and others. How do you tell the CEO he's walking on quicksand? Here are some ideas.

1. **Establish Your Role Early and Often.** Let the CEO and CFO know that you perceive your job as chief internal critic and that your value lies partly in serving as a surrogate investor, letting them know whether something will fly with the Street.

2. **Become the Corporate Historian.** When a new development is to be announced, remind the CEO and CFO of how it was handled before and how the investment community responded. Propose a plan of action that anticipates and compensates for that response.

3. **Remind the CEO of His Vulnerability.** Note the likelihood of embarrassment or heavy heat for presenting a development in an inconsistent manner. Make the point that an effort to avoid embarrassment near-term could explode immediately and most certainly will backfire later.

4. **Turn Lemons into Lemonade.** Give the CEO the ammunition to change near-term problems into long-term opportunities. Here, for example, is how one company reported its near-break-even results: *"A few years ago, before instituting aggressive cost controls, we would have posted a loss at this level of revenues."* This kind of perspective is important to the Street and important to the CEO in a potentially difficult situation.

5. **This, Too, Shall Pass.** Don't fall into the trap of overstating the good news, any more than you would understate the negatives. Remind the CEO that even in hindsight, you don't want to seem to overstate an opportunity or understate a lead time.

Each CEO is different and your approach must be customized. Some executives respond best to memos and others to phone calls. Some need to be approached well in advance so the idea can become familiar, while others should be prompted at the last minute.

Whatever the case, credibility can be built with consistent effort and protected easily, whereas rebuilding it is difficult to impossible.

down to a level where the relative valuation made sense. Why was the stock price still holding up? Needless to say, this is one of the better questions an IR executive can get. And the answer was very simple: People don't sell the stock because they believe in the company. The client's management is as expansive in explaining its problems as in talking about growth. Management is accessible and unafraid to say a mistake was made. This kind of credibility translates directly into a reduced investor perception of risk and a higher relative stock price.

The IR executive must apply special discipline in characterizing results, anticipating possible traps that could ensnare the company later. Similarly, the IR executive must keep track of all prior claims, so new situations aren't presented in ways that conflict with earlier statements.

The biggest trap arising from these conflicts becomes apparent at the time of greatest opportunity. When an analyst or financial reporter is ready to undertake substantial research, with a potentially favorable recommendation or profile article to result, the company's background kit will include annual reports, news releases, and other documents spanning a period of years. The person doing the research won't need a long memory to spot any inconsistencies. In fact, during the interview arranged with the CEO or CFO, these inconsistencies serve as a source of questions and possible embarrassment.

It should be clear at this point that information management is one of the most critical IR assignments. From required disclosure to aggressive marketing, a solid plan for information flow leads to stronger credibility and market support. In short, information reduces risk.

START WITH STRUCTURED DISCLOSURE

Although information management starts with a world view and works down into details, most firms find it easier to focus first on required disclosure when creating their information plan. In fact, IR executives will often label the information management plan a "disclosure policy."

Required disclosure, often referred to as "structured disclosure," is implemented through a variety of reports all public companies must file with the SEC. Events requiring disclosure include financial results—both quarterly and annual—as well as extraordinary events such as changes in management or share ownership. (See 2-2, *Required Disclosure.*)

While most disclosure events are clear, some are fuzzy. Words like *substantive, significant* and *prompt* invite internal debate among IR executives, attorneys, chief executives and others. When quarterly results are reported, there is no question about which core numbers *must* be included. There is, however, substantial room for discussion about added data and any comments to be made about the numbers.

The results of these discussions are reflected in *Management's Discussion and Analysis of Financial Condition and Results of Operations (MD&A).* The MD&A is required text in each annual report (Form 10-K) and interim report (Form 10-Q) filed with the SEC. In this section, management is expected to explain changes in financial condition and operating results and to comment on known trends likely to influence future finances.

Until quite recently, MD&A sections tended to follow the strictest letter of the law, but not its spirit. Compelled to describe three years of sales and earnings, many corporations would state, *"Sales rose 9 percent in 1993 versus 1992 and increased 8 percent in 1992 over 1991. Net income increased 12 percent in 1993 and 14 percent in 1992."* The text parroted the financial tables and insights were rare.

Increasingly, the SEC has pushed for more expansive discussion of results, trends and outlook. Simultaneously, the rise of investor activism and other trends have encouraged companies to explain more in these "required" discussions. In response, MD&A sections are being upgraded on a fairly widespread scale.

2-2   Required Disclosure

Forms filed with the Securities and Exchange Commission range from Form 1, Application for registration or exemption from registration as a national securities exchange, to Form X-17F-1A, Missing/lost/stolen/counterfeit securities report. Fortunately, most companies need only focus on a relative handful. Among the most important are:

S-1   General form for registration of securities prior to sale. (Actually, there are several S forms, each related to different types of securities or circumstances.)

S-4   Report on sale of securities by issuing company and use of proceeds.

3   Initial report on beneficial holdings of officers, directors and any holders of more than 10 percent of a company's shares filed within 10 days of obtaining that ownership level. (Updated through filing of Form 4 by the 10th day of the month following any changes and Form 5, an annual update due 45 days after the end of the fiscal year.)

8-K   Report on major developments between reporting periods. Such events might include acquisitions, changes in control of the company, changes in auditing firms and director resignations. Form 8-K must be filed within five or 15 days, with the time lag determined by the specific type of reportable event.

10-K   Annual report filed within 90 days after the end of the company's fiscal year.

10-Q   Quarterly report of financial results, due within 45 days after the close of each of the first three quarters of the fiscal year.

144   Notice of sale of certain restricted securities. (Stock held by certain insiders might be restricted in terms of the timing and amounts of any sales. Such shares are known as "144 Stock.")

14A   Proxy statement information requirements are covered in Form 14A. Preliminary proxies must be submitted to the SEC for review at least 10 days prior to distribution to shareholders, in many cases, and the final proxy must be filed with the SEC before being sent to shareholders.

The focus on MD&A reporting brings to light just one gray area in structured disclosure. Statements about outlook, for example, offer substantial debate potential. While it is clear companies must comment on known trends likely to influence future results, it is tough to determine exactly when a trend is known or its influence clear.

Consider a company whose largest customer might be affected by the bankruptcy of the customer's largest customer. Orders have not yet been reduced and it is not certain that they will be, but the likelihood is growing. Should the IR executive argue for full disclosure, including a worst-case example, knowing that the worst case is highly unlikely? Should the company wait until the true impact is clear, even though many months may pass before any announcement is made?

An example: A client in the middle of a stock offering road show learned that a significant customer might be lost. The customer's loss was not expected to influence annual earnings much, but the Street might wonder whether this well-known customer would be the first of many to jump ship. The investment bankers opted to change prospectus text to note the volatility of customer relationships, without specifying any customers. From a legal perspective, naming a customer could be more dangerous than being general. If one customer was named, but a different customer was subsequently lost, the company could have been accused of inadequate disclosure for failing to mention both firms.

A BUSINESS DECISION

Without question, the IR executive's role as chief credibility officer begins with required disclosure. Recently, added influence has been coming from an unwanted corner—shareholder derivative suits. These legal actions are filed on behalf of shareholders, claiming damages (lost stock value/missed profit opportunity) due to statements made, or not made, by management.

While shareholder derivative suits can be abusive—a 1990s form of ambulance-chasing—the fact remains that fuller disclosure is a strong defense against such actions. Recent studies by our firm and others support the conclusion that disclosure is a management issue—not strictly a legal matter. As with other business judgments, the risk/reward ratio must be considered, and recent research indicates that the risk/reward equation favors companies that disclose aggressively.

In the business-judgment model, the likelihood of a suit and the likely outcome of legal action are weighed against the improved market support that results from a more proactive disclosure policy. It now appears that additional market value achieved by proactive firms is much greater on average than legal judgments absorbed by firms that failed to disclose aggressively.

This new viewpoint finally brings disclosure theory in line with common sense. However, it is notable that in this specific case the company view can differ from that of its shareholders. A relatively stronger stock price may not provide immediate tangible benefits to the company, as it does for shareholders, but a legal judgment represents cash out the door. To the extent that the stock is being used for acquisition or other currency-equivalent purposes, the higher share valuation is of more immediate benefit to the company itself. Aggressive disclosure is the investment world's parallel to informed consent. The more information provided to the potential investor, the less likely a claim of misdirection will stand.

MOST DISCLOSURE IS UNSTRUCTURED

Although required disclosure focuses primarily on filed documents, most disclosure is unstructured. News releases, media interviews, meetings with analysts, and most shareholder communications fall into this category.

This disclosure, significantly, is also "required," although the burden is levied by the marketplace rather than the SEC. Prompt and broad dissemination of quarterly earnings, for example, can be achieved by simply delivering the latest 10-Q report to the

---

2-3   Minimum Standards for Non-Structured Disclosure

Non-structured or informal disclosure is the mechanism for selling the investment story. Carrying the message beyond the legalistic and heavily formatted SEC documents, such disclosure should include, at the minimum:

- News releases on financial results, dividend declarations and other developments that would be included in required SEC filings.
- Fact sheets and/or books explaining the company's investment message in language and form familiar to the investor audience.
- Quarterly conference calls with key followers to review results and answer questions arising from reported performance as well as conference calls following other major announcements.
- "Glossy" annual report and quarterly reports covering both the disclosure topics required in the 10-K and 10-Q reports *and* insights and highlights that add to investor understanding of the corporate investment appeals and opportunities/risks.
- Regular update interviews with financial newswire reporters assigned to follow the company, to help ensure both ample and accurate coverage of the company.

These are minimum standards for disclosure and don't begin to cover all of the steps needed for effective marketing of the company story.

SEC, applicable exchange, Associated Press, Dow Jones, Reuters, Bloomberg, Standard & Poors and a handful of other "disclosure points."

No law says a news release must be sent to the media, or that management must answer questions posed by analysts. No law requires a response to reporters' questions. Required disclosure, in fact, is a very limited arena.

If marketing consisted solely of *letting customers find you,* required disclosure would suffice. But selling the company's story requires more. The IR executive must meet the information expectations of the marketplace, and these expectations are set through competition. (See 2-3, *Minimum Standards for Non-Structured Disclosure.*)

If, for example, a company's competitors disclose business segments in detail, the company's IR effort will suffer for failure to do the same. If competitors issue regular news releases on significant contracts, pressure is created to follow suit. A company can decide to differ, of course, but that decision must be made with the risk/reward concept in mind. Failure to meet the disclosure standards of competitors, or the minimum disclosure standards of the marketplace, will almost certainly cost something in terms of market capitalization.

In fact, aggressive disclosure should be the preferred choice of IR marketers. Without question, information reduces risk by building comfort levels. Given two firms with identical earnings potential, the one that is more accessible to investors is likely to gain the stronger following—and value. The perception of reduced risk can lead to lower volatility in share price and, in turn, to lower bid-ask spreads, resulting in reduced transaction costs for investors.

WALKING THROUGH THE MINEFIELD

Disclosure policy focuses not only on the content of documents, but also on the ways in which information is communicated. Disclosure, by law, must be conducted on a level playing field. Quarterly financial performance and other news must be disseminated promptly and thoroughly to the investment community. For most companies, this is accomplished by issuing a news release (unstructured) to the three financial news wires (Bloomberg, Dow Jones and Reuters) and other disclosure points, as well as distribution of the release via fax, mail or messenger to local news outlets, key investment professionals who follow the company and other top targets.

Because companies must seek to be fair to all investors, it is illegal to provide an unfair advantage to one group by selective disclosure of material inside information that could affect the market for the company's stock. Included in this concept are several words—*unfair, advantage, group, selective, material, inside, affect*—that can be interpreted several ways.

Selective disclosure is suicidal, both legally and from a marketing perspective. Although each investor wants special access to management and special insights into operating trends, each investor also will resent the granting of such advantage to others. Keeping the field as level as possible is the best defense.

But that defense is more easily described than achieved. The company's closest followers may simply call more often and be willing to invest more time in getting to know the company, giving them greater insights that have nothing to do with selective disclosure. Likewise, a question asked at a meeting with brokers might elicit details not previously disclosed. And an analyst or broker might be a close friend and confidant of the CEO as well.

Fortunately, common sense can prevail. In regular reporting periods, such as quarterly earnings cycles, the company should take pains to cover all significant trends in its filed documents and news releases. Details can be given later to those who follow up, if such responses are given to all who ask, with minimal concern for liability, provided that the general situation has been disclosed clearly.

A company might, for example, announce in its news release a 50-percent increase in backlog. An analyst who calls might obtain some added detail on the kind of orders involved without creating a disclosure problem. *However,* if the margins anticipated from this backlog differ significantly from prior levels, management might be asking for trouble by enlightening only those who call and excluding the fact from the release. (See 2-4, *IR Quiz.*)

Without any further explanation, the investor would be expected to assume that margins in the backlog approximate historic margin levels. If this isn't the case, failure to disclose can lead to disappointment—and potential liability—later.

An example: One CEO tended to provide comments to callers based on whatever had just crossed his desk. On a good sales day,

2-4   IR Quiz

There are more right answers than wrong ones to the questions below. Here is some food for thought on information management.

1. In its second-quarter earnings release, Widgets of America indicated backlogs were up 20 percent. Since then, several orders were canceled and new ones added, so the backlog increase is closer to 18 percent. Should management disclose the shift in orders and the likely impact on backlog levels?

2. Jack in marketing tells his best friend and golfing buddy, Bill the broker, that he just made the biggest sale of his life, a five-year exclusive contract that will add 15 percent to his company's sales base. Ted, the IR executive, gets a call on Monday from Bill, asking for more details. What does Ted say?

3. In the case above, Ted knows the contracts aren't final and, in fact, could fall apart based on a critical issue. Ted wasn't planning to make any announcements until the ink was dry. Now what?

4. Management tells analysts its costs are controlled through hedging programs. Then a raw material, the cost of which hasn't changed in five years—and therefore isn't hedged—quadruples in price. The ultimate impact on next quarter's numbers is uncertain, but will be negative, and analysts are unconcerned about the run-up because they assume pricing was locked in under the hedging program. When does this become a disclosure event and how does management handle the assignment?

During the Senate's Watergate hearings, the crucial question repeatedly asked was: *"What did he know, and when did he know it?"* Disclosure policy and shareholder derivative suits rest on the same questions of management.

he talked about new orders. On a bad day, he complained about quality at the plant. We attempted to compensate for this free-wheeling approach by adding much more detail to releases and supplying the CEO with a single sheet covering the major facts and trends we had disclosed.

21

MANAGING EXPECTATIONS

The information management challenge is easiest when it involves facts, especially historical information. Disclosure gets substantially more difficult when it concerns the future impact of current or past developments. Here, the challenge is one of managing expectations.

Expectations arise with each statement made by a company. Silence itself can create expectations as well. A company that posts 40-percent sales increases in the first and second quarters will generate expectations that third-quarter gains will be similar, unless otherwise indicated. A company that announces a record backlog level creates the assumption that those backlogs remain firm, unless management declares otherwise later.

In the absence of developments, it would be ridiculous to provide daily updates to the investment community *("No orders canceled," American Widgets declares!!)*. Even if minor developments occur, management should avoid excessive announcements. Too many updates can create a forest-and-trees phenomenon, with analysts unable to discern significant developments among the details.

More sensible is the use of three primary tools to manage expectations: *perspective, earnings models* and *forecasts.*

Perspective entails detailed discussion of the company's operating environment or basis for decisions. Management decisions should be described in context, giving the investor a more informed view. For example, management can report that the coming year should be better than the year just ended and leave it at that. But the company protects itself and informs investors better by adding perspective to the statement: *"If the rebound in housing starts continues at approximately the same pace as in the past three months, management expects 1995 results to exceed those of 1994."*

Perspective also includes consideration of relative importance. A company's best known subsidiary might receive a disproportionate share of media attention, but add relatively little to earnings. That perspective is important, lest the market overreact to changes at the well-known subsidiary.

Finally, perspective can be provided through written policy. Firms that pay a dividend, for example, might publish a policy explaining the basis for payments (X percent of prior year earnings, Y percent yield on share price, etc.), giving investors a reasonable measure on which to base expectation of future dividends. Policies on forecasting, financial reporting and other matters can also lend valuable perspective.

The *earnings model* is a financial format that can be used to explain the impact of different inputs. (If interest rates go up a point, the cost to the company is $X. If sales rise 10 percent, and no other changes occur, earnings per share rise 15 percent.) Analysts armed with the earnings model can input their own assumptions as to direction of interest rates, sales, earnings and other factors.

An example: For one client company in an agricultural commodity business, we added to the annual report a grid showing the earnings impact of various changes in commodity prices, based on historic cost structures. The large number of variables kept it from serving as a forecast while at the same time providing substantial value in showing profit sensitivities.

Forecasts are the most direct vehicles for managing expectations. In forecasts, the company reveals its own estimates of future sales, costs, margins, product mix and other variables. Forecasts can include projections of financial results or major operating developments. In the early 1980s, software and personal computer companies would often announce major new products as soon as possible as a means of getting customers to hold off on making other purchases until the products were available. Because so many of these "major new products" never reached market, the industry soon dubbed them "vaporware." This problem is particularly acute for small or development-stage firms, including many high-tech and biotech companies, whose shares trade primarily on the potential of new or future products. Delays or cancellations

23

2-5 How to Forecast

Forecasting is very difficult, as one wag stated, especially when it involves the future. Companies that opt to provide thorough insight to investors through forecasts can increase investor support if the forecasts prove accurate—and raise the risk of legal action if the predictions fail to materialize. Effective forecasting is an art and its foundation includes these elements:

1. **Background.** Woe to the company that simply projects its numbers. No forecast should be made without a detailed explanation of the assumptions and earnings model used to generate the outlook. The amount of detail can vary, based on the type and specificity of forecast. This perspective is critical both for the investor who wants to check for reasonable foundation and for defending potential suits. Background information creates informed consent.

2. **Ranges.** Pinpoint numbers assert a certainty that no company can claim. A firm that projects on January 1 that its yearly earnings will be 19 cents per share is kidding itself. Forecasts should be delivered in ranges, with broader ranges for numbers further out on the time line. If the range becomes so wide it's meaningless, skip the forecast.

3. **Updates.** Forecasts should be updated regularly, either at the end of a quarter or along with reported results. A company with a consistent forecasting schedule might announce its estimate for the period just ended, and adjust its full-year forecast when a quarter ends. A forecast that hasn't been updated is presumed to be current.

4. **Predictability.** Predictions are based on predictability and the company that has none should avoid forecasts. This applies especially to firms with complex revenue recognition, such as construction companies, or those whose results are heavily skewed toward one quarter.

5. **Publicity.** The company's decision to forecast and the policy for updating the forecast should be stated clearly.

Forecasting is an effective way to manage expectations and is relatively low in risk, if handled in a common-sense manner. Forecasts should be based on conservative estimates, with reasonable focus on things that can go wrong as well as right.

change the income stream outlook dramatically, so any forecasts or other guidance provided entails substantial risk. (See 2-5, *How to Forecast.*)

Many companies already provide forecasts on a selective basis to analysts and major holders of stock. Terming it "guidance," these firms might review the analyst's research report prior to publication, for example. In addition to checking the factual presentation, the company is asked to pass on the analyst's estimates of future earnings.

CFOs often will give the numbers a nod, acknowledge that the analyst is at the high or low end of the possibility range, or provide some other guidance regarding the estimate. While the analyst is free to reject a CFO's pressure to tone down or bump up a number, management's guidance is usually accepted.

This steering process serves a useful purpose in that it avoids substantial discrepancies among analyst forecasts. But it also can put the company in a selective disclosure situation. There is, in fact, no legal basis for sharing insights with analysts and not others. Guiding the analysts, then, is a delicate exercise and should only be undertaken by companies that set clear standards, with advice of counsel, regarding the level of additional insight to be provided.

This, of course, is contrary to the view held by many chief executives who will express one of the following sentiments:

1. The analyst controls our stock price and we have an obligation to make sure he is well informed.
2. The analyst is the only one interested enough in our company to call us regularly, so why shouldn't she get more information?
3. This is how the game is played.

All three statements are correct and perfectly logical. In fact, the analyst is an influential and important conduit to investors. The analyst will be more likely to call with insightful questions. And, absolutely, guiding analysts is the norm, not the exception, in the investment world.

On the other hand, rules are rules, and the logic of helping friends does not pass muster in the securities environment. Here, information is power and unequal empowerment is simply prohibited.

No CEO/CFO should enter into discussions with analysts, shareholders or in-laws without a clear knowledge of prior disclosures and the limits of information that can be passed on even in social situations. *(Note: If a "social" conversation leads a listener to make a quick financial decision, then the discussion wasn't really "social" in the first place.)*

The reality is not likely to change. Insiders will continue to discuss significant issues with outsiders—including analysts, major shareholders, barbers, caddies and brokers. No set of internal rules can prevent leaks.

In this environment, full and proactive discussion of developments, trends and potentials is the greatest possible shield. If the corporation discusses substantive issues promptly and disseminates the information fully, the risk of subsequent damage from loose lips is reduced dramatically.

UNDERSTANDING THE AGENDAS

Effective information management would seem, on its face, to be a positive without detractors. Who, after all, could argue with a policy that reduces risk and adds to market capitalization?

The answer, of course, is lots of people. While the IR executive approaches disclosure policy with an eye toward long-term credibility and market capitalization, many other players have different agendas. For example:

Attorneys, as described earlier, tend to be very risk-averse, and often adopt the most conservative approach to issues. Business decisions are not their focus; legal decisions are.

Investment bankers, as also noted, tend to focus on their relationships with their largest customers, the institutional investors, and will attempt to direct corporate policy in ways that support this priority. While their guidance can be crucial, the basis of their viewpoint must always be considered.

Analysts want special insights and access to management, which can give them an edge in marketing their research to institutional clients and others. Often, analysts will decline invitations to full-scale presentations, partially because everyone receives the same information at such events.

Auditors/Accountants tend to focus on risk-avoidance, much the same as attorneys. Their belief system revolves more around the historical numbers, which they consider real, than the future-oriented trends that guide investment.

Reporters, like analysts, seek special insights and relationships. They tend to view the company's reports as the "official line" and therefore suspect, while granting greater credibility to outsiders whose views are considered more *objective.*

Corporate executives, no matter what department they're in, tend to focus on the needs of their departments first. They often are especially sensitive to the ways customers might react to various announcements—and to insights competitors might gain from disclosure.

Regulators look for portrayals that differ from the presentations being made to them. A regulated utility, for example, must continually cite need to regulators and prosperity to investors—a veritable tightrope dance.

Families of employees, especially top executives, want their friends to say nice things to them based on what appears in the local press. They can be a major source of complaint when news coverage is unfavorable.

Each approaches the information stream from a different perspective. For the IR executive, however, effective management of information depends not only on artful implementation, but just as certainly on how well the constituent groups can be coordinated.

3

FINANCIAL ANALYSIS:
THE INCOME STATEMENT

One of the great myths in the investment world is that *the numbers speak for themselves*. Chief executives often suggest that, if they can generate consistently stronger earnings, this feat alone will propel improvement in the stock price. It's a seductive line of reasoning, based on an assumption of rational and efficient markets.

But the stock market is neither rational nor efficient in the short term and, in the case of individual stocks, might not be so over the long term, either. In some ways, the takeovers of the 1980s were made possible by long-term discounts assigned to stocks that became targets of leverage-minded buyers. Very few targets had a history of selling at or above their peer group valuations.

Equally important, the *numbers-as-spokesmen* concept assumes people will actually be paying attention when these numbers are announced. Likewise, it assumes that investors will be compelled by the simple announcement of numbers to take action on the stock.

In fact, inertia is the norm in the investment market. Worse, the idea that strong earnings will propel investment assumes management can consistently deliver such results. The likelihood of consistently higher, quarter-by-quarter numbers is, in fact, relatively slight. Even the best managed companies encounter snags when their performance is measured in 90-day increments.

Truly effective investment strategies that rely solely on reported results also must depend on the still-uncertain practice of time travel. Financial results are historical, not prospective, and only cogent analysis and interpretation can give them any voice at all. By themselves, "the numbers" are no more chatty than the Sphinx.

Finally, it is worth noting that *the numbers are merely a proxy for what happens on the plant floor, in the customer's purchasing department or in the supplier's warehouse.* While dollars are a common denominator for all financial statements—making it easier to compare apples and oranges—something is *always* lost in translation. This is an important point because the investor relations executive will sometimes need to explain why the figures on the income statement fail to tell the real investment story.

Fortunately, financial analysis for investor relations purposes is a discipline that can be learned, at least on a basic level, by most IR practitioners. While no one will become a Chartered Financial Analyst by reading this book, the careful reader will identify new opportunities to present the corporation's story in a more compelling manner.

THE INCOME STATEMENT

The income statement is organized in a logical manner, moving downward from the plant floor to the corporate office, the bank, the tax collector and, eventually, the shareholder. The first items on most income statements are revenues, direct costs of goods sold, selling and administrative costs and so on. Approaching the bottom of the list, categories focus on the corporate side, including interest paid to finance debt, taxes recognized, etc.

Let's move through a typical income statement to look for sources of investment appeal.

SALES/REVENUES

The word *sales* typically refers to products or services sold, although some firms use *revenues* to include both products and services and such other inflows as royalties. No matter. The first item on the income statement represents the flow of funds the company will have available to pay bills, return a profit to shareholders and so on.

Sales can be accounted for in several different ways, including the intuitively obvious moment when cash is actually received. Many firms recognize a sale when a product is shipped to the customer, but a firm involved in a long-term project, such as building construction, might recognize sales on a percentage-of-completion basis. The company registers revenues, whether received or not, as the costs of the project are incurred. Some firms recognize sales upon receipt of a firm order, a practice that is considered somewhat aggressive in most circles. Clearly, sales recognition isn't necessarily the same as cash coming in the door.

In addition, the sales/revenue figure is usually a net number, reflecting both the gross level of sales and some minor deductions for freight and certain discounts.

Sales also are net of intracompany transactions. If Division A buys raw materials from Division B, that transaction will be canceled out in the consolidated results.

A relatively small number of companies break out sales by division or market on the income statement, although segment reporting usually appears in the annual report footnotes and financial review. Especially among smaller firms, management tends to resist extensive segment reporting because of concerns that competitors will learn too much. In fact, competitors usually learn much more of a sensitive nature by talking to customers than they glean from the company's financial statements. However, the sensitivity often has a strong basis in fact and should be considered seriously by any IR professional. A product line or segment with strong margins, for example, might be a strong point with shareholders but a disaster for the saleswoman whose

31

customer wants a lower price. A balance must be struck between the potential to add value for the company and its shareholders and the risk of lost sales or other negative impacts.

In the sales category, the biggest issue is trends, and not all trends are strictly financial in nature. Because the sales number represents thousands of visits by sales staff or manufacturers' reps to customer offices, all sorts of qualitative issues can be reflected in sales.

For some companies, the trends are clear and long term in nature. For others, the sales figure changes from year to year with few, if any, underlying patterns. While the latter presents a challenge from a story-creation standpoint, it is also relatively rare. Few companies truly bump along with no patterns, buffeted by daily changes in markets and customer preferences. Usually, the patternless sales issue is greatest when a company is operating near or below its breakeven point, especially during periods of recession. In most instances, some case can be made that sales trends offer insight into the future. Here are a handful of investment messages that can be generated from the sales category:

1. **The Pipeline Effect.** The *pipeline* represents all the middleman stations between the manufacturer and the final consumer. Often viewed from a retailing perspective, the pattern is no less real for companies selling product to original-equipment-manufacturer (OEM) customers. In times of economic growth, the pipeline expands to ensure that end-user demand is met. When a market is weak, inventories in the pipeline are reduced to conserve cash. When a new product is introduced, initial sales will reflect pipeline fill, which can be positive or negative. An aggressive IR executive might note, "Initial orders were for 300,000 units, and that's simply to stock the store shelves," while a more conservative spokesman might say, "Our first 300,000 units represent shipments to customer inventories, rather than sellthrough, so we don't expect this sales surge to continue."

   On the other hand, a company experiencing lower sales can often point to pipeline shrinkage as a cause. This indi-

3-1   Income Statement

	1993	1992	1991
			Year ended June 30,
Net Sales	$ 123,406,511	$124,850,694	$114,361,543
Cost of Sales	88,764,419	89,745,016	82,193,129
Gross profit	34,642,092	35,105,678	32,168,414
Expenses:			
Selling and shipping	17,070,261	17,368,489	16,127,571
Administrative and general	6,574,659	6,862,240	6,485,128
Restructuring expense (Note 4)	1,529,000	—	—
Total expenses	25,173,920	24,430,729	22,612,699
Operating income	9,468,172	10,674,949	9,555,715
Other Income (Expense) — net (primarily interest)	(915,040)	(437,016)	(1,219,467)
Income before income taxes	8,553,132	10,237,933	8,336,248
Income Taxes (Note 8)	3,035,000	3,603,000	2,857,000
Net Income	$ 5,518,132	$ 6,634,933	$ 5,479,248
Net Income Per Share (Notes 4 and 13)	$ 1.04	$ 1.26	$ 1.06
Weighted Average Shares Outstanding (Note 13)	5,324,502	5,254,130	5,159,197
Dividends Per Share: (Note 13)			
Common stock	$ .66	$ .60	$ .545
Class B common stock	$ .60	$ .536	$ .488

See accompanying notes to consolidated financial statements.

cates that the problem is not one of product acceptance or consumer demand, but simply inventory adjustments among all the middlemen. *An example: A consumer electronics client experienced a significant decline in demand for certain products even though the consumer market continued to increase. The source of the contradiction was consolidation at the retail level, where store closings led to a contraction of retailer inventories (pipeline). Emphasis of this point provided some assurance that the company's markets still offered potential for profitable sales, once consolidation slowed within the pipeline.*

2. **The Pipeline Effect—II.** The pipeline has added dimension when it's the product development process. Products still in development are of intense interest in some industries because they are the source of future growth. That's especially true in high-technology industries or other markets where product lives are relatively short. *An example: A company reports each year on the percentage of sales that result from relatively new products, demonstrating that the research pipeline is filled with potentially strong sellers. In addition, by showing the pattern of sales growth for new products, the company gives early indication of likely trends as new products reach market, or recently-introduced products mature.*

3. **Market Share.** Changes in market share provide some of the strongest indications of sales opportunity. A company increasing its penetration of the market is usually offering a product and, by extension, a product line that meets the needs of the ultimate user. The astute IR executive will examine market share issues in detail to determine whether changes are predictive. In some cases, share growth reflects a temporary aberration such as a long strike at a competitor's plant or a temporary swing in currency valuation that changes relative pricing for a competitor's product. Investment theses based on market share are strongest when they involve clearly defined markets, measurable improvements and consistent or long-term patterns.

4. **Industry Trends.** It's always important to compare the company's performance with industry trends. Is the industry growing or shrinking? Is the company focusing on a specific market segment that is growing, shrinking or less price-sensitive than the industry? Are competitors increasing or decreasing? Is the cost of entry high, so competitors who exit tend to stay out, or is it so low that any middle-manager with a good severance package can become a threat? Because each company competes with its industry peers in the investment market, it's important to distinguish your firm—favorably, it is hoped—from its peers.

   Industry trends should be measurable and current whenever possible. As a rule, megatrends make a good story but have relatively little impact on sales. Megatrends unfold over time, giving competitors and new entrants an opportunity to change marketplace dynamics. Thus, a company with a 20-percent share of the retiree market for its industry could anticipate a doubling of sales as the market doubles. In all likelihood, though, the market's growth will attract new competitors, leading to a smaller nominal growth rate and a smaller share of a larger market. It's also worth noting that megatrends are just one factor in sales trends. In some cases, the megatrend is overwhelmingly important, but in most instances, the day-to-day business issues are what count. A good IR executive will incorporate megatrends carefully and selectively into the investment story to avoid overpromising.

5. **Product Mix/Features.** To what extent does the sales increase reflect a change in product mix? Product mix shifts can reflect new products, changes in product features or technologies, totally new markets penetrated, and so on.

6. **Same-Store Sales.** A classic analysis vehicle for retailers, the review of same-store sales applies equally to many other firms. How much of sales growth reflects increased penetration of existing customers? Is this a leading indicator? *An example: A client breaks out its stores by relative age, demonstrating that a store increases sales and profitability as it ages.*

As a result, analysts can impute certain sales and earnings patterns based on the expected maturation of newer stores. When new stores are added, analysts can use the earnings model to create their own estimates of consolidated results.

Let's apply this to other industries. A company selling to automakers adds a new car company as a customer. How do we state the potential for sales? Here, history is largely predictive. Can the company show that its pattern with other automakers is one of increased year-to-year sales? In some higher-technology markets, product life cycles include predictable patterns of experimentation and ultimate acceptance among customers. Thus, the *same-store* approach would focus on products by age and distribution maturity, providing insight into the normal life cycle to be expected.

7. **Backlog.** The backlog of unfilled orders is a major indicator of sales trends as well. This is particularly true for firms with a relatively long lead time for project completions, including construction-oriented companies, capital goods firms and so on. But there is not usually a straight line relationship here. Backlogs grow both when orders increase, indicating that sales growth will follow, and when facilities near their operating capacity. When backlogs stretch too far, companies can fall victim to phantom orders, essentially a customer maneuver to maintain space in the production schedule. Companies often talk about firm backlogs, focusing only on signed contracts or discounting their numbers to some extent to account for these phantom orders.

In addition, very long backlogs can lead to shifts in orders to competitors whose product can be obtained faster. Shifting patterns of business can also make a difference in how much work flows through backlog. A company that both builds and repairs equipment will have a backlog for new equipment orders and no backlog for repairs. Changes in backlog here might or might not be indicative of future sales growth for the company as a whole.

Likewise, in multidivisional or multi-market companies, it's important to identify exactly to what extent sales come out of backlog. If the percentage is relatively small, say 25 or 30 percent, discussions of backlog might not be meaningful.

Finally, on the downside, backlogs also can grow when a weak economy leads customers to postpone delivery of product. *An example: Early in 1993, a major airline postponed delivery dates for new jets. The decision had no impact on the total backlog of the aircraft manufacturer, but the action clearly reduced near-term sales expectations. Another example is a client who received a firm contract order for nearly $20 million, equal to nearly three-quarters of sales. But this particular project wasn't scheduled to be delivered for more than a year. Consequently, we emphasized that its near-term impact on sales was zero.*

8. **Promotions/Advertising.** Sales growth resulting from special promotions or advertising present the same potential trap as the pipeline effect. The IR executive should be alert to any strong dependency on promotions. Does the advertising or other marketing program have a long tail, influencing sales for an extended period, or is it transitory? Is the market responsive solely to special promotions (rebates, coupons or television ad campaigns)?

9. **Sales Staff.** Do sales increases reflect changes in sales staff? Such changes could include a shift from internal staff to manufacturers' reps or a change in commission structure, territory size, etc. If increases in sales force are usually a good predictor of demand, the IR practitioner has one more bit of ammunition in hand. *An example: A client experienced a significant level of productivity from new salespeople several months after adding them to staff. We emphasized this point, along with the number hired in the past year, to indicate potential for sales growth.*

10. **Proprietary Technology/Brand Equity.** To what extent do sales come from products that cannot be duplicated? These could include proprietary or patented products or brands for which loyalty is particularly strong. How much time before the patents lapse? Have patents been challenged and suc-

cessfully defended? Is there a history of product extension, with brand loyalty transferred to the new product? Is product extension planned?

11. **Run Rate.** Annualized sales levels often provide greater insight than numbers for a specific year. While an acquisition at mid-year might increase a company's sales base by $100 million, only $50 million will be recorded in the acquisition year. An IR executive can make a strong case that sales should improve another $50 million as the company benefits from a full year's ownership of the subsidiary. The run rate is an important issue for any company growing through acquisition or in a high-growth sales trend.

12. **The Grid.** The grid is a time-honored and largely specious bit of overextension used to predict sales potential. Basically, a company lays out all of its product lines on one axis and puts its customers on a second. An "X" marks the spot where a particular customer and product line meet. "If we can get all our customers to buy all our products," the reasoning goes, "sales will rise 2022 percent without adding a single customer."

	Customers							
	A	B	C	D	E	F	G	H
Products								
1		X		X		X	X	
2		X	X		X		X	X
3	X		X		X		X	
4	X	X		X		X		
5		X	X	X			X	X

The problem with this analysis is that no company ever, ever fills the grid. It's fine to discuss increased sales to existing customers and a company is right on target in talking about increased numbers of products so sold. But it's a mistake to create the "all products to all customers" model exemplified by the grid because it sets an unrealistic goal in the minds of investors who follow this line of reasoning.

Key Ratios to Consider Relative to Sales
- Sales/employee.
- Sales/dollar of assets employed.
- Sales/customer.
- Sales/share.

Each of these ratios should be viewed both in terms of trends and in comparison to peers. (See 3-2, *Sources of Sales.*)

COST OF SALES/GROSS PROFIT

The line just below sales usually shows the *cost of goods sold* or *cost of sales*. This category encompasses direct costs of the product, including labor, materials and overhead burden. Subtracting cost of goods from sales yields gross profit, which is not only the first measure of corporate profitability, but also one of the most critical.

The cost of sales is especially critical because it is the measurement of manufacturing efficiency. (To avoid excessive verbiage, we'll use words like *manufacturing* even though some companies are in distribution or fabrication or deal in a technical service.) How much direct cost does it take to create a dollar of revenue?

As in the case of sales, this direct-cost figure warrants significant attention. From a static perspective, how are costs broken down? From a more dynamic perspective, what are the trends and is there any predictability? Here are some points to consider.

1. **Overhead Burden.** The first trap here is the overhead burden. Because, for example, machines are used up in creating the product, some percentage of both the cost (depreciation) of each machine and the factory itself is allocated to the cost of each unit produced. In slow sales periods, the relative cost per unit will increase because certain costs of operating the plant are spread over fewer produced units. If

3-2   Sources of Sales

Dozens of variables influence the sales number, and contradictory trends might cancel each other to create the erroneous impression that no change is occurring. When reviewing sales performance, the IR executive should consider the following sources of change.

1. More/less sales of the same products.
2. Price increases/decreases.
3. New territories not served previously or withdrawal from markets.
4. New products/product retirements.
5. Products that expand the line/replace old items.
6. Sales growth/decline on a per-customer basis.
7. Increased/decreased inventories in pipeline.
8. Increase/decrease in number of customers.
9. Supply constraints at company/competitors.
10. Changes in accounting for sales recognition.

For the IR executive, the sales number requires intense examination because it is the figure that flows most directly from the commercial marketplace. When reviewing sales, here are some thoughts to consider:

1. Is there a consistent trend to the numbers?
2. Does the trend result from industry patterns, general economic patterns or company-specific issues?
3. Is the trend of the past several years predictive of future performance?
4. Is there a change in the customer mix—a shift from retailers to wholesalers or from one group of retailers to another, a move from domestic to international or from one part of the country to another?
5. Is there a change in the source of sales, such as from manufacturers' reps to direct sales force?
6. For a multidivisional company, has there been a change in the kind of sales in the mix, such as sales accounted for on a percentage-of-completion basis versus those booked when a specific product is shipped?
7. If the company reports both sales and other sources of revenues, is there any shift between the categories, such as increased royalties from licensing and decreased sales of manufactured product?

capacity utilization rates have been low, each incremental dollar of increased sales should add a relatively high percentage to gross profit.

Consider a factory producing 100 widgets and applying all its overhead costs to those widgets. Assume that costs are split evenly between direct (direct labor, machinery depreciation, raw materials) and indirect (other labor, plant depreciation, etc.) expenses. Widget number 101 is then only half as expensive to produce as widgets 1–100 because the first 100 absorbed all the indirect cost. The accounting presentation isn't that simple, of course, but the message for the IR executive is clear. Incremental sales volume should be more profitable than the prior base. Likewise, declining sales will have a disproportionately negative effect on cost of goods sold.

Capacity utilization becomes a negative when usage rates are very high, however, because costs are being spread over almost as many units as the company can produce. Plant expansion might be necessary, which is a good indicator of sales potential while at the same time signaling greater near-term costs.

2. **Mix of Costs.** The cost of goods sold includes many costs, each of which might offer potential in the IR message mix. Trends in the type or cost of materials used, the scrap rate of production, internal recycling or other cost-reduction programs, changes in product design that shift the material content of the product—all can be indicators of earnings growth. Likewise, the mix of labor and capital equipment offers possible investment messages, as in cases of highly automated lines that reduce overall costs/unit or employee training programs that improve productivity.

Finally, the IR executive should be aware of the value-added components of these costs. Many activities in the factory add no value to the product, even though they're essential. Eliminating valueless steps can reduce direct costs without hurting quality or sales. In fact, increased efficiency can reduce lead times (and backlogs!) and improve customer satisfaction.

Key Ratios to Consider Relative to Cost of Goods Sold
- Cost of goods sold/sales (direct costs as a percentage of sales).
- Gross profit/sales, or gross margin (profitability of direct manufacturing, production).
- Costs of goods sold/total costs (indicative of how critical manufacturing expense is in total cost structure and often a signal of potential for improvement through cost reduction).

RESEARCH AND DEVELOPMENT, ENGINEERING

A company with heavy research or engineering programs often breaks out these expenditures on the income statement. (In the energy industry, expenditures for exploration might receive similar treatment.) For high-technology or highly engineered products, spending on research or engineering is the equivalent of capital spending, although accounting rules treat it differently.

These costs can cover a broad range of activities and entail a long payout period. A product developed through pure research, as in biotechnology, might take years, while value attributable to applied engineering might make its appearance within weeks or months. For the IR executive, it's critical to analyze such things as the type of research and development conducted and the patterns of results. Some points to consider:

1. **Investment/Return Patterns.** Is spending focused on relatively few large projects with potentially strong returns or on a large number of smaller projects, each offering moderate returns on investment? Is the research consolidated, so one research effort will generate several new products over time, or is it project specific, so crossover benefits are few?

2. **Pure/Applied Research.** Is the company pursuing *RE-SEARCH* and development or research and *DEVELOPMENT?* When results are achieved, how much lead time elapses before the added value appears in a salable product?

3. **Research Productivity.** How many new products or how many dollars of sales result from the research spending? Is this pattern changing? As a research program matures, its productivity might increase because so much of the legwork and obstacle removal has already been done. *An example: One client with substantial research expenditures plotted out resulting productivity according to new products developed. A clear, non-linear pattern demonstrated that research productivity was increasing. We bolstered that argument with examples of product sales resulting from the research effort.*

Key Ratios Relative to R&D Costs

- R&D as percentage of sales.
- Cumulative sales/cumulative R&D expenditures.
- Percent of current sales resulting from R&D investment.

SELLING, GENERAL AND ADMINISTRATIVE EXPENSE

The selling, general and administrative (SG&A) expense category takes us out of the factory and into the office. Once the product is made and product development (R&D/engineering) cost is absorbed, how much does it cost to sell the product, manage the business, heat the executive suites, and so on?

Ideally, this category would be covered in two lines on the income statement: one for marketing and sales of product (including bad-debt expense) and the other for corporate expense. Intuitively, a company that spends more to market the product and less on the corporate jet is likely to do better over the long term. But the number isn't usually broken out, so the IR executive will have to work with those numbers that are available. Here are some points to consider.

1. **Corporate Staff.** What percentage of the total employee force is reflected in the corporate offices or other non-operating capacities? The employee number is tricky because some firms use temporary workers on a project basis and others use manufacturers' reps instead of a direct sales force, and so on. But the order of magnitude should be reasonable and there should be some comparability among industry peers. Decentralized companies should have fewer executives in the corporate office than centralized firms do. *An example: To illustrate one client's decentralized approach to business, we emphasized that the corporate office included less than 20 people, while consolidated sales topped $600 million.*

2. **The Sales Force.** Is it an internal sales force or does the firm use agents or, more commonly, a combination of the two? Are sales direct to end-users or through distributors? Is there any predictability of sales per salesman? Has the number of salespeople or the mix of them changed? Is more being done with telemarketing or customer-initiated electronic-ordering? If so, is there a trend toward lower costs per unit of sales? Are commissions increasing or decreasing, either for the company alone or as an industry trend?

3. **National Accounts/Small Accounts.** Larger buyers demand lower prices, so gross margins tend to be lower when selling to them. However, they also tend to need less salesmanship per unit purchased, so the impact on SG&A is lower. Conversely, a sales call to a customer who will buy one unit, instead of 10, will never cost a proportionately lower amount. Often, as a company shifts its customer mix from smaller buyers to larger ones—especially in a consolidating customer market, the impact can be positive on one line and negative on another within the same income state-

ment. *An example: A client acquired a firm that sold largely to pharmaceutical companies, while the client's traditional business had been in low-volume transactions with medical labs. The new sales mix showed a lower gross profit, due to the volume sales, but lower selling costs per unit of volume.*

4. **Bad-Debt Expense.** Many companies include write-offs for bad debt in the SG&A category, so weak finances in customer industries can lead to an increase in this area. Are allowances and write-offs adequate or are unpleasant surprises lurking around the corner?

Key Ratios Regarding SG&A

- SG&A as percentage of total costs.
- Sales per sales rep (full-time equivalents).
- Corporate staff as a percentage of total staff.

EQUITY IN AFFILIATES/MINORITY INTEREST

Now, we're moving away from the core business. When a company owns a minority interest in another firm, or in a joint venture, the results of the other firm appear as a single number: earnings or loss attributable to the company's ownership percentage. Conversely, if the company in question owns the majority interest in another firm and consolidates that firm's results with its own operating results, this line of the income statement usually includes the amount of profit or loss that can be claimed by minority partners. *An example: A client's largest operation was 30-percent owned by another firm. The client company consolidated the operation's results on its income statement, reflecting all sales and costs as its own, and then subtracted out 30 percent of the earnings or loss in the "minority interest" category.*

These joint ventures and minority investments, or the presence of minority partners, usually get only minimal attention, but they deserve careful consideration from an IR perspective. Two points to consider:

45

1. **Purchase Opportunity/Obligation.** Many joint-venture or partnership agreements include provision for one party to buy out the other, either by choice or upon demand, using a specified pricing formula. These arrangements can prove advantageous or costly, depending on market conditions, industry outlook and relationship with the venture partner.

2. **Risk!** Especially in a partnership, or when the company is the minority owner and not the operator of the venture, the arrangement can present substantial risk. *An example: A client took on a partner in a small business related marginally to its core activities. The partner defrauded customers of the venture and, under the "deep pockets theory" of jurisprudence, our client was assessed several million dollars in damages.*

Note: Equity in affiliates or minority interests can appear in different locations in the income statement. In our example, we include it as part of operating expense, but in some situations, it will be shown as a line item after the operating income subtotal.

SPECIAL PROVISIONS

Special provisions encompass one-time expenses of a substantial nature such as costs of a plant-closing in a continuing business. Auditors are reluctant to allow companies to break out certain one-time charges, but companies should seek to highlight them or list them separately when it provides a more apples-and-apples comparison and when the special provisions are substantial. Because these charges are unusual, the IR executive is likely to look at them from two perspectives.

First, how would the income statement look without the special provision? Backing out that number, can a case be made that this special charge masks other trends?

Second, how does the special situation affect the firm's outlook? If facilities are consolidated, for example, what should the impact be on capacity utilization or productivity at remaining facilities? "If we had implemented the present structure last year," the IR exec might explain, "the same level of sales would have translated into 30-percent-higher net income."

Even if a special provision can't be broken out on the income statement, it is quite appropriate for the company to discuss the number in its financial review, press release, quarterly report or other outlets.

OPERATING INCOME

After expenses related to running the company are eliminated, what's left is operating income or income from continuing operations. Because the operating-income figure includes more activities than gross profit, it is both more and less useful as an indicator of potential performance.

It's less useful because operating income can increase when a company cuts back on advertising or research, or trims commissions to the sales force. Thus, increases in operating income can come through shortcuts that lead to long-term declines in sales and, ultimately, in profitability.

At the same time, operating income is much more holistic. It measures the company's use of resources to generate sales. While efficiency on the plant floor is important, proper allocation of resources throughout the company is a litmus test for management.

Analysis of operating income follows the same process described for other categories. Comparisons with industry peers and the company's own history are critical. Analysis of changes in the expense mix, from materials to joint ventures, is essential.

Key Ratio Relative to Operating Income
- Operating income/sales (operating margin).

INTEREST EXPENSE (INCOME)

Interest expense represents the cost of financing the company, putting it outside the overall operating environment. Interest expense is usually shown as a net number, although some firms include lines for both interest income and interest expense.

Interest costs are discussed in the following chapter on the balance sheet, where they are tied to capital structure. For now, we might simply note that because overall capital structure can vary widely among otherwise similar companies, interest expense may be higher for a company that is actually in better condition than its peers. Because interest expense is a tax-deductible cost and dividends are not, for example, the income statement doesn't offer much opportunity for meaningful analysis of corporate cost of capital.

Key Ratio Relative to Interest Expense

- Interest coverage (net income/interest expense).

PRE-TAX INCOME/TAX EFFECTS

Subtracting interest from operating income, for many companies, leads to pre-tax income. In some companies, particularly those with odd tax situations, pre-tax income is the surrogate for net income.

In the case of a company with substantial tax-loss carryfor-wards, for example, or one that has a volatile history of tax credits and subsequently, tax rates, the pre-tax number might offer the clearest indicator of trends.

The income tax provision, which is subtracted from pre-tax income to yield net income, is an estimate of all taxes, both currently due and deferred, owed on the taxable income for the period being reported. Taxable income reported to taxing authorities may differ markedly from "book" income reported on the income statement. This difference can result both from timing differences in recognition of income or expense under varying regulations and from permanent differences, such as the reporting of expenses that are not tax-deductible. In the annual report footnotes and/or financial review, companies provide a breakout of reasons why the tax provision differs from statutory tax rates.

The IR practitioner is not likely to be an expert in all the nuances of Generally Accepted Accounting Principles (GAAP) applied by the Financial Accounting Standards Board (FASB) to public companies, or possess comprehensive insights into the Internal Revenue Code, which directs reporting for taxation purposes. Nevertheless, new accounting standards and special factors affecting the specific company should be a subject of inquiry.

As a rule, income tax data are of little value for the IR executive because tax rates tend to be applied equally for all companies in a common jurisdiction. However, there are always opportunities to focus on special situations.

1. **Tax Loss Carryforward.** A company with substantial losses can use those losses to shelter future income from taxes. If the carryforward is great enough to shelter more than a year's worth of income, it creates an investment merit. This assumes, of course, that the company is likely to profit in the years ahead.

2. **International Sales.** Some international activities qualify for tax benefits, and any change in sales mix in the international arena can lead to changes in the effective tax rate for a company.

3. **Deferrals.** On the income statement, the tax line is a provision for income taxes, but it doesn't represent cash out the door in most instances. The subject of non-cash expenditures is covered in more detail in Chapter 5, which treats cash flow statements. For now, we can note simply that the IR exec might wish to focus on any unusually high variations between the provision and the actual payout of taxes.

Key Ratios

- Pre-tax income as a percent of sales (pre-tax margin).
- Effective tax rate (taxes/pre-tax income).

EXTRAORDINARY ITEMS

When a company closes a major operation, sells a subsidiary or experiences some other development that changes the nature of the business, the item might be classified as *extraordinary* and appear below the pre-tax income line. From an accounting perspective, this distinguishes the development from the company's ongoing activities. Although all sorts of expenses might be unusual or one-time in nature, the *extraordinary* category in financial reporting is used only for a limited number and type of developments.

The extraordinary item is often presented net of tax effects. For example, if the loss on sale of discontinued operations generates tax benefits of $500,000, those benefits are applied to reduce the loss that is recognized. In this way, the operating income and income-tax provision are insulated from the extraordinary item.

Although extraordinary items always require explanation, the IR executive will focus—as was true with special provisions on the operations side—on the impact on future activities. If an unprofitable business is being closed, for example, the IR practitioner will note how much more profitable the company would have been in prior years had that unit been excluded, and develop a model for the company's sales mix and margins going forward.

NET INCOME/EARNINGS PER SHARE

Finally, we get to the bottom line—the accountant's version of corporate efficiency. When it comes to net income, the IR executive is faced with the challenge of simplifying results. Following review of all individual activities that lead to earnings, the analysis is boiled down to a few key points.

It is certainly helpful to identify a few major trends influencing earnings. This makes the company easier to understand and follow, hence lower in perceived risk, and it makes the communications job clear.

In addition to the earnings number itself, investors focus on the level of earnings per share (EPS). All other things being equal, any change in the earnings-per-share level should be reflected in the price of the company's stock.

The EPS number also is affected by the number of shares outstanding and significant changes in this category must be tracked. A company that acquires another firm through a stock transaction might double its earnings, but triple the number of shares outstanding. Thus, existing shareholders might see some dilution of their stake in the company's profits. On the other hand, a company that buys back shares of its own stock might increase earnings per share as the number of shares outstanding declines and net income remains relatively stable.

(Earnings per share are not the same as return on the shareholder's investment in the stock. Total return to shareholders combines share-price appreciation with dividends received, making it somewhat independent of precise changes in earnings levels. Shareholders buy their stock at different prices, so depending upon the date and time of purchase, each shareholder has a different cost basis—and a different rate of return on investment.)

The job of the IR executive can be complicated by a few common issues related to net income and earnings per share. Although these are readily understandable for most investors, they do require some investment of time.

1. **Classes of Stock.** A company that issues both common and preferred shares will have two net-income numbers, one for net income attributable to common shares and one for true net income.

2. **Dilution.** Stock options available to executives or conversion privileges for debentures or preferred shares can create a significant difference between shares outstanding today and the shares that would be outstanding if everyone exercised all option/conversion privileges. Historically, companies reported both primary (current) earnings per share and a fully diluted EPS number that assumed all potential shares were outstanding. More recently, firms have been more likely to show earnings on a fully diluted basis only.

51

3. **Share Issuance.** A stock offering or other share issuance will lead to some shift—often a reduction—in earnings per share. Timing is one important source of reduced earnings per share. There is usually some delay between the time a company obtains funds and employs them profitably. Thus, a company might issue shares in the first quarter, but begin getting its intended return on the proceeds of the offering only six months later. Likewise, acquisitions in which stock is used as the currency can lead to near-term disruptions in earnings per share, even though the long-term benefits are expected to be substantial.

4. **Share Repurchase.** A stock buyback might be appropriate for a firm with excess cash and an undervalued security. The repurchase of shares counts as a direct reduction to the shareholders' equity account, so each dollar of stock bought on the open market cuts equity by a similar amount. However, the smaller number of shares outstanding after the repurchase should help the company generate a higher level of earnings per share, which can help boost the price of remaining shares outstanding. In addition, the smaller *stockholders'-equity* base will give the company a relatively higher return on equity at any level of earnings.

Key Ratios Relative to Net Income

- Earnings per share.
- Earnings as a percent of sales (net margin).
- Price of a share/earnings per share (p/e ratio).

4

FINANCIAL ANALYSIS: THE BALANCE SHEET

The balance sheet seems at first blush to be a daunting document, but it's really simple. Briefly, it summarizes what the company owns or has claim to (assets) and how those assets were financed. Everything the company holds in the way of assets is either funded with some kind of borrowings (liabilities) or the investment or retained earnings of shareholders (equity). One side must, by definition, balance the other.

Unlike the income statement which starts on the plant floor, the balance sheet starts with cash, moving essentially from the things that can be turned into cash most quickly to those that can be turned into cash more slowly.

ASSETS

We'll start with the left side of the balance sheet, the debit side, which includes all the assets the company has gathered to run its operations. Assets include everything the company owns, such as plant and equipment, and everything the company has a claim to, like receivables, deposits or pre-paid services.

Current Assets

The first category encompasses current assets, so named because it is assumed they can or will be converted into cash within a year. These include receivables which are expected to be collected in a month or two, inventories which the company expects to turn into sales shortly and, of course, cash itself. Let's review the different categories.

Cash and Marketable Securities. This includes cash, or rather the money in the company's checking accounts. Excess cash might be invested in money market funds, federal treasury securities or even corporate debt. As long as these non-cash investments are liquid enough to be turned into cash very quickly, they are essentially cash equivalents. Cash is, of course, the original fungible asset and its availability is essential.

However, cash levels will vary on a seasonal basis for most companies. A firm that sells consumer products will have a low cash position and a need to borrow in advance of fourth-quarter (Christmas season) shipments, and then become cash rich as payments are received. Cash is used to purchase materials that become inventories. Then products are sold to create receivables and receivables are collected in the form of cash.

Receivables. Receivables are the monies owed on products already sold. Usually, the receivable number on the balance sheet is discounted to an extent for "doubtful accounts." The company doesn't project which customers will fail to pay their bills, but the allowance for doubtful accounts assumes that some historically derived percentage of customers will, in fact, fail to meet their obligations. Receivables offer significant insights into how the company is being managed. For example:

1. *Relative Changes.* Receivables are most significant in relation to sales. If sales rise 10 percent, receivables should rise similarly. If receivables increase faster than sales, it could mean that the company is building sales by offering increasingly generous payment terms, or the company has begun selling to more marginal customers—people who are less likely to be able to make payments, or that the economy is slowing, making money tighter. Relatively higher receivables mean the company is turning sales into cash at a slower rate, which could mean the firm will need to borrow more to finance future inventories, increasing interest expense.

2. *Concentration.* While companies seek to increase their sales to existing customers, it's never a great idea to be too dependent on any one customer. A customer with too much clout can demand unprofitable concessions, or leave the seller with an unmanageable burden if the customer fails to pay when due. If receivables begin to grow relative to sales, it is often better, from a total risk standpoint, for that growth to be spread among a large number of customers rather than concentrated on just a handful.

3. *Allowance for Doubtful Accounts.* How aggressively is the company discounting its receivables? If receivables grow faster than sales, it means that bad debts are more likely. Is the company increasing the percentage discount for doubtful accounts, or is management leaving the company open for unpleasant surprises?

Receivables usually should be compared on a year-to-year basis as well as in relation to sales. Because most companies experience some form of seasonality in sales, receivables are likely to vary as well. That makes the numbers most comparable on a year-to-year basis as opposed to quarter-to-quarter.

Key Ratios Relative to Receivables
- Percentage past 30 days.
- Percentage past 90 days.
- Days' sales outstanding (receivables/daily sales).
- Receivables turnover (annual sales/average receivables level).

Inventories. Inventories include raw materials, work-in-process and finished goods. Like cash and receivables, inventories usually vary with seasonal trends. The level of inventories reflects the company's ability to forecast sales and manage resources. Like receivables, inventories are most accurately compared on a year-to-year basis, rather than quarter-to-quarter, if the company has seasonal sales trends. When reviewing inventories, the IR executive should note the following:

1. *Inventory Mix.* Is there a change in the relative mix of inventories among raw materials, work-in-process and finished goods? Has the company expanded its raw material supplies in advance of cost increases, which would be a nominally good move, or have delays in the factory led to a worrisome increase in semifinished parts?

2. *Sales Trends.* Do finished-goods inventories reflect current sales mix? Or has the company been caught with significant amounts of inventory for discontinued or slow-selling product while supplies of the top-selling products remain short? Similarly, do inventories match sales trends at the final customer level, net of any pipeline effects?

Inventories are evaluated using one of two primary methods: LIFO or FIFO. The method used is far more significant in periods of high inflation—or deflation—than in periods of relative pricing stability. LIFO stands for *Last In, First Out,* which means that the company assumes the last item purchased for inventory is the component that actually moved into the final product. FIFO stands for *First In, First Out,* and assumes that the first item placed in inventory is the first unit used on the production line.

A number of physical models demonstrate the differences. A company selling food will move product through the processing facility in the order received to minimize spoilage, so the food processor, physically speaking, will have a FIFO flow. A company that sells gravel will put new gravel on top of its storage pile and physically sell the last gravel added before getting down to the bottom layer—a LIFO flow.

However, the accounting treatment need not match physical reality. Inventory valuation choices flow from pricing more than from physical movement of product. Consider the 1970s, when soaring energy costs contributed to rapid inflation in the United States.

American Widget Corporation buys polyethylene resin, an oil derivative, and converts that resin into children's toys. On January 1, resin costs 37 cents per pound, but by December 31, the price has moved up to 60 cents per pound.

Under FIFO, American Widget recognizes an average cost of 40 cents per pound for its resin because the accounting is weighted toward the first units purchased. Under LIFO, which assumes the last items in inventory are the ones sold, the average cost recognized is 50 cents per pound.

Under FIFO, American Widget gets to recognize substantial profit margins, and relatively higher taxes, because the inventory accounting system tends to overstate margins in a high-inflation environment. The company's inventories, however, are valued at a near-market rate because the accounting assumes the most recently purchased inventories are still there. (Net balance sheet impact: higher values for inventories and equity.)

Under LIFO, however, the profit margins and taxes recognized are lower. The company assigns a higher product expense to the cost of goods sold in our high-inflation model. At the same time, inventories are recorded at well below the current market value. That's because the accounting assumes all those 37-cent resin packages are still in the warehouse. (Net balance sheet impact: lower inventory value and lower equity.)

LIFO adds one extra complication. When a company reduces inventories, valuations can be misleading because the firm might be reaching into a very old and undervalued LIFO layer. After three years of high inflation, for example, American Widget experiences a slowdown and trims inventories from an average of one million pounds to just 500,000 pounds. Suddenly, this LIFO-based company might be selling product that, from an accounting standpoint, has a four-year-old cost attached to it. Cost-of-goods-sold plunges, due to LIFO accounting, even though no other change in pricing or efficiency has occurred.

The impact of inventory valuation methods must be footnoted on the company's annual financial statements, and IR executives should review the differences between inventory methods applied by their own firms and competitors.

Finally, inventory accounts must be considered in relation to supplier arrangements. A company that has adopted just-in-time

4-1   Inventory Analysis

Although inventories take up just one line on the balance sheet, many companies break out the inventories in the footnotes that accompany financial tables in the annual report (10-K) or quarterly report (10-Q). Inventories for most companies include the following.

Raw Materials   These are often basic materials like plastic resin or lumber that will be crafted into finished products. Raw materials can also include high-value components, such as proprietary circuit boards prepared by an outsource vendor.

Work in Process   Materials in the production process (no longer raw but not yet completed) include in their valuation some component of labor and factory overhead. The cost of equipment and labor to work on these items is added as the materials move through production.

Finished Goods   Products ready for sale constitute the finished goods category. This grouping also can include obsolete products, discontinued lines and other products that have little chance of being sold.

As materials move through the production process, increased value is assigned to them to reflect the resources dedicated to production and/or fabrication. Inventory categories should not necessarily rise and fall together, especially for firms that have a highly seasonal sales cycle. In addition, implementation of inventory management systems and rapid delivery programs with vendors can lead to internal variations in the relative levels of one inventory category versus another.

---

type programs with its own suppliers might be able to maintain relatively low inventories compared to peers that must warehouse proportionately more raw material. (See 4-1, *Inventory Analysis.*)

Key Ratio Relative to Inventories

- Inventory turnover (sales/average inventories).
- Days sales in inventory (inventory/daily sales).

Deferred Income Taxes. Expenses which must be recognized under Generally Accepted Accounting Principles, although not currently deductible for tax purposes under the IRS code, can give rise to future tax benefits or deferred tax assets. Conversely, expenses which can be deducted under the IRS code earlier than under GAAP can give rise to deferred tax liability, which appears on the other side of the balance sheet. Changes in tax rates or the accounting rules applied to deferred taxes can influence this number.

Prepaid Expenses. Prepaid expenses, like rents or deposits against purchases, qualify as assets because the company has a claim to future services. For most companies, such prepayments represent a relatively small amount of total assets.

Fixed (Non-Current) Assets

While current assets are expected to change into cash within a year, non-current or fixed assets are expected to have lives beyond a year. These categories are made up primarily of property, plant and equipment, and the value of intangibles like goodwill and patents as well as equity investments or long-term notes receivable from subsidiaries, joint ventures and so on.

Property, Plant and Equipment. The property, plant and equipment (PP&E) account, like receivables, is a net account, adjusted for depreciation. On the income statement, the use of equipment and facilities is charged to sales in the cost of goods sold. Similarly, this decline in asset value is reflected on the balance sheet. Depreciation might be recognized on a slightly different basis for financial (book) reporting purposes than for tax purposes, and the actual wear and tear on a machine might not match its depreciable life under GAAP. But these numbers are a proxy for reality—not reality itself.

The IR executive looking for investment appeals will consider the following relative to property, plant and equipment.

4-2 Balance Sheet

| | Year ended June 30, | |
Assets:	1993	1992
Current Assets:		
Cash and equivalents	$ 630,681	$ 2,606,648
Accounts receivable, less allowance of $477,000		
and $453,000 for doubtful accounts and cash discounts (Note 11)	17,697,575	16,354,196
Inventories (Note 2)	23,041,884	21,806,743
Prepaid expenses	1,262,860	1,327,725
Refundable income taxes	778,037	—
Total Current Assets	43,411,037	42,095,312
Property and Equipment:		
Land and improvements	2,053,694	1,307,797
Buildings	16,294,147	15,120,271
Machinery and equipment	54,909,159	46,301,558
	73,257,000	62,729,626
Less accumulated depreciation	24,424,756	21,631,484
Net Property and Equipment	48,832,244	41,098,142
Other Assets	4,703,687	5,139,486
	$ 96,946,968	$ 88,332,940

| | Year ended June 30, | |
Liabilities and Stockholders' Equity:	1993	1992
Current Liabilities:		
Accounts payable	$ 5,384,193	$ 5,743,428
Accruals:		
Income taxes	—	655,679
Other taxes	961,753	893,623
Compensation	2,076,060	2,019,636
Retirement plan contributions	1,067,610	803,800
Miscellaneous	657,078	564,824
Current portion of long-term debt	—	3,000,000
Total Current Liabilities	10,146,694	13,680,990
Supplemental Retirement Benefits (Notes 5 and 6)	1,353,512	1,238,852
Long-Term Debt, less current portion (Note 3)	12,750,000	3,000,000
Deferred Income Taxes (Note 8)	8,820,800	8,345,800
Total Liabilities	33,071,006	26,265,642
Commitments (Notes 5, 6 and 7)		
Stockholders' Equity (Notes 9 and 13)		
Stock:		
Common, $2 par – 6,000,000 shares authorized;		
2,918,428 and 2,611,876 issued	5,836,856	5,223,752
Class B common, $2 par – 4,000,000 shares authorized;		
2,403,567 and 2,190,922 issued	4,807,134	4,381,844
Preferred, 2,000,000 shares authorized and unissued	—	—
Additional paid-in capital	23,689,539	15,568,272
Retained earnings	30,044,186	36,545,656
Foreign currency translation adjustment	(501,753)	347,774
Total Stockholders' Equity	63,875,962	62,067,298
	$ 96,946,968	$ 88,332,940

See accompanying notes to consolidated financial statements

1. *Replacement/Market Value.* Are values understated on the balance sheet, because inflation has increased the market value of assets or for other reasons? Because conservative accounting rules require that facilities and land be valued at cost (less depreciation) or market, *whichever is lower,* a 50-year-old facility might be valued at a fraction of its real value. *An example: A client operating a few hotel properties listed those properties on the books at historical cost, less depreciation, or roughly $15 per share. However, the properties were worth closer to $50 per share at market. We emphasized the hidden value in the balance sheet in our communications with investors, ensuring that shareholders would know enough to reject unfairly low buyout offers.* Many buyouts of the 1980s depended on the enormous gap between book value of assets and their true market or replacement value.

2. *Age of Property.* Older properties might be undervalued, but newer properties are likely to be more efficient. A case can be made that plant and equipment installed more recently than for industry competitors gives the company an edge in efficiency, precision or maintenance. *An example: One client with a relatively new refinery was able to note a substantial cost advantage in environmental compliance when compared with peers operating older facilities.*

3. *Additions to Plant.* Is the total value of plant and equipment declining or growing? Is depreciation being matched or exceeded by capital spending? Is capital spending going into replacement of existing operations or does it represent a redeployment of assets into newer technologies, new regions or new markets?

Intangibles. When operating assets are acquired for more than their fair market value, the difference is known as goodwill. Some of the excess of purchase price over fair market value might be assigned to specific intangibles categories, such as patents or non-compete agreements. The rest is simply goodwill.

These values are depreciated as well, although the term used for intangible assets is amortization. As with other assets, the true, fair-market value of intangibles might exceed book value.

It's also worth noting that intangible assets might not decline in value at all. The value of a brand name, for example, can continue increasing in the marketplace, even though reductions are reflected in the financial statements.

Investments. Unlike marketable securities, these investments will be longer-term in nature. Usually they include equity investment in unconsolidated subsidiaries or joint ventures, advances to these subsidiaries or other affiliates, or loans made to executives or others.

LIABILITIES AND SHAREHOLDERS' EQUITY

Everything the company owns or has a claim to is, in turn, owed to or claimed by someone else. Either the claim is made by a creditor or by an owner (shareholder) of the company. Now we turn to the right side, or credit side of the statement, where liabilities and shareholders' equity balance the value of assets.

Current Liabilities

Just as assets that are expected to turn into cash within a year are considered current assets, payments due within a year are considered current liabilities. Here is a rundown:

Accounts Payable or Trade Payables. Accounts receivable for one company are accounts payable for another. This payables category represents dollars owed for raw materials as well as to the people who fixed the drill press and the caterer for the company picnic. Like receivables, payables should rise or fall in line with sales. If payables increase at a disproportionate rate, it might mean that the company is getting more favorable payment terms for its purchases, but it also might mean a cash crunch is slowing payments. (The payables account should always be viewed in conjunction with trends in the cash, receivables, and inventories accounts.)

Accrued Expenses. Accrued expenses are those recognized on the income statement but not yet paid, including salaries, pension-fund contributions, rents, insurance and so on. Accruals usually reflect a relatively short-term difference between the date on which the liability is recognized (accrued) and the date on which it is paid.

Accrued Income Taxes. Taxes always get special mention. Like accrued expenses, these are taxes recognized as payable and expected to be paid within a short period of time, certainly within the coming year.

Billings in Excess of Costs on Uncompleted Contracts. For companies that recognize sales on a percentage-of-completion basis, profits are recognized along the way as well. Until the project is completed, the receivable on one side of the balance sheet, or in some cases value assigned to inventory, is offset in part by a liability reflecting the extent to which these assets exceed costs.

Current Installments on Long-Term Debt. Although long-term debt is, as would be expected, a long-term liability, installment payments due within a year are current liabilities. In some instances, timing and progress of debt renegotiation might lead to a long-term obligation becoming, at least temporarily, a current liability, even though finalization of a new long-term agreement is expected. Technical default on a loan covenant, for example, might lead to a reclassification of the long-term debt during the time new loan terms are negotiated.

Amounts Due to Affiliates. Obligations to affiliates create a liability. Obligations that must be met within a year are current liabilities.

Long-Term Liabilities

Like long-term or non-current assets, long-term liabilities are those that aren't expected to be settled within a year. Primary among these are:

Long-Term Debt. Bonds, debentures, bank loans of more than a year's duration, including mortgages, all fall in the long-term debt category. For the investor relations executive, the level of long-term debt is a focus of study, along with the trend for debt over several years. Equally important are the average interest rates on this debt, whether the debt covenants preclude or limit dividend payments or major capital expenditures, and whether a renegotiation is due within a year or two. While high debt might be perceived as a risk factor, low debt relative to peers can be viewed as unacceptable as well. Analysts often argue that a company with low or no debt is missing an opportunity to maximize returns on equity through leverage. On the other hand, a company with low leverage can claim to have ample access to expansion capital, especially when compared to more highly leveraged competitors.

Deferred Taxes. This category is similar to the accrued taxes category under current liabilities, except that it reflects taxes that aren't likely to be paid for more than a year.

Other Long-Term Liabilities. These liabilities could include leases, commitments to affiliates, or other non-debt, non-tax obligations.

Shareholders' Equity

Anything not owed to someone else is owned by the shareholders. Shareholders' equity is the difference between total assets and total liabilities. The equity accounts of the company reflect a number of additions to equity and might reflect more than one type of stock. In general, the following are the equity accounts.

Common Stock. When stock is issued, it carries a par value, often a few cents or a dollar per share—a quaint anachronism. The common-stock account will be equal to the par value times the number of shares issued. If the company has more than one class of stock, such as a common and preferred or a voting class and a non-voting class of common, there might be two lines on the balance sheet to reflect this.

Additional Paid-In Capital. Because stock is almost never sold at par, this account tracks the added amount received through sale of the shares. Thus, if a share sold at $10 in the initial public offering and had a par value of $1, the company would record $1 in the common stock account and $9 under additional paid-in capital. Together, these two accounts reflect the amount of money raised in offerings of shares for sale to the public, along with adjustments related to share repurchase and other events.

Retained Earnings. This is the big one—or it should be. Retained earnings represent the cumulative amount of net income earned by the company—minus a handful of specific reductions described below—since the company's birth. While most companies have a positive balance in the equity account, a start-up company might actually have enough losses to create a negative equity situation. That means that more than 100 percent of all assets have been pledged to someone other than the owners of the firm.

More recently, new accounting rules create increased potential for negative net worth for some companies. Especially for older firms with high levels of unionized workers, a requirement (FASB Statement 106) that potential costs of retiree healthcare benefits be recognized immediately has led to enormous one-time, non-cash charges. For an established firm in an ailing industry, it is not difficult to imagine a retiree healthcare charge wiping out all of the firm's equity. The company can continue operating, of course, in spite of that (non-cash) development.

Some charges do not flow through the income statement but are reflected directly in the retained earnings account, the most common of these being dividends, currency translation, or repurchased stock.

While interest paid on debt is considered an expense and limits the tax liability of a corporation, dividends are considered a distribution out of retained earnings and therefore an after-tax distribution. This is the source of the common complaint that dividends are twice-taxed—once on the way into the retained earnings account and again when received by the shareholder.

Currency translations, including adjustments to the book value of assets involved in international operations, also will be

65

charged directly to retained earnings or reflected in a separate entry in the equity category. Although these adjustments can be major, the true impact on the actual operation might be minimal. For example, a stronger dollar might reduce the translated value of a foreign facility, but that foreign facility might fare better because it is locally based, insulating its sales from U.S. export competition. Unless the profits of the foreign operation are repatriated, the translation effect can actually be misleading. Such currency translations for foreign operations truly become significant when an operation is closed or sold, but the interim adjustments can have conflicting meanings.

Shares repurchased by the company are charged directly against the equity account as well. The purchase price is charged against the common stock paid-in-capital and retained earnings accounts.

Treasury Stock. Treasury stock includes shares repurchased on the open market by the company, usually for stock options, Employee Stock Ownership Plans (ESOPs) or other programs. Because the purchase represents shares in the company, the payment is deducted directly from retained earnings. A treasury stock entry may appear as a charge against equity.

BALANCE SHEET ANALYSIS

For the investor relations professional, the balance sheet is the source of corporate growth and survival. A solid balance sheet can provide credibility when a company bids on a major project or staying power through a prolonged recession. The age of assets or the favorable interest rate or terms on debt can be presented as competitive advantages in making the investment case for the company. Here are some commonly applied mechanisms for balance sheet analysis.

1. *Working Capital.* The difference between current assets and current liabilities is known as working capital, and the quotient of current assets/current liabilities is known as the current ratio. For most companies, a current ratio of more than

one is desirable. Usually, a negative working capital position (more current liabilities than current assets) indicates a problem, although some companies can operate quite well under that condition. For example, a distributor might collect on sales in three weeks while its payment terms to suppliers are net 30 days. That means receivables would average three weeks of sales while payables would run closer to four weeks. Likewise, a restaurant might turn "inventory" into cash in a few days, but payment terms might be net-30. The IR executive should focus on the industry norms for working capital and identify any differences in payment terms that give her company an advantage.

2. *Debt/Equity*. High levels of equity as a percentage of total capitalization provide stability and survival capacity. At the same time, the use of debt (leverage) to increase the level of capital employed can provide a strong boost to returns to shareholders. The right balance depends not only on industry factors and the company's competitive position, but also on the general economy. Debt provides earnings leverage only after interest costs are paid. In times of weakness, dividends can be skipped, but interest obligations are not postponable. *A vastly oversimplified example: The leveraged buyouts of the 1980s led to some of the spectacular bankruptcies of the early 1990s because the leverage employed to purchase the companies stripped the firms of their staying power in weak markets.*

Key Ratios Related to Balance Sheet Analysis
- Working capital (current assets minus current liabilities).
- Current ratio (current assets divided by current liabilities).
- Debt/equity (long-term debt/shareholders' equity).
- Equity/capitalization (equity as a percentage of equity plus long-term debt).
- Debt/capitalization (long-term debt as a percentage of equity plus long-term debt).

5

FINANCIAL ANALYSIS: CASH FLOW

The dollars in the financial tables are a proxy for what happens on the plant floor and in the marketplace. Similarly, the income statement approximates the inflows and payments of cash to run the company. However, the income statement varies from actual cash in many instances. For example, while costs of overhead are attributed to each unit produced, buildings and equipment aren't purchased one increment at a time.

The cash flow statement seeks to explain the differences between the income statement and the checkbook, and the IR executive will look for ways to use this statement in proving the investment thesis. To understand how, let's look at some of the components of a cash flow statement.

THE CASH FLOW STATEMENT

In years past, it was the norm to start with the prior year-end working capital and review all account changes leading to the new working capital number one year later. But that table proved confusing in that it began with a computed number (current assets minus current liabilities) and ended with the same. More recently, the standard has been to use the indirect method of cash flow analysis. Beginning with net income, the table includes the following:

Non-cash Items Related to Operations. Several expenses recognized on the income statement are accruals that do not as yet represent cash payments. Likewise, some income recognized by the company is also accrued but not received. These include, in part:

- Depreciation of plant and equipment
- Income taxes booked but not yet paid
- Accounts receivable
- Allowances for doubtful accounts
- Amortization
- Provisions for restructuring, severance, etc.

In other words, the cash flow statement corrects for the timing difference between recognition of an event that results in cash being received or disbursed and the event itself.

Investing Activities. Although purchase of assets requires cash, the income statement doesn't recognize the expenditure because it isn't an expense. Instead, one asset (cash) has been exchanged for another (equipment). The income effect (overhead expense) comes as the asset is used (depreciation) in making product or other applications. The second section of the cash flow statement records cash used to purchase operating assets (excluding materials used in making the product), cash involved in making or collecting on certain loans or other instruments, and cash from purchase or sale of property.

Financing Activities. Adjustments relative to operations match up with the current assets and liabilities portions of the balance sheet, and the investing activities section of the cash flow statement applies more or less to the long-term asset part of the balance sheet. Financing activities adjustments tie into the long-term debt and equity accounts. (This is an oversimplified explanation, but the general rule applies.) Thus, the third section of the cash flow statement addresses activities related to capital formation, including:

5-1 Cash Flow Statement

	1993	1992	1991
		Year ended June 30,	
Operating Activities:			
Net income	$ 5,518,132	$ 6,634,933	$ 5,479,248
Adjustments to reconcile net income to net cash from operating activities:			
Depreciation	4,350,764	3,941,018	3,753,479
Amortization	669,731	800,825	786,908
Deferred income taxes	522,000	216,000	437,000
Supplemental retirement benefits	116,942	82,781	85,522
Changes in operating assets and liabilities:			
Accounts receivable and other receivables	(2,271,821)	(791,439)	2,665,908
Inventories	(1,629,062)	2,286,198	(1,357,565)
Prepaid expenses	39,844	(28,792)	53,008
Accounts payable	(285,154)	1,526,119	(977,084)
Accruals	(104,930)	1,904,919	(964,425)
Net cash from operating activities	6,926,446	16,572,562	9,961,999
Investing Activities:			
Additions to property and equipment	(12,515,093)	(8,381,278)	(4,433,286)
Sales of property and equipment	112,109	117,005	1,864,647
Payments for other assets	(285,804)	(1,016,164)	(907,232)
Net cash for investing activities	(12,688,788)	(9,280,437)	(3,475,871)
Financing Activities:			
Additions to long-term debt	9,750,000	—	—
Payments on long-term debt	(3,000,000)	(3,950,000)	(2,450,000)
Proceeds from issuance of common stock	507,097	603,878	175,363
Cash dividends paid	(3,360,108)	(2,988,661)	(2,664,356)
Purchase of common stock	(6,930)	(3,993)	(977,792)
Net cash from (for) financing activities	3,890,059	(6,338,776)	(5,916,785)
Effect of Exchange Rate Changes on Cash	(103,684)	(196,561)	23,005
Net Increase (Decrease) in Cash and Equivalents	(1,975,967)	756,788	592,348
Cash and Equivalents, at beginning of year	2,606,648	1,849,860	1,257,512
Cash and Equivalents, at end of year	$ 630,681	$ 2,606,648	$ 1,849,860

See accompanying notes to consolidated financial statements.

- Sale or purchase of the company's stock
- Issuance or payment of long-term debt
- Payment of dividends

Recently, a further refinement of the cash flow statement has been promoted by many. Instead of beginning with net income and making adjustments for non-cash expenses or incomes, this cash flow approach begins with sales. Thus, the first item under cash flow from operations is *cash receipts from sales of goods and services*. In fact, this is a true cash flow statement, rather than a mechanism for reconciling net income statements to cash.

In either case, the first and foremost question answered by the cash flow statement is: Does this company generate cash from its operations? It might seem a simple question, but the answer can be deceptive. A high-growth company, for example, will always be cash short on an operating basis because it is consistently ordering more materials to fill orders, investing in new equipment and so on. A more mature company might have more limited demand for new equipment and raw materials, making it a consistent generator of cash—a cash cow.

The cash flow statement also provides an insight into the ability and likelihood of a company to continue paying a dividend in spite of one year's net loss. Companies that pay dividends tend to be consistent cash-generators, and can be positive on the cash flow side even in years when the net income level drops below zero.

The cash flow statement also highlights the company's investment posture. Are capital expenditures keeping pace with depreciation of plant and equipment? Is most investment coming in the form of capital spending or acquisitions? On the financing side, is the company shifting from debt to stock or vice versa?

6

FINANCIAL ANALYSIS: MAKING SENSE OF IT ALL

In the preceding chapters, we reviewed the financial statements briefly and identified in each section key ratios related to each category. In this chapter, we focus more directly on the financial-analysis component of investor relations. Here, we'll look both at the ratios analysts consider and at alternative ways of presenting a company's financial and operating appeals.

FINANCIAL COMPANIES

Our analysis thus far has focused essentially on a manufacturing model, which broadly covers distributors, service organizations and other non-financial enterprises. To keep the analysis brief, we have excluded insurers, banks, brokerage houses and other financial institutions.

In an accounting sense, the accounts and analysis for financial firms differ from those for manufacturers. However, from a philosophical point of view, there is essentially no difference. Let's look at a bank, for example.

Banks are in the business of distributing money. A distribution firm finds manufacturers looking for a sales conduit to the ultimate consumer and matches them up with a customer look-ing for sources of goods. The bank makes money on the spread between the cost of the goods from the source and the price of the goods to the user.

Just as the distributor takes responsibility for the product obtained from the manufacturer, and must focus on collecting payment from the end-user of the product, the bank recognizes its liability for funds received (deposits and borrowings) and focuses on collection of funds advanced to others (loans).

Net-interest margin, the difference between the bank's cost of funds and the interest received on loans extended, is essential-ly the gross profit. Out of that profit, other expenses are covered. Fee income, or non-interest income, is a second category of rev-enues, just as royalties or licensing fees are to a manufacturer. The percentage of revenues coming from each category, as well as the relative profitability of each and the trends in these cate-gories, are all grist for the IR mill. Consider the similarities among categories.

Assets/Liabilities. For a bank, loans are an asset because these are funds owed to the bank. Deposits, on the other hand, are a liability because the bank's customer has a claim to that money. Different types of deposits, like various raw materials, have different cost structures. While checking accounts have high transaction levels, the interest paid to depositors is low or zero. Time deposits or funds borrowed from other banks or the Feder-al Reserve Bank have higher interest rates but relatively lower transaction expense. Loan pricing, like product pricing, is estab-lished based on a number of variables. Although the risk of non-payment is a more critical component of product pricing for loans than it is for a tennis racket, the payment terms of a loan and the payment terms provided to any buyer of widgets from a manufacturer both reflect estimates of repayment probability.

The jargon may differ but the concepts are the same. Thus, although this volume doesn't focus specifically on the financial statements of financial firms, the lines of reasoning included for non-financial companies are instructive.

FINANCIAL RATIOS

Financial ratios focus on two primary issues: efficiency and financial condition. Efficiency refers to the level of returns generated from a specific input, while financial condition describes the relative safety of an investment in the company.

Efficiency Ratios

Efficiency ratios include the standard profitability ratios that are the most commonly used in financial analysis.

1. *Net Margin or Return on Sales (Income/Sales)*. This refers to the percentage of sales left as earnings after all expenses are paid.

2. *Return on Assets (Income/Assets)*. This focuses on the company's efficiency in utilizing assets. The comparison in such a formula is always with a risk-free investment such as Treasury Notes. If a U.S. Treasury Note pays a guaranteed 6 percent, with no risk of default, a corporation must meet the test of generating a far greater return through operations than would have resulted if all the assets were simply converted to cash and parked in T-Notes. (The asset figure can be beginning assets, ending assets or average assets. Although many firms focus on either beginning or average assets, few compute a return on ending assets. Major changes in asset levels during the year, such as those resulting from acquisitions, can make one calculation much more appropriate than another.)

3. *Return on Equity (Income/Equity)*. Because the equity figure will be lower than total assets, return on equity (ROE) will be larger than return on assets (ROA). Like return on assets, this ratio is inferentially compared with a risk-free investment. (The equity figure can be beginning equity, ending equity or, more commonly, average equity. Major changes in equity levels during the year, such as those resulting from stock offerings or mergers, can make one calculation much more appropriate than another.) In rare instances, a firm

75

6-1   The DuPont Formula

The financial picture comes together through the DuPont formula, which combines income-statement and balance-sheet ratios to yield return on equity—the final measure of corporate efficiency.

In this process, numerators and denominators cancel each other out until the only remaining ratio is income/equity or return on equity (ROE). Specifically:

Income/Sales   Net margin (efficiency of sales and costs)

$\times$

Sales/Assets   Asset-turnover (efficiency of asset utilization)

$\times$

Assets/Equity   Leverage (how the assets are financed)

$=$

Income/Equity   Return on equity (return on shareholder ownership interest)

An example: One of our clients uses the DuPont Formula as a critical measurement tool, moving back from its ROE goals to individual categories of performance. In this client's case, low sales margins are the single source of shortfall in reaching the ROE goal. Hence, from an IR standpoint, the challenge is to explain how net margin can be enhanced.

---

may have negative net worth, yielding a meaningless number for ROE. (See 6-1, *The DuPont Formula*.)

4. *Gross Margin (Gross Profit/Sales)*. Because this number represents the most direct costs of running the business, it is an indicator of potential earnings. Companies with low gross margins need to keep other costs in line or raise volume if they are to generate a profit. Gross margins can vary dramatically from one industry to another. Grocers tend to have low gross margins, but might turn over inventory dozens of times each year, while capital goods manufacturers will likely have higher gross margins and lower inventory turnover.

5. As*set Turnover (Sales/Average Assets)*. Asset turnover reflects the company's ability to utilize assets to generate sales. All

other things being equal, higher turnover equals greater profitability. In a low-margin business, high asset turnover is critical for building net income.

6. *Inventory Turnover (Sales/Average Inventories)*. Inventory turnover is a more direct measurement of asset utilization because it focuses on both sales and the products or materials to be sold. Some analysts prefer to compute this number based on the formula: cost of goods/inventory. This alternate formula compares costs with costs.

7. *Operating Margin (Operating Income/Sales)*. Before adding in the costs of financing the company and other special expenditures, the operating margin shows how efficiently the company is managing its core business.

8. *Pre-Tax Margin (Pre-Tax Income/Sales)*. The pre-tax margin might be the most important measurement of earnings efficiency for companies with unusual tax status or an extraordinary item on the income statement.

9. *Tax Rate (Taxes/Pre-Tax Income)*. The tax rate indicates how much of pre-tax income the company will be able to reinvest in operations. A lower tax rate theoretically leaves more of earnings in the company, available for reinvestment. (Because some taxes are deferred, the tax rate alone is not a true measure of funds available for reinvestment. Cash paid in taxes, however, is disclosed in the annual report.)

10. *SG&A as a Percent of Sales*. This overhead measurement is used by some firms to show that a relatively small amount of corporate cost is expended in the executive suite. Not surprisingly, firms with bloated overhead seldom focus on this number.

11. *Research as a Percent of Sales*. This figure indicates how aggressively sales dollars are being plowed back into the research that will lead to future products and sales. It is a particularly important indicator for high-technology companies and especially important in comparison with industry peers.

77

Financial Condition Ratios

Ratios that measure financial condition usually compare balance sheet items or compare a balance sheet item with one from another financial table.

1. *Current Ratio (Current Assets/Current Liabilities).* The current ratio is the most commonly used formula for measuring near-term liquidity.

2. *Debt/Equity (Long-Term Debt as a Percentage of Equity).* This measures the relative importance of debt and equity as sources of capital. Companies in more cyclical industries should use more equity, relatively speaking, than those in more stable markets.

3. *Days' Sales Outstanding (Receivables/Average Daily Sales).* The Days' Sales Outstanding (DSO) figure tracks a company's ability to collect payment from its customers. A significant increase in this number can indicate a likely increase in bad debt and/or an increase in interim financing costs as lines of credit, rather than customer payments, are used to generate the cash needed for operations.

4. *Interest Coverage (Net Income + Interest Expense + Taxes/ Interest Expense).* Interest coverage is an important point of focus for firms with high debt levels, and less so for low-leverage companies. A high level of interest coverage can indicate ample capacity to take on—and support—additional debt. An alternative formula for interest coverage is *(net income + interest expense + taxes + depreciation and amortization)/(interest + principal repayment).*

NON-FINANCIAL MEASUREMENT

Although the financial ratios are the most obvious source of insight into a company's performance, they are not the only resource available and are not always the most compelling. Remembering that the financial statements are merely a proxy for the company's operations, the IR executive should also focus on several non-financial measurements.

1. *Sales/Employee*. The most efficient companies will have a high percentage of workers involved in the direct tasks of making and selling product rather than in administration, leading to a high sales/employee level. Companies with heavy capital investment or other means of leveraging worker output, as in software or engineering firms, can also have high sales/employee levels. Firms often focus on the trend here as well as in the nominal level, and comparisons with peers are common.

2. *Sales/Customer*. A firm that is increasing its penetration of existing accounts might want to highlight that progress by computing average sales per customer account.

3. *New Products*. New products are the source of increased sales or, at least, will replace sales falloff as older products lose favor with customers. Product development can be analyzed along a number of lines, including:
   - New products introduced each year.
   - Percentage of sales from products introduced in past two or three years.
   - Products resulting from R&D or engineering programs.
   - Size of market addressed by new products versus market addressed by existing lines.

4. *Market Position*. While market share is the most obvious point to emphasize, market position also can include quality leadership, low-cost–producer status, technology advantages, etc. Firms will often identify their niches by focusing on the customers they serve. For example, a firm might identify itself as selling to 10 of the top 12 retailers in its market or note that it has the only brand carried by several major customers. Customer loyalty, measured in average years of service, can also be a plus.

5. *Accounting Rules*. A company that uses different accounting than its peers might want to emphasize that point. For

79

example, if industry peers recognize sales when a product is shipped, but your company recognizes sales only when payment is received, the distinction should be emphasized. However, if that approach doesn't provide benefits from either an operating basis or in the investor relations arena, it might be sensible to shift to the same accounting approach used by the rest of the industry. In most cases, *being more conservative than the rest of the industry provides no benefit, but being less conservative can be costly in terms of market support.* Similarly, a change in accounting rules, such as the shift in accounting for retiree healthcare benefits, can have a greater or lesser impact on a company than on its peers.

6. *Core Earnings.* For companies that are active in the acquisition arena or are continually restructuring, the focus on core earnings can yield real benefits. Core earnings are the earnings of the company's established continuing operations. *An example: One client with substantial investment in start-up operations began breaking out the total sales and operating income of mature businesses and the total sales and income or losses of the startups, highlighting the continuing growth and profitability of the core operations.*

7. *Normalized Earnings.* A company that is recognizing unusual charges or recovering from a difficult year might wish to present investors with a view of normalized earnings—how the numbers would look in a more normal year. Consider a firm that had just reduced staff by 200 people, absorbing $8 million in severance costs. In its releases, slide shows and other presentations, the company would almost certainly wish to note that, "Absent these charges, earnings would have been $XXX higher." Normalized earnings also can be used to demonstrate the difference between one economic period and another. "Hurricane Zelda destroyed the orange crop, leading to a 180% increase in our costs for concentrate. If more normal costs had prevailed, gross margin would have been X percent and earnings would have been $XX instead of $YY."

6-2   Quality of Earnings

While analysts focus first on the level of earnings for each company, financial analysis also covers the quality of those earnings. Earnings "quality" is defined loosely as the linkage between management's actions and the results achieved. Quality can be very subjective, with each investor drawing a different conclusion.

Consider the following situations and make your own assessment of earnings quality:

1. Widget Corporation of America dips into a LIFO layer on its way to reporting unusually high margins for 1994. Do the strong results represent quality earnings?

2. Widget Corporation has maintained an underperforming subsidiary for several years, asserting that a one-year rebound in the cyclical business would justify the investment. The rebound comes and 1994 ROE zooms to 28 percent. Is this long-term investment classified as quality?

3. In 1995, that cyclical business posts a loss again. Would the same analysts who discounted the unusually high 1994 results add back some imputed ROE for this unit?

4. A four-week labor dispute leads to lower sales for American Widgets, but margins improve due to labor concessions that end the lockout. Even though disruptions due to the strike lead to a loss, should the company get any credit for the quality of earnings going forward?

Quality can be a fuzzy issue, but the conceptual basis is clear enough. Predictability, strong linkage between intent and result, likelihood of repetition—all combine in the quality analysis.

Conversely, a company experiencing unusually strong results will also want to reference its normalized earnings level. If, for example, settlement of a lawsuit leads to a windfall gain, the company will want to explain that impact to avoid creating unrealistic expectations for future performance. (See 6-2, *Quality of Earnings.*)

8. *Security.* Any protection from competition, including patents, an established distribution network or a high cost of entry into the market, deserves analysis and inclusion in the investor relations arsenal.

9. *Time Bombs.* The IR executive should focus on risk factors as well, including pending lawsuits, environmental problems and other potential negatives. To the extent that these risks can be measured and explained, it is essential that the IR professional provide these insights.

10. *Corporate Culture.* This can include a focus on the number of years a company's top managers have worked together, the number of operating units, the efficiency of centralized operations and/or the entrepreneurial approach taken to decentralized operating units. Measurements can include the size of the corporate staff as a percentage of the total staff, number of key people promoted from within rather than hired from outside, etc. Insider ownership of shares, although not strictly a culture issue, does provide some measurement of management (and employee) commitment to the shareholder. Broad distribution of ownership among management and employees is a greater positive than heavy ownership by two or three insiders.

    A caveat: Corporate culture works for a relatively small number of companies. While every firm has a culture, few have cultures that measurably influence long-term performance in any positive way. Often, the CEO's view of the culture is less than reality-based as well. A solid culture story can be very effective; however, that culture must be reflected throughout the organization and not simply on a business plan. In short, the culture must truly be a source of progress or strength.

11. *Not Invented Here.* Some measurements can be adopted from other industries. For example, the same-store sales measurement used by many retailers can be utilized for a firm in the distribution business or a bank. New bank

branches might move through the same type of maturation cycle as shoe stores or hamburger stands, for example, leading to relatively predictable patterns of profitability.

SEGMENT ANALYSIS

Many companies operate in several different industries and the SEC requires that such firms review their results according to each line of business, or segment. As a rule, managements will jump through hoops to prove that their businesses are all tied to the same industry segment as a means of avoiding this requirement.

The primary motive behind this avoidance is competitive fear. Particularly for smaller companies with limited product lines, extensive disclosure can give a competitor valuable insights into the cost structure or margins for specific products. The added costs of accounting and tracking different segments also play a role in management's concern.

For the IR practitioner, however, segment analysis is a valuable tool for proving the investment story. For companies that do report on a segment basis, all of the financial analysis approaches just discussed can be applied effectively to each segment. In addition, for conglomerates and other multisegment firms, the IR director might wish to adopt more of a *portfolio management* approach to reporting.

In this approach, the company is presented as a portfolio manager that has invested (usually 100 percent) in several attractive businesses. The holding company is managing investments, each of which has specific appeals, and the combined appeal of all is greater than the sum of its parts.

Sometimes, a firm that is organized along the portfolio manager/holding company model will spin off one or more subsidiaries, at least in part, to gain increased value for its ownership position in the now-public subs.

7

ANALYZING THE STOCK

After reviewing the financial and operational aspects of the company itself, the IR focus moves to the "product line" offered to investors. This includes any equity or debt instruments that provide an opportunity to invest in the company.

COMMON STOCK

For most public companies, common stock is the only investment vehicle. Stock represents equity or ownership in the company and is the fundamental source of financing. Even though borrowings are an important source of funds for corporations, it is the core equity component that gives the company its start—and its underlying strength.

The analysis of stock begins with the security itself. The marketability of a company is influenced strongly by the structural characteristics of its shares, including the following.

1. **Shares Outstanding.** The first issue, of course, is how many shares are out there. A firm with relatively few shares outstanding, less than five million for example, will general-

ly be less attractive to large institutional investors than one with higher share numbers. The number of shares already outstanding is an important consideration both when developing an IR targeting effort (institutional, retail, global, etc.) and when contemplating new financing alternatives. For a company with a relatively small number of shares in the market, a stock offering might be preferable to a debt offering simply because of the benefits provided in terms of added market exposure, IR targeting options, trading liquidity, potential new support and so on.

2. **Float.** Often more important than the number of shares outstanding is the number of shares available for trading. Commonly referred to as float, the shares available for trading will be the difference between total shares and the number held by such non-trading holders as corporate insiders, Employee Stock Ownership Plans, various trusts and other long-term investors.

3. **Classes of Stock.** While most companies simply offer common stock, another type—preferred stock—is frequently encountered.

   Preferred stock has a higher priority claim to dividend payments and the assets of the company in any reorganization or liquidation. Preferred stock is essentially a hybrid of stock and bond. While preferred shares, unlike common shares, often have a set dividend (comparable to interest on a bond) and a priority claim to assets, the issuing company also has more flexibility regarding the payment of those dividends than would be the case with interest payments to lenders. Investors who purchase preferred shares often have different goals or investment parameters than those who buy common stocks. For example, reduced risk or higher current income (dividends) might be goals of the preferred-share buyer, while the common-stock investor often is more focused on capital appreciation.

   Preferred shares also come in a variety known as *convertible preferred,* which generally provides for conversion into common shares. This convertibility kicker can offer added returns to investors if common-share prices appreciate sharply.

A second major distinction, one that increased in importance during the takeover craze of the 1980s, is that between voting and non-voting shares of common stock. In this comparison, we also include voting and super-voting shares. Primarily as a takeover defense, or to preserve the voting majority of a founding family or other insider group, some companies have divided their shares into voting and non-voting classes, or a class that has one vote per share and another super-voting class with 10 or 100 votes per share. Whatever the case, the normal practice is that those holding stock as of a specific date can vote their shares. But if the stock is sold, the new buyer receives the other class of stock, identical in every way except that it has a lesser or no-voting privilege. In relatively few cases, voting shares can be sold and retain their voting privilege. The net effect of this dual class approach is that, over time, the founders, insiders or other long-term holders amass greater voting power and control over the corporation. Many major investors will refuse to invest in companies that have non-voting stock because they view the proxy (vote) as the doomsday mechanism needed to oust a poor management or maximize the value of their investment. Dual classes of stock can be a barrier to exchange listing, diminishing their appeal, as well.

Some firms will provide some added compensation for holders of non-voting stock, including higher dividends, as a means of increasing the appeal of these shares.

4. **Restricted Shares.** Some shares of stock may be restricted in a trading sense, such as stock owned by insiders, investment bankers or other affiliates during a period following a public offering. In some cases, the restrictions flow from SEC Rule 144, which describes the timing and number of share sales permitted under specific circumstances or from voluntary "lock-up agreements" between key holders and the

87

company, other investors, or other third parties. Although restricted shares are not a major issue for most companies, the IR executive should be aware of restrictions imposed by Rule 144 or any lock-up agreements—and the timetable for possible sales of such shares.

It is not uncommon for insiders to begin selling some stock once the restriction period expires and that can send an unwanted message to investors: management is bailing out of the stock. When restricted shares are about to become available for sale, an event usually tied to a public offering but also linked in some cases to acquisitions made for stock, the company can see its shares come under pressure from short-sellers. These individuals, anticipating that 144 holders will be unloading some stock soon, might sell into the market in advance of any "insider dumping."

5. **Exchange Listing.** Whether and where the stock is available for trading is an important issue, although its importance is declining. Historically, companies would issue shares in the over-the-counter (NASDAQ) market or, if large enough, on the American Stock Exchange and ultimately seek to move to the New York Stock Exchange. As the over-the-counter market increased its stature and capabilities over the years, many large firms simply opted not to switch to a traditional exchange. As a result, regional exchanges and independent operators began making inroads into the trading environment by making markets in shares traded by other exchanges or over-the-counter at a lower (narrower) bid-ask spread than available elsewhere.

For the IR executive, the issue of exchange listing is one of transaction costs and pricing volatility. It is in the issuing company's best interests to have a relatively narrow spread between the price paid by the ultimate buyer and the price received by the ultimate seller of shares. High transaction costs, as one might expect, limit the attractiveness of an investment. Likewise, the IR executive seeks venues with low volatility so pricing doesn't change with every order.

In addition to the structural characteristics of the stock, each company has its own market trading patterns. These include such fundamental matters as overall valuation, based on the company's financial strengths and growth prospects, and trading characteristics, which might reflect such factors as float or transaction costs. Here is a quick review of trading issues to be addressed:

1. **Liquidity.** How many shares must be traded in order to move the price of the stock one dollar? That's the classic definition of liquidity and it's as good as any. A liquid market is one in which buyers and sellers can get in and out without moving the price of the stock by a large amount. Clearly, companies with more shares in the float have the potential for more liquid markets than those with fewer shares. But the number of shares outstanding doesn't tell the whole story. Among the other key factors are:

   - *Average Trade.* If a stock is held mostly by institutions, the average size of a trade might be 10,000 shares instead of 300. A market that is liquid for small investors might not be conducive to the needs of institutions.

   - *Average Daily Volume.* A cyclical company might have less active trading than a high-growth technology stock, so the average number of shares available in a day can be higher or lower regardless of the number of shares outstanding.

   - *Consistency.* Does the stock trade infrequently in relatively large blocks or does it trade on a consistent basis with smaller average-order sizes? The more consistent or predictable the trading pattern is, the more liquid the stock.

   - *Traders.* A large volume of transactions can be spread across a wide range of locations, limiting the true liquidity in any one instance. For example, an over-the-counter stock might have 15 market-makers, each willing to take some part of a transaction. But none of the market-makers may be interested in taking a position large enough to handle any specific transaction. Most commonly, this is an argument cited by stock exchanges in their search for companies to list. With one market-maker, the exchange specialist, committed to buying and selling shares, the argument goes, liquidity will invariably improve. (It's also important to note that public orders must be handled first on an exchange, while market-makers can trade for their own accounts first in an over-the-counter environment.)

- *Costs.* The bid-asked spread, the difference between what the buyer pays and the seller receives, is both a cause and effect in the liquidity equation. An over-the-counter market-maker might set a high spread on a particular stock, believing it to be a relatively illiquid security and, therefore, riskier for the market-maker. Investors, in turn, might shy away from stocks with high transaction costs because these costs simply increase the hurdle rate of return for the investment, and that caution reduces liquidity further.

2. **Beta.** The beta is a derived, historical number that measures how much a general market price move has influenced the price of the specific stock. Stocks with betas greater than 1.00 tend to rise or fall more than the market, while those with a beta below 1.00 are less volatile than the market. The closer the beta is to 1.00, the more closely the stock price will move with the market. Because the beta is a product of so many other functions, addressing the beta directly as an issue is one of the least productive venues an IR professional can choose.

VALUATION ISSUES

The market is an amorphous combination of analysts, individuals, fund managers, investment publications, general economic circumstances, consumer sentiment, and happenstance. Although we generally refer to the market in the context of people trading stocks, it is difficult to imagine a definition broad enough to include all conceivable influences at work in establishing stock prices.

For purposes of simplicity, however, we'll focus here on the most common valuation tools utilized by investors. Generally, because the share of stock is the common denominator in investment decisions, valuation will focus on how much is being paid for the percentage of corporate value or returns inherent in a share of stock. The most commonly applied ratios are:

Price/Earnings. This refers to the price of a single share divided by earnings per share. The p/e ratio measures the relative cost of acquiring the earnings stream represented by each share of stock. p/e ratios usually are stated based on historical (trailing) results, but can also be calculated based on projected EPS. Companies expected to generate rapid increases in future EPS will tend to command higher p/e rations than firms with similar EPS levels but lesser growth prospects.

Price/Cash Flow per Share. Cash flow is a better indicator of performance than is earnings for many companies, such as those with no earnings, high depreciation and amortization levels, unusual tax credits or other circumstances. As noted previously, a company's cash flow can be far stronger or weaker than reported earnings, so the cash-flow ratio is a second measure of investment return.

Cash-flow analysis is a consistent tool, but it seems to go in and out of style among analysts, or at least among financial writers. On February 7, 1987, a *Wall Street Journal* headline read: "Stock Analysts Increase Focus on Cash Flow." Two years later, the July 24, 1989 issue of *Business Week* declared: "Earnings, Schmernings—Look at the Cash." Early in 1993, the focus shifted to cash flow again, this time to discounted cash flow as a measurement of return on investment.

In the discounted cash-flow example, valuation is determined in much the same way as for a debt security. Cash flow per share is translated as a cash stream justifying—at a stated discount rate—a specific share-price level.

Price/Book Value. Each share of stock represents a claim on a specific percentage of a company's equity or book value. In some industries, such as banking, it is quite common to focus on the relative market value of shares in relation to equity, rather than in relation to the earnings stream alone.

Price/Sales. Because sales are the initial driver of all investment returns, several analysts and fund managers look for companies with relatively low price/sales ratios.

Yield. Yield is the historic or projected return to shareholders of dividends as a percentage of share price. For companies paying a dividend, the payment of cash to shareholders represents a relatively certain return on investment, whereas stock price improvement is less of a sure thing. Of course, dividends can be increased or decreased, but the presence of a dividend tends to create a lower risk perception, all other things being equal.

In some circumstances, analysts will focus on the valuation of a company by a standard other than those commonly used. For instance, a firm might be measured at its breakup value, which is the sum of all parts if broken out and sold separately. A marginally profitable company might consist of one very successful subsidiary and a weak sister that is dragging down consolidated results. An investor might believe the successful subsidiary alone is worth more than the value assigned to the entire parent company and buy with the expectation that the weaker unit will be sold or closed.

Similarly, a company with a number of subsidiaries might find that few analysts want to follow all of its myriad industries. As a result, the company receives less aggregate investor interest and support than would be the case if its subsidiaries were traded individually. An investor might see a bargain here and invest with the hope that the company will spin off or sell some of its subsidiaries, enabling investors to realize the underlying value of the firm.

The valuation approach that is most appropriate for any given company can change over time and, as a matter of IR marketing strategy, it might be desirable to create pressure for such a change. At one time, break-up value can represent a much stronger pricing model than the earnings stream for a company.

Likewise, a company in a highly competitive market might be well served by increased focus on cash flow, rather than immediate earnings, to demonstrate that the company is generating adequate funds to ensure survival in tough times.

SHARE DISTRIBUTION

Adding to the complexity of the IR challenge is share distribution. Who owns the stock and why? Whatever the level of shares outstanding and the amount of float, the trading characteristics and valuation of the stock will be influenced strongly by the distribution of shares. Distribution is both geographic and demographic in nature, and the IR executive is always seeking ways to improve valuation by shifting distribution patterns.

In common discourse on shareholder interests, no distinction is made among shareholders, but the fact is that different shareholders may have competing interests. For example, an arbitrageur will have a substantially shorter investment return horizon than a person who holds shares in a 401(k) plan. When investor relations executives focus on the goals of shareholders, the usual emphasis is on long-term holders, people who expect to make the stock part of their retirement nest egg. This is probably an excessively long time line for the average investor, but it is usually appropriate from a planning perspective.

On the demographic side, shareholders can be described as experts and amateurs, long-term and short-term, and desirable and undesirable. (An undesirable shareholder might be an individual holding three shares received as an inheritance. Unless the person can be encouraged to invest more in the company, the costs of servicing this shareholder will outstrip any negative impact from the selloff of these holdings.) For our purposes, we'll divide our shareholders into three basic groups: insiders, institutions, and individuals (retail). Market makers, exchange specialists, trustees and other holders might technically be shareholders from time to time, but we'll ignore them here because we are focusing on the ultimate consumer of shares as an investment.

Insiders. Insiders include members of management or the board of directors, some high-level employees, members of the founding family who are still involved in company issues, and venture capitalists or investment bankers who have opted to retain an interest in the company post-offering. Although not all will be privy to inside information at any one time, they are considered insiders.

The IR executive hopes for a favorable balance of insider holdings, neither too high nor too low. If insiders hold more than half the shares, or (through a special voting class of stock) more than half the proxies, many investors will see the lack of corporate democracy as a negative. All too frequently, firms with very high levels of insider ownership are managed as if they were private companies for the benefit of insiders, with only limited attention paid to the needs of outside shareholders.

Too high a level of insider holdings also will tend to soak up the float that can add to liquidity and reduce transaction costs. High levels of insider holdings create a significant takeover defense, even for companies with relatively low market valuations and/or financial performance.

On the other hand, a low level of insider holdings tends to separate the goals of management from those of shareholders. Managers who own relatively little stock in the companies they manage might be more interested in near-term factors that can build immediate compensation than in activities that build shareholder value over time. Stock options are one way to encourage increased focus on the shareholders' interests, of course, but it is this author's opinion that there is absolutely no substitute for actually owning a substantial amount of shares.

What is the right level of insider holdings? As is commonly found in investor relations, there is no single correct answer. While insider holdings in general are measured when considering liquidity and other trading factors, the most critical type of insider ownership is that of active management and directors. Because these individuals make the decisions affecting shareholders most directly, it is their holdings that should receive the attention of investors.

Here, too, there is no magic number. In a company with 50 million shares outstanding, officers and directors might hold only 3 percent of the stock, while a 20-percent level might be more appropriate in a company with just five million shares. The number of shares held might reasonably be lower if compensation plans truly tie executive pay to long-term investment market valuations. Although nearly impossible in the real world, an optimum approach would be to link shares held to the net worth of top management. For example, one could make the case that 25 to 35 percent of the chief executive's net worth should be tied to the company's stock price. There's no reasonable way to track or enforce such a practice, but the logic of linking management and shareholder interests is clear.

Potentially the worst insider situation is a company under the control of one group but actively managed by another. In such a case, the managers might begin to serve only the major inside holders, maximizing their own short-term earnings in the process at the expense of other shareholders. Such abuses are rare, but they do occur.

While not legally classified as such, ownership by individual employees, retirees and their families is a form of insider holding. Although the situation would technically qualify as retail ownership, the relationship with the issuing company constitutes a special type of insider interest. Marketing shares to employees and others with a special connection to the company will be treated later.

Institutions. Institutional ownership covers a broad range of investment possibilities, from pension funds to mutual funds to private pools managed by individual investment advisers. Institutions are defined by the fact that they invest funds on behalf of someone else. Institutions own more than half the shares on the New York Stock Exchange and account for well over half of the trading volume in stocks every day. Institutional investors—either the fund managers themselves or the investment advisers they select to direct their portfolios—are widely courted because they control such large collections of funds.

At the same time, institutional ownership is a double-edged sword. As institutions begin buying up shares, they can soak up the float that previously made for trading liquidity. Institutions tend to move in concert, following the general trends of investment community sentiment, so a company can face dramatic price declines when several institutional investors decide to head for the door. In the past few years, they have become restive, and increasingly seek an active role in the direction their companies take. While this is touted as classic corporate democracy, many institutional investors seem to be taking a course of action closer to bullying.

Institutional activism is still in its infancy, so we are likely to see both an increase in activity and numerous excesses before the system adjusts to this new reality. Because so much money is invested via institutions—including some multi-billion-dollar pension funds for state employees and other retirees—the managers of these funds claim they cannot simply vote with their feet by dumping shares of underperforming companies. As a result, they say, their role must be to foment change leading to stronger corporate performance and ultimately to higher prices.

Fortunately for the IR professional, the investment marketplace is populated by thousands of institutional investors and investment advisers. In an effective strategy, institutions with the proper size and investment approach are targeted as long-term supporters.

One last point worth noting is that many of the largest institutions are index funds which simply invest in a market basket of stocks chosen to replicate overall market activity. IR marketing to many such funds is largely wasted effort. Purchases and sales reflect computer models rather than company fundamentals. However, in some instances, a company can work to be included in a specific stock index, leading in turn to increased demand from the funds that replicate that index. Although most indices are based on strict numerical criteria, a company could prove its case for inclusion ahead of other possible firms in some indices.

Keeping on good terms with major index funds also can provide benefits in proxy contests. Although this is largely defensive, it is certainly an action to be considered by any firm with substantial institutional ownership.

With index funds, particularly, it is essential to track all databases for errors. A company can be dropped from an index, or have its share level reduced among index funds, based on numbers picked up and reported inaccurately by various reporting services.

Individuals. The class of individual or retail investors includes both individuals and investment clubs and could be interpreted to include some portfolio managers who handle limited amounts of investment dollars. One could claim all portfolio managers are institutional investors, were it not that the smallest of funds tend to have characteristics more similar to those of an individual.

Individual investors have lost much of their clout on Wall Street in the past decade. Their share of total trading volume and share holdings has declined relative to that of institutions. Their role in the takeovers and restructurings of the 1980s was relatively muted, reducing their profile and—for corporate boards—their perceived power. In addition, many individual investors now choose to buy mutual funds rather than individual stocks, placing the ultimate stock selection decision with an institution.

As a result, many chief executives believe that institutions are the key for IR marketing—creating an opportunity for the insightful executive willing to pursue individuals. We're often asked by clients if there are enough retail investors left in the market to make a difference. The consistent answer is "yes." While there aren't enough retail investors to own every share of every company, there are certainly enough to add several p/e ratio points to any individual stock.

Individual investors tend to have stronger loyalty, holding shares longer on average than institutional investors. But it's generally a bad idea to overgeneralize about such things. Some institutional investors focus on long-term holdings, just as many individuals focus more on trading stocks than holding them.

97

GEOGRAPHIC DISTRIBUTION

Share distribution can also be classified according to geography. Although most stocks ultimately have national or international distribution among shareholders, it is common for some factor to lead to pockets of local concentration.

Such a pocket could include a large concentration of retired employees who participated in a stock purchase plan or the customers of a regional brokerage firm that acted as an investment banker. In some cases, the presence of many companies in an allied field in one region can lead to purchases of stock in many competing companies in that area.

Whatever the reasons, geographic distribution is an ongoing point of interest to the IR strategist. Finding the reasons for a particular concentration can lead to new opportunities to expand holdings in a similarly situated region. Likewise, finding areas where the company is unknown offers opportunity for new penetration.

Geographic distribution studies commonly focus on the question of international investor contact. With all the talk of global securities markets, it is tempting to look to the world at large as a beckoning source of investment dollars. For all but the largest or other specially situated firms, the U.S. market provides as much opportunity as is needed, with minimal complications.

However, a global IR approach can be utilized effectively by those companies willing to make the investment of dollars and management time.

COMPETITIVE ISSUES

Whatever the valuation method used by investors, each company is just one of thousands of investment vehicles available at any time. This means the investor relations executive must focus not only on her own company but also on competing investments. It's not enough to prove that Widgets of America is a good investment. The effective IR executive also has to be ready to explain why it's a better investment than U.S. Widgets, Widgets of North America and Widgets 'R Us.

Internal Competition. Equally significant, the public company with multiple classes of stock or other investment vehicles might end up competing with itself in drawing some investors. A company with both common and preferred stock, for example, needs to focus not only on which investors to pursue, but also on which security to offer as the right investment vehicle for each target. Some companies, in an initial public offering, will sell units rather than straight stock. The units usually include both a share of common stock and some number of warrants to buy further shares at a specified price during a specified period. In the mid-1980s, we struggled to build liquidity for clients whose stocks competed with both units and warrants in the post-IPO market. Ultimately, warrants were exercised or repurchased by the company, leaving common stock as the only vehicle for investment. But while the units and warrants were being traded, the companies' trading liquidity suffered.

Likewise, the listing of options on a company's stock can lead investors to focus more on the option than on the underlying shares. In the best of cases, options reduce risk for institutions and other holders by enabling these investors to lock in gains (premiums) through options strategies.

Commercial Competitors. Once any internal competitive issues are addressed, the IR challenge moves to industry peers. Certainly, investors focused on a particular industry will choose among firms within that industry. To market a specific company effectively, the IR executive will study both the financial performance and the market trading characteristics of competitors.

In this peer-group analysis, the IR executive is seeking some edge, some incremental benefit that accrues to his company. That edge could be a higher return on equity, stronger cash flow per share, increasing market share or lower cost of labor. Efficiency should be a key area of focus. Does the company achieve the same return on equity with lower leverage (risk) than its peers? Is cash flow stronger at the same sales level? Are receivables collected faster or inventories turned more quickly?

99

On the stock-trading side, the IR executive could focus on a relatively lower valuation, indicating upside potential as the relative valuation gap disappears, or perhaps on the lower bid-asked spreads for the company's shares.

Investment Peers. In addition to industry peers, each company has dozens or hundreds of investment peers. These are companies similar to it in size, growth rate or other respects that appeal to specific investors.

For example, some investors prefer companies in a turnaround to high-fliers, and some look for investments that have a relatively low price/earnings ratio or high cash flow per share. Others look for investments in a particular price range or with a particular market capitalization (price/share × total shares outstanding) minimum or ceiling.

While industry peers represent the most obvious group for comparison, investment-peer analysis helps to identify a much broader and deeper pool of potential investment dollars.

SUMMARY

In the past several chapters we have reviewed basic means of analyzing the company and its investment characteristics. From the number of employees with 10 years' experience to the level of cash flow and percentage of insider holdings, every facet that defines the corporation can provide potential ammunition for an investor marketing effort.

Thus, the investor relations professional is more likely to face a challenge of excess options than limited possibilities when crafting the marketing plan. At first glance, it would seem the list of possible strengths and marketing edges is too great to allow for significant trimming. However, such trimming is essential.

For example, many competitive advantages identified for any one company will ultimately prove to be of little importance in the minds of targeted investors. Relatively few will be seen as strengths unique to the issuing company and hold a cause-and-effect relationship with either stock price or financial performance. (Advantages that are interesting but not necessarily of investment merit can be highlighted in media relations efforts or annual reports and other communications, so they are not without value. Those used in the investor marketing effort, however, must be linked to stronger results and, ultimately, potential investment returns.)

In addition, investors will focus on only a few points at a time. Although the most thorough analyst will become familiar with dozens of key strengths, the simple fact is that the stock will sell on the basis of a relatively limited but compelling story. A broker might tell a client to buy a stock because it looks like earnings will rise 25 percent per year for the next five years, without explaining all the market-share and technology data that support that outlook. Or, having explained the reason for the earnings outlook, the broker might not focus as well on the corporate culture or the level of cash flow per share.

No matter. The point is to amass enough ammunition to make a bulletproof case for a company's stock. Understanding the lay of the land is just the first step in that effort.

8

ANALYZING THE
CORPORATE CULTURE

Having studied a handful of the financial and structural issues that drive the investor marketing program, we'll now examine the extent to which corporate culture can be measured and used to attract investors. To complete the picture, we'll also look at ways in which the corporate culture can work against IR effectiveness and credibility.

First, let's clarify our terms. Sociologists define culture in a context of socially transmitted patterns of behavior, artistic expression, human interaction, and so on. In the corporate sphere, culture is created or influenced through both formal and informal direction, including company policy and the office grapevine.

Corporate culture almost invariably flows from the top down. The direction and messages come from corporate management and are transmitted and filtered on their way through the organization. Even among those firms that encourage great autonomy at the lowest levels of the organization, that autonomy is achieved with the direction or acquiescence of senior management.

Two words in the preceding paragraph should have sounded an alarm in the minds of readers. The first is *filtered* and the second is *acquiescence.* Both represent a painful reality for managements that intend to lead their firms effectively.

All messages are filtered in some way as they travel from sender to receiver. Even in one-on-one conversation, the speaker's words might not represent what the speaker means, and the listener might interpret the words to mean something other than the speaker intends or the words indicate. Each party also brings preconceived notions to the conversation, including views on how the other person will respond, what the hidden agenda might be, who else might be involved in the equation, and so on.

If this is true of a single conversation, it is most certainly the case in a large organization. Each memo, employee newsletter or staff meeting is followed by an examination of tea leaves and play of tarot cards. "Sure he said that," the conversation at the water cooler goes, "but that's only because he wants us to. . . ."

Interestingly enough, the people at the water cooler understand one another far more clearly than they do the official speaker. As peers, they are likely to share the same perceptions and filter the boss's message in roughly the same way. Their understanding reflects the true corporate culture as *filtered* through the layers of staff.

Our next troubling word, *acquiescence,* points to a key reason why management's view of the same culture often differs from the post-filtration reality. Quite frequently, management will call for one policy and then acquiesce to a variety of non-conforming practices. Because people learn best by example, it is not the policy but the practices that inform the culture. Thus, a company can aggressively advertise its commitment to customers. Its written guarantees and employee handbooks can be as customer-focused as humanly possible. But if employees see managers waffling on customer complaints or trying to dodge responsibility when problems develop, the impact is total negation of the stated policy.

For the investor relations executive, corporate culture is both a tool and a trap. To figure out which is which, it's important to identify three key points.

1. What are management's views of the culture?
2. Do employee actions reflect the same viewpoints?
3. Does the culture have a significant impact on the company's success?

A negative answer to question two eliminates culture as an IR tool for the vast majority of companies. All too frequently, the messages top management believes it is sending are filtered and corrupted along the way from policy to practice. As a result, the CEO might believe a collegial atmosphere of give and take exists, when in fact the middle managers are enforcing a more militaristic structure.

It doesn't take much variance between intended and actual culture to invalidate its use as an IR marketing tool. Culture is difficult to prove and sell, and a relatively small number of investors will increase their valuation of a company based on a favorable culture. These are very attractive investors because they constitute a core group of "true believers" who are likely to hold their shares in good times and bad. But they also need significant evidence to become "defenders of the faith" and that means the culture must be consistent and pervasive.

The last question on culture concerns its impact on the company's success. We can define success very broadly here, using such factors as lower employee turnover, greater customer retention levels, and so on. But whatever the benefit, it must be a demonstrable result of the culture. (See 8-1, *Measuring the Culture.*)

If the culture is one of lifetime employment and career-building, the average length of employee tenure might be a key measurement. Likewise, it might be beneficial to indicate how many years top managers have invested in the company or the entry-level positions in which they started. If the focus is on decentralized management, the average size of operating units or the relative size of the corporate or divisional headquarters might be important.

Whatever the measurement, the cause-and-effect factor is vital. Without it, the investor relations effort will be less effective because the audience is being directed to focus on factors that are irrelevant to the company's true investment story.

In times of corporate trauma, such as restructuring or other reversals, culture can be cited as a defensive mechanism. The culture linking employees to one another and the company becomes a fundamental force for the firm's recovery.

Playing the culture card in difficult times requires some previous discussion of the culture as a source of strength. A company that has never mentioned this investment merit will seem to

---

8-1 Measuring the Culture

Every company has a culture, but few can prove that it provides a benefit to investors. Measurement requires only a handful of common-sense questions.

1. If the company's culture is allegedly based on internal innovation, how many senior officers have been promoted from within? How many patents or new ventures have been created by employees with the company five years or more? Ten years or more?

2. If the culture is supposedly one of collegiality, how common is it for individuals to transfer among the various subsidiaries or between departments within an operating unit?

3. For the top three investment appeals in the marketing arsenal, can a cause-and-effect relationship be shown between the claimed culture and the investment strength? (For example, can a company with high sales growth demonstrate linkage between the sales increases and cultural characteristics?)

4. Do the company's numbers (turnover, patents, management tenure with company and executive/staff ratios) differ from commercial competitors in any way that reflects the culture?

Answers to questions like these will eliminate corporate culture as a discussion point for most IR programs, enabling the IR executive to focus on more fertile opportunities.

---

be groping if the subject is first raised during a restructuring. Credibility flows from citing effective culture, in perspective, on a consistent basis during favorable periods.

This analysis makes corporate culture a dead end for all but a handful of public companies. Culture is difficult to isolate as an investment merit, difficult to demonstrate as a *source of financial strength,* difficult to sell to most investors, and difficult to describe.

From an IR marketing standpoint, corporate culture should rank no higher than fourth on the list of investment merits. Strengths like low turnover or internal innovation that flow from the culture can rank higher, but the culture itself should not be a lead appeal.

9

CHECKING OUT THE COMPETITION

Every company competes against every other company for investor dollars, and firms with multiple classes of stock or both debt and equity issues can run into internal competition when it comes to the specific security to be marketed to an individual target.

A thorough competitive analysis can help the IR executive focus more effectively on targets to pursue and tools to use. Because the investment market is far larger than any single firm's capital requirements, and because the tools available for marketing a company are so varied, the potential approaches and targets are essentially limitless. The investor relations job is one of continual refinement—selecting and discarding options until the matchmaking singles out those opportunities with the highest potential.

Simultaneously, refinement helps identify the investors most likely to become substantial long-term supporters, the messages most likely to convert those potential investors into shareholders, and the right channels to reach them and convince them to act.

For a company with multiple classes of securities, the marketing effort should include both an umbrella set of messages for all investor audiences and specific marketing approaches for each individual security. For example, buyers of preferred shares tend to differ from buyers of common stock in that they place greater emphasis on current income (dividends) and safety.

INDUSTRY PEERS

Commercial competitors provide a valuable source of leads for any investor relations effort. Just as consumer products companies seek to identify owners of competitors' products and convert them at repurchase time, a publicly held company can target owners of competing firms as potential investors.

The comparisons with product competition are intuitively obvious, but critical distinctions limit the value of detailed comparison between IR marketing and product marketing. Products, from cars to corn flakes, tend to be purchased sequentially. In other words, a consumer usually doesn't buy a new car until the old one is gone or ready for trade-in. But an investor does not necessarily sell one security prior to buying another. The mix of subjective and objective issues related to consumer product purchases is far different from that of investment vehicles.

Still, competition in the commercial marketplace can offer substantial opportunity in the investment arena. Investors who own competing companies already have indicated some belief that the commercial market offers growth potential. They have indicated confidence that companies in the specific industry can grow profitably. (See 9-1, *Finding Industry Investors.*)

It is the IR marketer's challenge to convince the holder of a competing company's stock that his company is a superior investment. Doing so requires an analysis of competitors similar to the internal analysis described in previous chapters. It also requires a refinement of the message to create a compelling argument for superiority, as well as a thorough analysis of the reasons why the investor bought the competitor's stock in the first place.

Commercial peers, after all, are not always investment peers. The fact that a small consumer electronics firm competes with a

---

9-1   Finding Industry Investors

Investors in competitors can be identified through a relatively straightforward series of steps.

1. Review the 13F filings of institutions owning shares of commercial competitors. These quarterly filings are required for institutions managing more than $100 million in assets.

2. Conduct a media clippings search, using a clipping service or database, to find articles on competitors and comments from investment professionals claiming expertise on the competitor companies.

3. Search databases and industry guides for analysts who have earnings estimates on competitors.

Focus on industry investors, while simple, can backfire for the IR executive. In some instances, analysts and others welcome the opportunity to check on one company's progress, but only to increase their ability to track the other firms they are supporting. In not-so-extreme situations, information provided to a key follower of another company will be repeated to that competitor as a means of checking the competitor's own claims.

---

division of a global telecommunications giant doesn't make them competitors from an investor viewpoint. And while a manufacturer completing a financial restructuring competes with one that has remained consistently profitable for decades, their investment appeals may be vastly different.

Those differences can create opportunity or irrelevance. A small biotech company competing with an industry giant might be positioned as a pure play for investors who bought the larger company as an investment in an emerging area of research. An underperforming firm in a growing industry can be positioned as a relatively inexpensive means of entry into this investment market, with higher upside potential if the company can put its house in order.

In the case of financial analysts, adding a commercial competitor to the research universe is a way to leverage the analyst's time. For example, the same industry data and economic trends will influence both competitors, and the analyst might benefit professionally from being recognized as an expert on a specific industry. Thus, analysts who already focus on a specific industry are primary targets for the IR effort.

Likewise, funds that focus on the same industry, or own several competing companies, are evidencing a belief in spreading their bets to profit from industry trends. Here, too, the IR executive can achieve significant progress with a well-crafted message.

On the negative side, the investor who owns a competitor might believe her portfolio is appropriately weighted in the industry and might not want to commit a greater share of her holdings to the sector. In such a case, the IR executive must either convince the investor that greater weighting is appropriate or that one stock should be sold to buy another.

INVESTMENT PEERS

As a result, the search for market support cannot be limited to holders of competitors' shares. The small firm competing with a global entity might have too small a float level to attract the kind of investors who like industry giants. The only company in an industry to pay a dividend can appeal to investors who look for current income, while a firm with undervalued assets can appeal to those who focus on breakup value.

For several reasons, investment peers provide far greater opportunities than industry peers and should always be part of the targeting equation. First, it is impossible to imagine a company that doesn't have more investment peers than industry peers. This means the universe of potential shareholders is far larger when the focus is on investment parameters. Second, while a company might compete in only one industry, its investment merits might make it attractive to several types of investors. Third, investors who focus on similar types of investments are

9-2 Finding Peer Investors

The search for peer investors begins with the selection of key investment merits. Once the IR executive has determined the appeals forming the basis for investor marketing, the search focuses on investors who respond to those appeals.

1. Create a screen of public companies, focusing on the combination of investment appeals. In most instances, several peer companies can be identified with close match-ups on all, or nearly all, investment merits.

2. Conduct the same type of research used to find industry investors, including 13F filings, analyst reports and news articles.

3. Set targeting priorities. An investor owning several investment peers is most likely following an investment selection process favorable to your company. Those investors who own the most investment peers should constitute the "A List" for targeting purposes.

4. Make the connection. When contacting the A List of investors, note their investment in companies A, B, C, etc., and suggest a pattern indicating potential interest in your own firm.

5. Test your assumptions. If none of the A List investors respond to your company, reconsider your investment appeals. Fundamental assumptions regarding investment merits could be incorrect, leading your marketing effort in the wrong direction.

less likely to see their portfolios as fully invested in the company's industry. (See 9-2, *Finding Peer Investors.*)

Investors can be divided and subdivided into dozens of groups, but here are some of the primary types of approaches and parameters that can be identified.

Growth   Companies or industries that offer high growth in sales and/or earnings appeal to specific investors. Such companies tend to sell at high relative valuations (price/sales, price/earnings, price/book) due to the fact that they are expected to provide a more rapidly increasing stream of revenues or profit and, consequently, stock price appreciation. In the 1970s and 1980s, growth companies were those offering sales gains that averaged 15 to 20 percent per year. With lower inflation during the past several years, a growth company might be one with 10 to 15 percent increases, if those increases are likely to be continued for a large number of years. High-technology companies usually are viewed as growth plays.

Value   In what is usually the opposite of a growth play, companies that are bought on a value basis tend to be those that have underperformed financially or are otherwise out of favor. A value play is one in which the price is at a relatively low level when compared with assets, equity, cash flow or earnings. Turnarounds often fall into this category, as do stocks in cyclical industries when those industries are out of favor in the market.

Income   Investors who focus on income want greater assurance of a return on their investment, and the presence of a dividend provides some of that assurance. Income investors generally focus on companies that pay relatively high dividends, so the simple fact that a company has a dividend doesn't make it a natural; however, the greater assurance that investors will receive a cash return can be a marketing edge when addressing other investors.

Turnaround   A company in a financial recovery, or expected to begin one, can offer substantial opportunity for investors. Turnaround companies often have some appeal as value plays, although the earnings growth story is the closer model. Turnarounds often are unattractive to growth investors, even if earnings growth is likely to be very high, because the track record of performance is spotty.

In addition to the type of play the company represents, the investor will focus on other parameters, including size of company and trading liquidity. Some investors focus only on the largest firms, while others look for undiscovered smaller companies. Some investors seek only companies with solid track records for return on equity or net margin, while others are willing to look at speculative issues.

Likewise, the peer analysis will focus on both financial and securities performance. It is the combination of these factors— financial trends, stock valuation, liquidity and so on—that makes for effective investor marketing.

For the IR executive, the matchmaking process requires hardheaded analysis of investment peers and a realistic assessment of which peers (or investors in peer companies) are the most deserving of further attention.

10

AUDIENCE PERCEPTIONS

After completing all the internal analysis and comparing the company with peers of all types, the investor relations executive still isn't quite ready to develop and implement a strategy for marketing the company. Before the plan can be created and launched, it's essential to measure existing attitudes about the company and its peers.

The IR executive is armed with details and insights about the competitive strengths of the company, the culture, and the outlook for sales and earnings. She now understands the compelling competitive reasons for buying her company's shares and exactly who should buy the stock.

But is anyone listening? Worse, will anyone be willing to accept the story as she wants to tell it? Further research is needed to test the investment thesis. As discussed in Chapter 9, the IR executive must present the core message to targeted investors, selectively at first, to prove the point.

Audience analysis includes several targeted groups, ranging from existing shareholders to third-level investor targets to news reporters to commercial lenders. The opinions of each audience create the foundation or identify obstacles in the marketing effort.

10-1   Why Shareholders Might Not Know You

Current shareholders are the logical first choice for testing an investment message. These are, after all, the people who proved their interest by putting up investment dollars. The appeals that drove their interest, by extension, should be presented to other like-minded investors.

However, study of current investors is far from foolproof. As a group, they might provide fewer insights than a sample of investors who focus on industry competitors or investment peers. Among the sources of this dissonance are:

1. **Inherited Shares.** Whether the holder is an individual or an institution, the person responsible for the shares today might not be the person who made the purchase decision. Such an individual might hold the stock simply because no sell decision has been made.

2. **Limited Insight.** Even for investors who made the buying decision, the purchase could have been based on erroneous or limited information. For example, a person who buys a multidivisional company based on its retail operations might also be one who would have invested more heavily, or not at all, given a true understanding of the industrial divisions prior to purchase.

3. **Changing Circumstance.** The company's new investment message might relate to changing opportunities unknown to current holders. Even for holders unencumbered by the limited insight described above, the value of history-based viewpoints can be minimal.

4. **New Blood.** The search for new investors might be the key to IR marketing and new investors can translate into a different type of buyer. Firms with heavy retail ownership, for example, might seek to increase institutional following, but the hot buttons for institutional buyers can vary from those influencing individual investors.

Keeping current holders happy is an important goal for the IR marketing program and shareholder views should be sought on a regular basis. Still, existing holders offer only part of the insight needed to market shares effectively.

Current shareholders are the first stop in this research. Why did these people buy the stock? What characteristics did they ascribe to the company and do they believe those characteristics still apply? Do they own other stocks and do those fit the industry or investment peer group that the IR executive has identified as offering the greatest potential?

Where did current shareholders learn about the company and what means do they use to keep track of it now? Are they considering selling the stock or buying more—and why?

Clearly, the study of existing holders provides an immediate opportunity to determine which messages are being received and which are being acted upon in the investment community. It enables the IR executive to focus on changes in the type of investor who is attracted to the firm. Is the company becoming more of an institutional stock, more retail, or more of a value play? Are investors relying on industry trends as their guide or on outdated notions of how the company works?

Do they know how the company compares with its competitors or the relative valuation of the shares when compared to investment peers? Do they have a particular goal for price appreciation or a timetable for selling the stock—or buying more? (See 10-1, *Why Shareholders Might Not Know You.*)

Just as the corporate culture analysis seeks to determine whether messages sent are being received intact, the analysis of current shareholders focuses on the messages received and acted upon by the investor audience.

Primary investment community targets are the next group to study. Having identified those investors who own the stock of commercial competitors or investment peers, the IR executive then seeks to gain insights into the views held by these targets.

With these prospects, the IR executive should make some distinction based on industry knowledge. Those who have invested in commercial competitors might be expected to know more about the IR executive's company than those whose investments are defined by stock market characteristics.

117

10-2   How To Ask Questions

Investor surveys should begin with the general and move toward the specific. Questions should be designed to create an information tree, a pathway of sorts through the investment decision process. The first question "Do you still own the stock?" leads to one or two second questions: "Why did you sell?" or "Do you have plans to change your level of ownership?" An information tree would look much like the figure below.

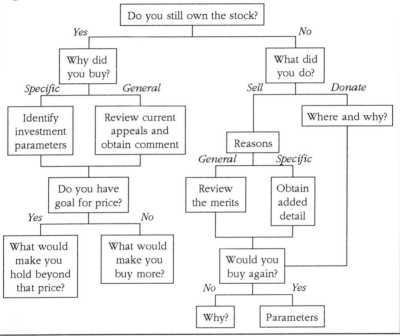

Again, the search is for messages received. Do the investors know the company? Have they even heard its name? Do they have an opinion of the firm and its investment merits, and does that opinion match the reality the IR executive has identified? (See 10-2, *How to Ask Questions.*)

The audience analysis should also include members of the news media whose assessment of the company and its management can play a key role in the perceptions of the company by other audiences. Reporters, who love to do surveys and hate to work on a "not for attribution" basis, will tend to resist participating in such interviews and often will demand that they and their views not be identified to management. That makes the survey process a bit more difficult, but the study is necessary nonetheless.

As with investors, the review of viewpoints should include several types of reporters, including those who cover a particular news beat (industry) for a business or trade magazine, those assigned to cover the company by newspapers or broadcast outlets in the headquarters city or near a major plant, and those who cover key industry peers in other cities.

Reporters who cover a commercial competitor in another city can be important opinion leaders on the IR executive's firm. Quite often, these reporters get their insights from the competitor's management and those assessments end up in print.

Employees are another important group of opinion leaders, at least locally, as are vendors and customers, local officials in cities where the company has facilities, bankers and others. While each of these groups is less critical (in most cases) as an audience to be studied, the IR executive should be alert to significant differences between the messages the company wants to send and the views held by these groups.

Divergent views can present a trap for the IR effort. Analysts following the company and reporters doing interviews often will ask questions of distributors, employees, vendors, customers and others with commercial insights into the company's affairs. An analyst covering Company X might also follow its largest customer, Company Y. In the course of discussions with Company Y, the analyst is likely to ask whether Company X is fulfilling its role and whether orders are likely to stay at historic levels. Likewise, assertions regarding competitors can be checked out by analysts or reporters.

Several grains of salt should be kept on hand for this audience survey effort. Quite often, the people who know the least about the company will have the strongest opinions, or the per-

119

son with the least potential to help the stock will also be the one most available for comment. Investment analysts and reporters who are trained and paid to communicate ideas are likely to be more articulate than other respondents, leading to an over-weighting of their views. The group studied might or might not be large enough and the questions specific enough to lead to valid conclusions.

Moreover, the result of the study might be inconclusive. Messages sent might be received intact, but not generate excitement either way. Those who don't know the company might not provide valuable insight into how to market the stock to them. The difference between those who like the culture and those who don't might not be meaningful. (See 10-3, *Sources of Error.*)

In advance of a forceful and clearly defined marketing effort, it shouldn't be surprising to find that the targeted audiences have only a vague perception of the company and its investment merits. In fact, an undefined image can be a strength, particularly when compared with audience perceptions that are strongly held, but just plain wrong.

Ultimately, the IR executive faces a critical decision point. Should resources be expended to change perceptions or should an entirely new audience be pursued? The decision is complex, but basic guidelines should apply.

Inaccurate Perception   An inaccurate perception could be more or less favorable than the facts would demonstrate, and the audience might be open to education. Inaccurate perceptions usually can be corrected with minimal investment of resources.

Accurate Perceptions   Accurate but undesired perceptions present a different problem. A company with a history of internal management strife, for example, might accurately be perceived as unstable. In such a case, efforts to sell a new and improved corporation to existing audiences could fall on deaf ears. The company's history might be a less significant issue for a newer audience.

10-3   Sources of Error

IR executives should always be alert to the potential for survey error. Such sources can include any or all of the following.

1. *Self-Fulfilling Prophecy.* A company that pays no dividend is likely to find that its existing holders are not income investors. While the company might be the only firm in its industry group that doesn't pay a dividend, and its appeal might be much greater if dividends were initiated, the survey of holders probably won't reveal that point.

2. *Forced Answers.* Investment professionals hate to seem uninformed, so a direct question can generate an answer based on zero knowledge or thought. Particularly dangerous are questions along the lines of "Why haven't you bought the stock?" A question like that almost never brings a response like "I don't know" or "I'm too lazy to look into it." Instead, the respondent will feel compelled to think up an answer, valid or otherwise.

3. *Topics du Jour.* A major public policy issue, such as the latest Tax Simplification Act or environmental regulation, can be front of mind with many respondents when the survey is done. Because of this, survey responses can be overweighted toward these near-term issues.

4. *Audience Differentiation.* Each company has a relatively small cadre of articulate and close followers, a larger group of less-informed supporters and a very large base of potential investors. Formulation of questions and tabulation of the answers must take these differentiation points into account. Differences of perception among these groups can be critical to the IR marketing effort.

Inappropriate Investors   The existing audience might be responding to a story other than that being pressed by management. The firm might have attracted short-term investors who add to volatility in pricing and volume, for example, and the IR effort might be directed toward long-term holders. Or a high-growth stock might have drawn buyers who

121

will accept nothing less than 40-percent growth rates, giving farsighted management the incentive to pursue people willing to settle for 25 to 35 percent growth instead.

However the audience is chosen, the study of perceptions should always have both specific and general goals. Each survey should lead to a decision point and a choice among several options. For example, a study of existing holders might fill two needs: to predict the likely reaction among shareholders to several potential board actions and to identify information gaps that need to be closed.

From a resource allocation point of view, audience perception studies help the IR executive establish or reorder priorities for targeting efforts and investment merits. This critical research early in the marketing program can help avoid misdirected application of a limited budget.

11

SETTING GOALS AND BUDGETS

One of the most difficult aspects of the investor relations practice is the establishment of goals and measurement of progress toward their achievement. IR goals are, by their nature, both multiple and moving targets. Like valuation, they tend to be relative, such as a goal of trading at a price/earnings ratio higher than industry peers.

Goals also must be set within the substantial constraints of budgets and schedules. Some targets can be hit more quickly by spending more money on the IR program. In other cases, time is such a critical ingredient that spending more won't yield more rapid results.

For the IR executive, matching goals with budgets is just one of the dozens of balancing acts that make the job a continual challenge.

BASIC GOALS

The fundamental goals of virtually every investor relations program should be similar because the marketing of the company as an investment offers a number of basic benefits. A stronger relative valuation for the company's shares provides:

1. **A Lower Cost of Capital.** Just as lower labor costs or lower scrap rates are a competitive advantage, so is a reduced cost of capital relative to competitors. A high stock price translates into added fundraising capacity in a secondary offering.

2. **Compensation Currency.** A strong reception for the company's common stock in the investment community makes stock options an attractive form of executive compensation, enabling the corporation to attract top talent with less drain on cash and to structure compensation packages that ally executives' financial interests with those of other shareholders.

3. **Acquisition Currency.** A strong stock valuation provides an attractive non-cash currency for acquisitions, and limits the degree of potential dilution in any merger in which stock is swapped.

4. **Takeover Protection.** A high stock price is absolutely the best defense against an unwanted suitor. Corporations can put in staggered boards or poison pills or set up systems to include local impact or employee security in any analysis of a buyout offer. But the fact is that every board must negotiate in good faith with potential buyers or run the risk of expensive shareholder suits. A high stock valuation raises the minimum ante for any would-be suitor.

5. **Higher Profile.** This isn't a financial benefit, but it's no less real. A higher stock price leads to or flows from stronger recognition and acclaim in the public markets. Stronger investor support has ancillary benefits when employees are recruited, bankers are interviewed and customers are pursued. To the extent that people are attracted to winners, a high share price can provide benefits ranging from stronger employee morale to more attentive bankers.

6. **Shareholder Wealth.** "Shareholder value" became a mantra of sorts in the late 1980s and early 1990s, as the takeover/leverage craze died down and corporate manage-

ments began focusing more aggressively on the need to keep shareholders happy. In fact, nothing makes shareholders happier than a profitable investment.

RELATIVITY

Clearly, the benefits just cited make a higher relative valuation of the company's shares the single most important goal of an investor relations effort. But *relative* improvements must be defined clearly. In our own firm, we frequently cite a goal of achieving the *highest sustainable price/earnings ratio* for our clients—a constantly moving target. (We emphasize "sustainable" levels because near-term spikes or troughs do not reflect the success or failure of an IR effort.)

One reason the price/earnings target moves is that the market itself is moving. When the S&P 500 sells at an average trailing p/e multiple of 30, an individual firm shouldn't celebrate its p/e of 18, all other things being equal. On the other hand, that 18 p/e ratio might be quite respectable when industry peers are selling at an average price/earnings ratio of 14.

Likewise, a price/earnings ratio of 18 might be less than our goal, even if competitors are selling at 14, if it turns out that our client's earnings are rising rapidly and competitor earnings are falling.

The valuation of each company moves relative to its own corporate performance, relative to the market, relative to industry and investment peers, and relative to near-term imbalances in the number of buyers and sellers. Always, we seek to increase the supply/demand imbalance in favor of demand.

INTERMEDIATE GOALS

The long term is not only a moving target, but also one that is never reached. The horizon is continually moving back at exactly the same speed at which we approach it. For the IR director, fine-tuning of targets and strategies is a constant process, and progress is measured most readily against intermediate goals. Such goals might include some of the following.

Ownership Mix   A company with little institutional ownership and relatively high liquidity might seek to raise its institutional ownership mix to a higher percentage, as a means of soaking up some of the supply of outstanding shares and raising the long-term profile of the company. *In the reverse situation, we have worked with a number of firms to reduce their institutional ownership percentages, moving more shares into retail hands and raising the companies' relative valuations in the process.* Changes in the mix don't have to be focused solely on a shift from institutions to retail or vice versa. In some cases, we focus on increasing distribution within a category, such as by spreading ownership among a larger number of institutions, with fewer average shares held by each.

Geographic   Shares can be concentrated too much within
Distribution   one region of the country, leading to limited supplies of potential new supporters when other shareholders are ready to sell. *A special example of this situation applies in the Minneapolis/St. Paul market. With several strong brokerage firms in the region, many public companies work with each regional firm in turn, until essentially anyone who is ever going to own the stock already owns it or has owned it, and essentially all the brokers who are going to work the stock have already done so. In a condition I refer to as "Twin Cities Syndrome," these public companies end up with limited new investor interest and little excitement among local brokers.* Moving out-

side of a specific geographic region can provide a significant benefit in terms of new blood and upward price movement.

Valuation

While the highest sustainable valuation is a continually moving target, goals can be established and reached on an intermediate basis. For example, a company that is performing at about the average level for its industry can set a goal of matching industry price/earnings ratios or exceeding them by some reasonable level. On the other hand, a firm that is underperforming in comparison to its competitors might seek to limit its price/earnings discount to 10 percent or 15 percent of its peer group level. *In some cases, the company's goal might be to change the valuation model itself. A company whose earnings lead to a price below book value might focus investor attention on net asset value rather than earnings. Positioning the firm as an asset play could lead to a higher stock price in the near term than would be achieved based on earnings.*

Perception

In the stock market, perception is reality. Prices are set each day, or each minute, by changing perceptions of corporate performance, outlook, relative investment merit and so on. A frequently profitable IR approach is to focus on intrinsic changes in perceptions. To the extent that investors view a company as likely to default on debt, for example, share prices will be held back by this perceived risk. If the company can show that healthy cash flow or other strengths cause this risk to be minimal, the risk discount assigned to the company will decline and the share price will rise, all other things being equal. *Qualitative factors like perception can*

127

be measured through surveys and can have a major influence on valuation. Equally important, they do not require a change in company earnings or other fundamentals.

Volatility Price stability, or at least a relatively steady movement in price, is a goal in itself because volatility is perceived as a risk factor. Every buyer wants to be able to exit from his position without triggering a major price drop. High volatility in pricing increases the risk that such an exit will be overly costly, thereby reducing the likelihood an investor will buy the stock in the first place.

Certainly, these few examples are just a handful of the goals or measurements that can be established for the IR program. When establishing goals, the IR executive should focus on a few key factors.

Reality Goals should reflect realistically achievable targets. Goals that are too lofty defy effective targeting.

Measurability Achievements should be measurable so that the IR executive can make adjustments based on hard evidence.

Consistency Goals should not contradict one another. The pursuit of institutional shareholders can reduce share liquidity as the average size of trades increases and total shares outstanding remain constant. Thus, the goals of increasing liquidity while raising institutional holdings are often in conflict for smaller companies.

Timing The horizon for achieving the goals and the time frame for maintaining the level of achievement should be realistic. Time horizons that are too short tend to confuse short-term fluctuations

with real change, while too long a window
allows too many fundamental factors (industry
trends, market sentiment and corporate performance) to change in ways that would normally
lead to a reassessment of goals in any case.

Goals can be market-related or qualitative. A company seeking to raise its profile in the investment community might set a
goal of winning awards for annual report excellence or look for
opportunities to provide testimony to Congress or the Securities
and Exchange Commission on pending issues. Achievements in
both cases are readily measurable and both might provide benefits for the overall IR effort, even though neither is directly
focused on the immediate share price.

Certainly, qualitative goals are important to the extent that
stock market support and valuation depend on factors beyond
the strict financial figures. In investor relations, as in other forms
of marketing, the practitioner works at the margin, seeking to
gain the incremental edge that adds value beyond what would
otherwise be assigned.

If all companies are valued in part along a risk/reward continuum, valuation changes can result directly from changed perceptions of the relative risk and reward of a specific company.
The risk component can be reduced simply through more frequent and forthright communication, which adds to the comfort
level among investors. As expressed in our own corporate
mantra, "information reduces risk." More accurately, information
reduces the perception of risk, especially the risk that management will not be proactive on disclosure. In any event, the qualitative matters can provide substantial opportunity for improved
marketability and valuation.

BUDGETS—TIME AND MONEY

The investor relations executive is faced with a limitless array of
potential investors, investment messages, near-term and long-
term goals, communications approaches and other variables. Lim-

its on IR activity are imposed not so much by the market as by the most critical of scarce resources: time and money.

Of the two, time is the more limited. The chief executive and chief financial officer are committed to managing the company, dealing with dozens of constituent groups and sleeping every so often. The IR executive, likewise, has more than enough opportunities to keep busy 27 hours per day.

But there are only so many hours in a day and so many days in a year, and the sad fact is that the lack of time forces companies to narrow their focus from the optimal to the possible. It's important for the IR executive to manage expectations here, because the chief executive's expectations for achievement must be in sync with the goals that can realistically be attained within the constraints of available time.

Dollars, however, can be used to leverage the time available for an IR effort. Dollars can buy the time or resources of other individuals, whether this purchase includes database information that would otherwise be collected individually or extra staff to arrange meetings or write speeches.

Similarly, management expectations must match the reality of what can be achieved with the combination of time and dollars assigned to the IR marketing function. The effective IR practitioner analyzes time and dollars as a continuum. Time can replace dollars, and vice versa, and the goal of this resource allocation is to achieve the greatest impact relative to inputs.

Unfortunately, some of the IR budget has been spent before the first decision is made. As with other budgets, this one includes a hierarchy of expenditures that reduce strategic resources to well below the nominal budget level.

Entitlements First among these are entitlements, costs that every public company must incur. These include transfer-agent fees, filing costs, exchange listing fees, legal and audit fees related to the annual report on Form 10-K, annual meeting, and so on. For even the smallest public company, the cost of simply being public can start at $50,000 and soar to several times that amount.

Essentials   In addition, some expenditures fall into the category of essentials. Press releases announcing
quarterly results, phone calls to interested
investors and others who request information,
quarterly reports to shareholders, mailing list
maintenance and other selected activities are the
minimum standard for any company that wants to
gain recognition or support from anyone. Granted, some companies are discovered without
spending a dime on IR promotion, but they
almost always are discovered by accident and are
of interest because they are substantially undervalued. No farsighted management will want to
be "discovered" in such condition.

Marketing   Finally, the IR executive gets to the marketing
Plan   plan, which encompasses those activities that are
strategically or tactically organized and provide
the true value-added impact of IR marketing. The
marketing mix can include everything from
upgraded annual reports to conference calls with
analysts and product discounts for shareholders.
The most effective budgeting approach is to
begin by adding impact—or marketing leverage—
to those expenditures in the *entitlements* and
essentials categories. Quite often, the IR effort can
be advanced by adding a relatively small number
of incremental dollars, or time, to an activity that
will be undertaken regardless of its marketing
content.

As with other aspects of IR marketing, the budgeting process
is one of infinite variation. In allocating time and dollars, the first
stop is the make/buy decision. The IR executive must decide
which activities to undertake internally, utilizing the time of the
IR executive, CEO, CFO and available staff, and which to purchase externally, using dollars to leverage the value of internal
time.

131

A few examples of the complexity involved and opportunity afforded:

1. Although buying subscriptions to industry publications and specific periodicals can cost less than the monthly charges of a clipping service, internal time must be used for review, and the breadth of publications received is limited. On the other hand, clippings tend to be received on a delayed basis. While electronic clipping searches can provide much faster turnaround, this is the case only for those publications in a specific database. In a corporation that already subscribes to a clipping service via the marketing department, the IR director might be able to piggy-back on that arrangement at minimal cost.

2. Tracking of research reports on the IR exec's company and its competitors can be done through the investment of time, calling analysts and newsletter writers regularly and cajoling them for copies of their work, or by subscribing to services that track such documents.

3. Comparing the financial performance of peers, maintaining a record of peer stock activity, and otherwise following the competitive market can be achieved by obtaining annuals and other materials from each competitor and calculating the ratios by hand, or by accessing databases that already include these crunched numbers.

That leaves the biggest make/buy decision of them all: whether to staff all activities internally or hire an outside consultant for IR support. As with the other make/buy decisions, this one depends on the size of the budget, the availability of internal staff and support, expertise available to the company and hundreds of other variables.

Agencies provide value to the extent that they can effectively leverage the time of the internal IR person, whether that person is the director of public relations, the corporate secretary or the chief executive officer. The pros and cons of selecting an agency include:

Expertise   Just as a corporation will consult with an environmental attorney or a litigator when special needs arise, the use of an IR specialist can also add significant value. The agency executives assigned to a company will never know as much about the company as the insiders do, but they should always be expected to know more about the market, the media and investor targets than the in-house staff does.

Cost   For most companies, the total cost of hiring an agency is about the same as the salary, administrative support and benefits entailed in bringing IR staff on board internally. Agencies charge by the hour, as a rule, and the hourly rate will be far higher than the *nominal rate* for internal staff. When employee benefits and administrative support levels are added for the internal staff, however, the difference in costs narrows dramatically—or disappears. For smaller companies, the agency approach can prove more cost-effective, while larger firms ($1 billion in sales or higher, as a rule of thumb) should probably invest in internal staff for most needs and use outside resources primarily for special projects, consulting and surge capacity.

Flexibility   Agencies tend to offer greater flexibility in time and budget allocations. Likewise, an agency can assign different people, with differing levels of expertise, as company needs require. Resources utilized can vary sharply from one event to another, which is not an option available to a company with one person assigned internally.

Credibility   This is a two-edged sword. For many companies, affiliation with a well-regarded agency adds to their own credibility. For others, the use of an agency as an intermediary suggests to some targeted investors or the media that the company is becoming more

133

distant. The right balance can be achieved for each company, given appropriate attention to the issue.

Efficiency   Because an agency can pursue multiple targets on behalf of multiple clients, the cost of a program can be reduced in relation to results obtained. Various costs can be pro-rated among a group of clients, leading to lower total costs from the agency effort, even as the number of contacts or the effectiveness of those contacts increases.

The bottom line for hiring an outside consultant is added value. If the consultant can specify where its contribution will be made, and deliver on that promise, the buy decision makes sense. If the agency consists of order-takers who simply parrot management's view, the buy decision is probably a mistake. Similarly, if the outside consultant provides true leadership, making recommendations for strategy or change before they are solicited, for example, then the agency approach makes sense.

Again, the issue is leverage. How does the IR executive get the most impact from each dollar spent or each hour invested? Whether the make/buy decision centers on news clippings or annual report production, the right choice is the one that furthers the marketing effort the most and at the least total cost.

SETTING THE BUDGET

Exactly how large should an investor relations budget be? Predictably, there is no single answer. Nor is there a formula that can be applied uniformly. Each company has its own mix of challenges, internal staff, research-following, investment banker support and so on.

Among the systems that can be applied to establish budget parameters are these.

Percentage of Market Value. This is the simplest and it has the most intuitive appeal. Just as a fund manager might be compensated on a percentage-of-assets basis, this approach tends to treat market capitalization as an asset to be managed productively. As a rule of thumb, total spending on investor relations—including entitlements, essentials and the marketing plan—should be in the range of 1 percent of capitalization.

Thus, a company with 10 million shares outstanding at $8 per share would sink $800,000 into investor relations. If one recognizes that this cost includes internal salaries, outside resources, production and mailing of the annual report, and all the other factors that are part of IR marketing, that $800,000 budget is logical.

But what if the firm had 10 million shares at $45 per share? Would the same company then spend $4.5 million on investor relations? Probably not, and with good reason. The number of shares is the same and we can presume the number of shareholders will be relatively similar for each company. The size of the annual report isn't likely to increase fivefold simply because the stock is more expensive. The company won't start reporting results every three weeks instead of quarterly.

In fact, the primary value of the one-percent rule is that it focuses attention on the relatively low investment that can be made in investor relations when compared with other forms of marketing.

Percent of Value Increase. As a variation that's still based on market value, this budgeting approach attempts to link spending to return on investment. If the company's IR efforts are to lead to a market capitalization increase of $20 million, for example, the company might be willing to invest $1 million in the process. This kind of approach might make sense if the company anticipates a secondary offering in the future and wishes to ensure that the offering draws maximum interest.

However, the limitations of this approach are several. There's no way to predict exactly what will happen to market capitalization, no matter how much money a company throws into the program. If the stock market declines 20 percent and the company's shares decline only 5 percent, would the IR director still owe the firm a few million dollars to make up the difference?

Cost per Shareholder. Like market capitalization, the cost-per-shareholder approach makes sense in the middle, where budgets are reasonable, and falls apart at the extremes, where budgets become silly. Ditto for cost/share, which has no linkage whatsoever to the dollar value of shares, institutional/retail mix and so on.

Annual Sales. Here, the budget is based on sales dollars, but that's even more fuzzy a linkage than market capitalization. The size of a company's product line has nothing to do with its investor relations needs. In fact, a company with nationally known brands and a larger sales base can be a much easier sale for the IR department than a smaller company with unknown products.

Manufacturing Approach. We could also refer to this one as the profit maximization model. It recognizes that each company's IR effort includes fixed costs (entitlements) and variable costs (essentials and marketing plan) that can create returns as measured by several means. After covering entitlements, the budgeter reviews the efforts necessary to achieve the year's goals. For example, these might include three research reports, two feature profiles, a p/e equal to industry peers, and a 50-percent increase in the mailing list of qualified followers. The costs of these efforts are then estimated. Although there is no straight-line linkage between the efforts, the goals and a dollar return on investment, this approach makes the most sense because it focuses on controllable or predictable matters.

As with other forms of marketing, some things must be taken on faith here. It is intuitively clear and inherently logical that a company with more research reports will likely see greater demand for its stock and a relatively higher share value than a firm with fewer reports or no published research. Likewise, a company that is recognized favorably in the financial press is likely to draw more buyers than one that is unknown.

Although it is difficult to prove cause and effect here, significant circumstantial data can be generated. Certainly, one would readily accept this linkage: pursuit of a specific analyst's support, followed by a research report, followed by 400,000 shares being bought by customers of that analyst's firm and an improved price/earnings ratio relative to industry peers.

Exactly how should a budget be put together? This author's favored approach is based on the manufacturing model. Cover the entitlements first and then focus on those efforts that have the most impact on investor support. After investing in these higher-leverage activities, focus on some of the projects that improve overall marketability and the marketing environment but don't pay off in the near term. To the extent that costs and events can be combined to maximize impact per dollar expended, so much the better.

Even with this approach, the market capitalization number should be kept firmly in mind. That's because investment in investor relations can be far more profitable to shareholders than corporate investment in product and services. Consider the following example:

A company with sales of $200 million and a net margin of 5 percent has 10 million shares of stock outstanding. The company earns $1 per share and the shares trade at $15, for a price/earnings ratio of 15. Total market capitalization is $150 million (10 million shares × $15/share). If the company can use effective IR marketing to increase its price/earnings ratio from 15 to 18, without changing earnings or shares outstanding, market capitalization will rise to $180 million (10 million shares × $18/share) and shareholders will be $30 million richer.

If the company wants to increase market value simply by earning more money, without affecting the p/e ratio, it would take a 20-percent increase in sales, to $240 million, to add the same $30 million in market value. Most likely, an effective IR program will be effected more readily than a 20-percent sales increase.

The purpose of this exercise is simply to show the relative impact that an IR investment can have on raising the wealth of shareholders. But there are too many what-ifs attached to the comparison to make it compelling by itself. What if the market was rising anyway? What if the company's earnings rose 20 percent? Wouldn't that raise the price/earnings ratio in and of itself? Would the company need to invest in new facilities in order to expand sales 20 percent? Wouldn't that reduce margins in the near term? The list of questions is endless.

Further, each of the possible answers and formulas is too limited for universal application. IR marketing programs and the costs of being public cover such a broad range of possibilities that no company should rely on a simple rule of thumb.

However, the budgeting effort must have some starting point and the following thoughts should help. These guidelines for investor relations costs are directed largely at companies below the Fortune 500 level, with limited bureaucracy or gold-plating of operations. Orders of magnitude for IR costs include:

Entitlements Only Costs of complying with SEC rules should start at around $50,000 and move up into the $200,000 range, depending on the size of the company, number of shareholders, complexity of operations, number of significant corporate events, etc. These costs include expenses not normally associated with IR marketing, such as the year-end audit, transfer-agent fees, preparation and mailing of the proxy and other legal filings.

Responsive Mode For a company that plans to be responsive to inquiries and keep in touch with existing shareholders, but make no effort to attract new blood, add $25,000 or so to the entitlements number. This is really bare-bones IR, with most of the added cost tied into a few mailings, returned phone calls and some secretarial time.

Basic This is really the first category that qualifies as marketing. The basic marketing budget includes a real annual report, rather than a 10-K. It includes cultivation of a mailing and facsimile list of followers through personal contact and prospect mailings. It includes expanded disclosure in press releases, a couple of meetings per year in areas where primary investors are based, quarterly conference calls with followers after earnings are announced, and media contact with local reporters assigned to cover the company and the major financial newswires. Taking into account printing, staff, mailing, travel, lunches for key investors and so on, the basic menu should add anywhere from $125,000 to $225,000 to the entitlements package.

Mildly Proactive

In the mildly proactive program, which includes everything in the basic program, the company seeks new blood through regular prospecting within the investment community, prepares upgraded materials to market the company as an investment, holds meetings with brokers and analysts in cities where support is not yet extensive but opportunities are high, pursues feature coverage in media outlets rather than just keeping in touch with reporters already assigned to cover the firm, and generally lets the world know that the firm is interested in getting more support. For this kind of program, add $175,000 to $250,000 to the entitlements category.

Fully Proactive

This approach includes and expands on everything in the mildly proactive effort. The fully proactive company adds a shareholder hotline, possibly toll-free, for investor use at any time. Management participates in meetings with more investors and investor groups, the media relations effort is enlarged to include a greater variety of targets, the annual report is accompanied by a videotape, etc. With all these bells and whistles, add $250,000 to $300,000 to the entitlements budget.

While these examples cover some level of expenditures for staff, whether internal or external, nothing is allocated for the

139

CEO or CFO salaries to cover time spent in the investor relations effort. It's worth noting that none of these budgets, including entitlements, exceeds $500,000—and that makes investor relations a relative bargain for any company with a reasonable size or market capitalization. For a company with 10 million shares outstanding at $10 per share, even a $500,000 IR commitment is just one-half a percent of market capitalization, and probably a fraction of the value of top management's stock options.

When focusing on the budget, the IR executive should analyze the relative merits of fully burdened costing versus incremental expenditures. If the company has an internal IR staff, the expenditure for salaries and benefits should be included in the budget. Should an allocation be made as well for office rental for these individuals? Does it make sense to include a percentage of the chief executive's or CFO's salary (and bonus)? Should the cost of the audit be included, even though the audit number appears on another budget already?

Fully burdened costing has the advantage of highlighting the total costs of public ownership. Recognizing the base level of expenditures already required, the CEO might see each incremental expenditure as a relatively small percentage of the total and be more accepting of a proactive approach to investor relations. In addition, the inclusion of all public-company activities in the IR budget helps the IR executive to stake a claim to involvement in all areas related to public ownership. Whether that includes coordination of parts of the audit effort or working with attorneys to simplify proxy language, the presence of these projects on the IR budget creates an opening for greater internal involvement.

At the same time, the IR executive is not likely to gain real control of the audit, legal filings, rental costs and other numbers that would be added to a fully burdened IR budget. That means the IR effort would invariably appear several times as expensive as its marketing component would justify.

A two-part approach is probably best here. Clearly defined costs, such as the salary of the IR executive and her secretary, should be included in the overall budget, while items beyond the IR executive's control (legal fees, audit, etc.) should not. The budget plan should note how much the company must spend—with no real benefit—to be a public company, and make the point that the IR budget is a relatively low-cost means of generating returns on those expenses. In other words, *the IR program will help turn a cost sinkhole into a profit center.*

Granted, the profit won't show up on the income statement, unless a successful IR effort enables the company to replace debt with equity and reduce interest expense in the process. But the profit center approach can focus on improvements in market value relative to other companies and indices. It's also quite legitimate to argue that the investment in investor relations is similar to the cost (cash or opportunity cost) of a line of credit or an investment banking relationship. Each is designed to ensure that the company will be able to gain access to funds when needed. Investor relations is no different.

12

CHANGING THE COMPANY

Any good marketing department will consider changing the product, customer service, warranties, and other features to improve the marketing environment and sales level. The same is true of the investor relations effort, even though changing the product in this instance can include restructuring the company.

Marketing research includes customer feedback, and the response of targeted customers might indicate a need to change the product to a more accommodating form. While most of the investor relations effort seeks to match goals to the reality of the company, this chapter focuses on ways to change the company to meet the needs of IR marketing.

Changing the company isn't something that can be done too regularly, or the constancy of change can begin to damage credibility and the overall marketing effort. At the same time, companies that are open to change in ways that do no harm to the core business present themselves as more flexible and concerned about shareholder returns than do those that steadfastly refuse to make even the most basic changes.

Obviously, any IR executive who seeks to change corporate structure or practices should provide ample evidence of the need for the change. The evidence must show that the structural element is a critical impediment to marketing the company effectively and that another marketing approach or another target audience is not the answer. This isn't as challenging as some

---

12-1   Corporate Sensitivities

Any plan to change the corporation can place the IR executive in conflict with major powers. These could include the chief executive, lead investment banker, corporate counsel, influential directors, the chairman's spouse and other "experts." It is in the area of corporate structure and governance that IR executives must exercise the greatest sensitivity to political issues.

For many NASDAQ companies, the pressure to list on the New York Stock Exchange comes not from the IR department or institutional holders, but from an outside director. Scratch below the surface and find that this individual yearns to be director of an NYSE company. Whatever the merits of listing, the driving force might be personal, not corporate.

Similarly, the chairman's stock broker or closest friend might be the prime force behind a suggestion of stock split, dividend initiation or other action. The chief executive's son, quite an expert after two years at college, can provide the impetus for an acquisition program.

In almost all instances, reason will prevail. Acquisition plans and dividend policy will be reviewed by a broad array of experts and the decision reached will make sense for the corporation. Still, two risks are worth noting.

1. The decision will be based on opinions expressed at the country club, with emotion the dominant force.
2. A sensible decision will be reached, earning the ire of an influential member of the management family.

The issue of emotions is most significant in the corporate governance arena because egos are most at stake here, and because the line between right and wrong action is often less certain than for other business decisions. IR executives cannot avoid the risk attendant to these decisions unless they plan to relinquish their voice in corporate governance, but the investment of egos cannot be ignored either.

---

might suppose, especially in areas like stock splits or exchange listing, which do not require significant internal change. (See 12-1, *Corporate Sensitivities*.)

Following are some of the areas to focus on for structural change.

STOCK SPLITS/DIVIDENDS

Stock splits or dividends can be used to increase the number of shares outstanding for companies suffering from limited liquidity, to send a message of confidence in the company's outlook, and to provide an incentive for certain holders to sell part of their positions, thereby increasing the number of shares in the public float.

The difference between stock splits and stock dividends is largely one of size. Usually, stock splits are larger, such as 2-for-1 or 3-for-1 distributions. Stock dividends are commonly issued in 25-percent (5-for-4) or even 10-percent (11-for-10) denominations. In a financial sense, a stock split/dividend is the same as adding another quart of water to the soup. There are more shares, but the underlying value of the company doesn't change. Still, the stock split/dividend is a structural change that can provide real momentum in an investor relations program.

The first major advantage is improved liquidity. Higher float can accommodate increases in daily trading volume, which can lead to increased price stability. Lower price volatility, in turn, can reduce perceived risk, leading to improvement in average pricing. Splits tend to be more attractive to individual (retail) investors than to institutions, but that added appeal can translate into greater sponsorship by brokerage houses with a strong retail client base.

Splits also create the perception of wealth among many investors, and that perception is often rewarded with higher share prices. There are a number of reasons for this, the most obvious being that only companies experiencing growth will split their shares. These are the same companies that would likely see a price increase in any event. On the other hand, the message that this growth is likely to continue, increasing the street's perception of the company as a growth stock, is most clearly transmitted through the stock split.

In a survey of individual shareholders several years ago, the vast majority indicated a belief that splits offer investment opportunities and about a third indicated they had thought of purchasing a stock simply due to a split. This confidence is difficult to create with any other single action.

Although this same study indicated that nine out of 10 shareholders intended to hold or acquire more shares after a split, the split can be utilized to help free up some shares for trading. In this view, it is hoped that a significant stock dividend will lead some investors to sell off part of their holdings, adding to liquidity.

While it might seem contradictory to pursue a stock dividend in order to encourage selloff of shares, the goal of increased trading liquidity can justify such an approach. In this case, if the strategy doesn't work, it is only because shareholders decide they don't want to part with any of their holdings. If only all failed strategies worked out that well!

The reverse split represents a different spin on the same issue. Although a large number of shares can increase trading volume and liquidity, too large a float—and too low a price—can have a negative effect. For example, stocks trading below $5 per share, and even some trading below $10, can run the risk of being categorized as "penny stocks." Penny stocks, of course, are the highly speculative, overly promoted shares that often are the product of the worst practitioners in the brokerage business.

No management worth its salt wants its shares associated with this part of the business. And many brokers and analysts simply refuse to look at companies in the very low price ranges. While a low-priced company might be a diamond in the rough and its investment merit could be terrific, few investors are willing to search through all the truly worthless entities on the way to finding the hidden values.

For that reason, a management with a low-priced stock might undertake a reverse split. In a 1-for-4 split, for example, a company with shares trading at $3 each would end up with one quarter as many shares, each selling at $12 per share. Reverse splits are much less common than regular splits and dividends, as might be expected. As with a regular split, a reverse split sends a clear message to investors. By undertaking a reverse split, a company announces that its operations and opportunities should be judged by the same people and on the same merits as other, frequently larger, companies. It is, in a way, a rite of passage into the mainstream investment community.

However, a few cautionary notes are called for in this area.

Patterns Are Treacherous. Some high-growth companies get into a pattern of announcing a split after each September board meeting or at each annual meeting, setting up an expectation among investors as the next anniversary approaches. The first time such an anniversary passes with no split announced, investors might react as if the company had just declared growth opportunities ended. Why not? If split announcements have been a statement of confidence, the cessation of splits must mean that confidence is gone. For that reason, among others, it's best to consider splits at different times of year and not necessarily on an annual basis.

Penny-Stock Territory. Because many investors shy away from very low-priced shares, most companies will want to keep their share prices above $10. Since companies that split their shares generally do so when the price is high, the post-split price can easily be set to remain above that level. For example, a company with a $30 stock might declare a 3-for-1 split, giving each shareholder three times as many shares at $10 per share.

In most instances, the price of the shares will continue to rise, so that by the time of the split the shareholder might have three times as many shares at $11 or $12 per share. But the far-sighted investor relations executive would seldom recommend a 3-for-1 split like this one.

Stocks that are rising quickly can fall just as rapidly if investors sense any deceleration in the growth rate. In addition, overall economic trends or market sentiment can lead to a decline in overall market values, taking most companies down with the rest of the market. The sharp IR executive, recognizing this possibility, will lobby for a split percentage that leaves some cushion in the stock price.

In our $30 stock, for example, the IR executive might recommend a 2-for-1 split, bringing the average price down to $15 per share. If the market declines, it's still not likely that the stock will fall below $10. If the market continues to improve, and the company's finances do likewise, it's just a matter of less time until the next split can be implemented.

SHARE REPURCHASE PROGRAMS

Stock splits usually are implemented at relatively high prices, expressing management's confidence that corporate performance will justify further price increases. When the share price is depressed, the company might consider a share repurchase program.

Share repurchase is a clear statement by management that the company's stock is undervalued. By committing cash to buying shares, the company is telling investors its own stock is the most compelling investment available. (When the stock market plunged in October 1987, with the Dow Jones Industrial Average falling more than 600 points in two days, dozens of boards authorized share repurchase programs as a statement of confidence.)

Share repurchase is more common among mature companies than high-growth ventures. High-growth companies, by their nature, need to plow all available cash back into their operations. The ability to use cash to repurchase shares or pay a dividend suggests reduced growth potential to the investment community.

Share repurchase can be an effective IR tool for cyclical companies or those whose industries are out of favor. The message sent to investors is one of risk reduction: management will not let the share price fall below a certain level, so shareholders have a floor below which their stock is unlikely to drop. There are no guarantees that future buybacks will be announced or all authorized shares will be repurchased, but the authorization can reduce the perceived risk attached to price fluctuation.

Unlike stock splits, which can create value indirectly, share repurchase can have a direct impact on wealth for investors who maintain their position in the stock. When shares are repurchased, both the cash (asset) and shareholders' equity accounts are reduced by the same amount. Any earnings generated by the company are spread among fewer shares, leading to higher earnings per share and, all else being equal, a higher share price.

Consider a company with 10 million shares outstanding priced at $10 per share and earning $10 million or $1 per share. The price/earnings ratio equals 10. The company announces repurchase of 1 million shares, funded with internally generated cash. After the repurchase, the same $10 million of earnings is spread across 9 million shares, yielding earnings of $1.11 per share. If the price/earnings ratio remained constant at 10, the share price should increase 11 percent to approximately $11.10.

This same mechanism also leads to higher return on equity because the same level of earnings is applied to a reduced denominator of shareholders' equity. The impact on equity per share depends on the relationship between share price and the equity per share number.

If, in our example, equity per share was $10, equal to the stock price, the repurchase of 1 million shares would have reduced equity by $10 million to $90 million. The total return on equity would increase from 10 percent ($10 million earnings/$100 million equity) to 11 percent ($10 million earnings/$90 million equity). Equity per share would remain unchanged: $90 million/9 million shares = $100 million/10 million shares = $10/share.

If the stock was trading below book value, the benefit to continuing holders would be greater. If, for example, shares were trading at $5 each, the $10 million repurchase would reduce equity by the same $10 million, but shares outstanding would fall by 2 million. Earnings per share would increase 25 percent, and equity per share would increase as well ($90 million/8 million shares = $11.25 per share). Return on equity would also be higher at 11.1 percent and, if the p/e ratio remained at 10, the price of the shares would rise to $12.50.

The return on equity calculation is secondary in such instances. Because share valuation is most frequently linked to earnings per share and secondarily to equity per share, the repurchase that boosts EPS the most is preferred. Thus, stock buybacks are most attractive at lower prices. One added note: if borrowed funds are used to repurchase shares, interest expense on those funds would tend to reduce earnings, leading to some changes in the relative benefits of share repurchase.

ODDLOT BUYBACK/ROUNDUP PROGRAMS

There is one instance in which repurchase might be pursued at more elevated pricing: the oddlot buyback. Such programs are driven more by the cost of servicing small shareholders than by the market value of shares.

The cost of servicing a shareholder doesn't vary much with the number of shares held. The cost of printing and mailing annual and quarterly reports and proxy statements, and maintaining/updating names on mailing lists runs $6 to $10 per year, conservatively estimated. When a shareholder owns a small amount of stock, such servicing costs are excessive.

To reduce servicing costs and increase the number of round-lot holders, companies will often undertake buyback/roundup programs. In such programs, oddlot holders will be offered the opportunity to buy from the company enough shares to bring their ownership up to 100 shares, usually without paying a brokerage commission. Conversely, if the holder wishes to unload stock, the company offers to buy it back with no commission.

The holder of 15 shares worth $10 each might be hesitant to sell, recognizing the impact broker commissions would have on the proceeds of the sale. But the company's offer to return full value can compel the holder to liquidate his position and thus reduce the company's ongoing servicing costs.

In an oddlot buyback/roundup program, the company makes a market in its own stock for small holders. If the program works well, the firm ends up with fewer holders, each with a larger number of shares at a very low net cash cost and a lower total cost for servicing the shareholder base.

These programs also provide some benefit for companies considering an exchange listing. Because requirements for listing on the New York Stock Exchange, for example, include a minimum number of round-lot holders, programs that increase the number of such holders can bring marginal companies closer to the required level.

CASH DIVIDENDS

The initiation of a dividend sends a powerful message to the investment community, but it isn't always positive. Attention to the dividend, and establishment of a policy relative to its maintenance and amount, is clearly an essential aspect of investor marketing.

On the spectrum of investment options, the category of growth stocks is vastly different from that of income stocks. Similarly, investors who prefer one type are usually quite different from those who seek the other.

Growth stocks are defined by rapidly accelerating operations, with a continuous need for more cash to finance new inventories, facilities, salesmen and other resources for keeping up with growing demand. The faster sales are growing, the more cash-strapped a growth company can be because orders for product require cash up front for raw materials, labor, etc., before product can be shipped and payment received. Growth companies, as a rule, do not pay dividends.

Income stocks, on the other hand, are usually slow-growth or even declining companies with limited need to invest in new facilities, and operations that generate more cash than they need. They tend to have ready access to cash and relatively few attractive areas to invest it. These companies tend to pay such relatively high dividends that the yield (dividend as a percent of stock price) on the shares might exceed that of a passbook account or money market fund.

The underlying assumption is that a growth company should keep every dollar it generates because reinvestment of cash in that company will provide the greatest return to shareholders. For income stocks, however, the assumption is that the company should distribute all excess cash to shareholders, who can reinvest it for returns far superior to reinvestment in the company's operations. (Some companies will recognize this distinction internally by pulling cash from a mature operation, the so-called *cash cow,* to provide funding for higher-growth divisions of the same company.)

Dividends provide a significant benefit in that they offer some level of assured return to investors. While a stock might rise or fall, the dividend payment offers some compensation for the risk shareholders take in buying a company's shares. On the other hand, payment of a dividend creates a taxable event for the shareholder, whether the shareholder wants the cash or not. While a shareholder can decide when to take profits from the sale of stock, the dividend payment is at the option of the company alone.

In addition, the dividend is taxed twice, losing a substantial amount of its value along the way. First, of course, it is taxed as part of the company's net income. Then, the dividend is counted as income again by the shareholder. A dollar in pre-tax income could become a 65-cent dividend payment (after tax effects) to the shareholder, who then would pay an additional 17 cents in federal income tax—for a net benefit of less than half the original pre-tax dollar. Attempts to remove this double taxation have not generated much interest in Washington.

While a company that pays a dividend is demonstrating that its operations generate excess cash, that payment also shows that the company doesn't need to reinvest all of its cash in new ventures. Thus, a growth company that begins paying dividends is sending two messages.

1. Operations are stable enough that cash flow and profitability are likely to increase, cash will be utilized to pay down

debt, and shareholders still can receive a cash return on investment.

2. Growth is slowing.

Initiation of a dividend can actually lead to a decline in the price/earnings multiple of a growth stock because it suggests that the rate of growth is likely to slow. The growth premium included in the p/e multiple can decline after the dividend is announced.

However, the growth premium in the stock price might begin to fall off well in advance of a dividend initiation. Quarterly sales growth rates are likely to have slipped back in the periods preceding the board's decision to start a dividend. Publicly available numbers are likely to indicate that the growth rate is slowing, so the dividend announcement would simply validate that view.

The investor relations executive would tend to argue for debt reduction as the first and sole use of excess cash prior to any dividend initiation. Paydown of debt would tend to increase earnings and the lower debt, in turn, would lead to reduced perception of risk in the marketplace. Both would tend to have a salutary effect on the price of the stock. Debt reduction, most likely, is also a superior use of cash because it frees up the company's financial capacity to capitalize on additional high-growth ventures as opportunities present themselves later.

The analysis changes somewhat for a company with very low debt that is already paying a dividend or a firm whose board is absolutely committed to initiating dividends. Here, the IR executive is focused on dividend policy—the creation of a plan to set and maintain payments.

As with stock splits, dividends are expected to become a regular event, only more so. Dividends usually are paid quarterly and in equal amounts each quarter, although some firms pay an annual dividend or three regular dividends and a year-end "special" payment usually higher than the regular dividend.

In our firm's research, we have not seen a particular benefit to the use of special dividends. By holding back on the dividend payment during the year, the company can sweeten the payout further at year-end, but the investment community doesn't seem to give the company much credit for that added payment. In other words, it might be better for a given company to pay a 10-cent dividend each quarter for a total of 40 cents, than to pay three 5-cent dividends and a 30-cent "special" at year-end. Even though the payment of a special dividend makes the total payout higher, the investment community will tend to focus on the predictable quarterly payout, reasoning that next year's "special" dividend might be 40 cents or zero.

As a rule, companies should look to set their dividends at a rate that allows for regular quarterly payment out of free cash flow. In addition, the dividend should reflect some underlying pattern of activity. Some possible dividend policies:

Earnings Basis The dividend payment is set at a percentage of current or prior-year earnings. It's not the optimum approach because earnings will fluctuate from year to year while the dividend should remain relatively constant or rise at a reasonable rate. *One client traditionally set its dividend at 20 percent of prior-year earnings and the system worked fine until earnings began to fall. Then we ratcheted the payout ratio into the 25-percent range and, as earnings continued to fall, we were forced to depart completely from this standard because we also had set a goal of increasing the dividend each year.* For a growth company, setting the dividend payment at a low percentage of earnings sends the message that most of earnings will, in fact, be reinvested in growth.

Yield Basis The dividend is related to the stock price so that shareholders receive a specific cash return on the current share value. This yield approach is more common for income stocks, which compete with preferred shares and debt instru-

ments for investor loyalty. As with earnings, a lower share price can lead to lower dividend payments, with the yield remaining about the same.

Cash Basis Similar to the earnings basis, the company sets the dividend based on its ability to generate cash from operations. The payout can be a percentage of prior- or current-year cash flow, and it can be based on total cash flow, cash flow from operations, free cash flow or some other category.

Peer Basis If competitors are paying dividends, it's a relatively simple matter to set the dividend in the middle, or the lower end, or somewhere within the range of directly competing companies. A dividend that's consistent with peers suggests that the company is in just as good a financial position and just as capable of sharing the wealth as its competitors. *Targeting yield to peer averages can be tricky, however. In setting the dividend target for one company, we noted that a yield equivalent to peers would create much too high a payout ratio based on earnings for this underperforming company. On the other hand, a payout ratio based on earnings would leave the firm's dividend relatively skimpy on a yield basis. Fortunately, our time-line analysis indicated that dividends were declining on a yield basis and that investors were not much focused on dividends in that industry, so we recommended pegging the payment at the low end of the scale.*

Emotional Sometimes the dividend policy is based on emotion. The chairman wants the dividend to increase each year or all outside directors work for companies that pay dividends or the investment banker has institutional clients that prefer dividend-paying companies. Any or all of these reasons can lead to creation of a dividend, increases or decreases in the payout, and so on. For the IR executive, the negotiation must move the payment toward the most reasonable level from a marketing standpoint, against this emotional tide.

Whatever the general policy established for dividends, it's important not to allow near-term trends to have much influence. Investors' preferences will shift from growth stocks to Blue Chips and back over time, and the dividend might have little total impact. A growth stock that pays a dividend will not be perceived as a Blue Chip when big company shares are in vogue, and a mature company with a small dividend won't be confused with a growth company.

Because dividends are expected to be consistent, however, increases and decreases in dividends are generally perceived as permanent. That means that each increase in the quarterly dividend is assumed, for all practical purposes, to be the new floor for all future payments. It also implies that omission of a dividend means the company will never pay one again.

Of course, never is a long time, and some investors will buy into a firm that has canceled its dividend in anticipation of a price increase when the dividend is reinstated. Others will sell their stock, assuming that the canceled dividend is just the first sign of a continuing decline.

Omission of a dividend cannot be taken lightly. Because it is usually prompted by a severe earnings decline and a need to husband cash aggressively, such omission indicates that a company is in crisis. A board that is considering such a move should do so only if it anticipates that the dividend will be canceled for several quarters.

The dividend omission should never be announced as a quarterly event with reinstatement to be considered at the next board meeting. That approach leaves investors waiting for the next shoe to drop, and then the next and the next. Instead, it is preferable to say that the dividend is being omitted for the foreseeable future as a cash-saving approach and that the board will consider reinstatement when earnings/sales/cash flow improves. This approach gets the bad news out of the way quickly, avoids the water-torture impact of stretching the announcements out over time, and takes the dividend issue off the table as a discussion point for most investors.

A few other nuances worth noting:

1. Stock splits and dividends for companies that pay cash dividends should usually be accompanied by maintenance of the cash dividend on the post-split shares. If the dividend was 5 cents per share on the old shares, it should usually be 5 cents on the new shares as well. That creates a de facto increase in the dividend yield for each shareholder, providing some increase in wealth regardless of stock price action, and avoids the perception of a dividend decline when people check the number later in the newspaper stock tables. However, this is not a hard-and-fast rule. A company can reduce the dividend per share in proportion to the split amount and then increase the dividend later for added impact, or increase the dividend at the time of the split.

2. Different dividend policies can be created for different classes of stock. The most obvious situation is with preferred stock, which generally has a higher dividend yield and priority payment ahead of common stock. But some firms have non-voting and voting classes of common stock, often as a result of efforts to maintain family or insider control. In some cases, the non-voting shares receive a higher dividend payment, largely to compensate for the fact that voting power is concentrated elsewhere.

3. Companies that pay dividends can look into creation of a dividend reinvestment plan under which shareholders have dividends reinvested into whole or fractional shares of stock. Such plans, known as DRIPs, usually allow current holders

to buy new shares with no brokerage commission and sometimes at a discount to current market value. While dividend reinvestment plans can be costly from a paperwork and management standpoint, they do create a base level of demand for new shares of stock.

EXCHANGE LISTING

The battle for supremacy in stock-trading is moving so quickly that this section of the book will be obsolete before these words are stored on a floppy disk. As of this writing, the National Association of Securities Dealers Automated Quotation System, commonly known as NASDAQ, has overtaken the American Stock Exchange as the nation's second-largest trading arena, behind the New York Stock Exchange, and electronic-trading and special deals of all sorts continue to eat away at the traditional exchange business.

In the traditional exchange environment, a specialist handles all trading in a specific listed stock. The specialist is required to buy when there are too many sell orders and sell when buy orders are in abundance—the cost of holding a monopoly to trade and set the price of a listed stock. The specialist system can offer substantial benefits in liquidity by consolidating all trading at one site. In addition, the traditional stature of the large exchanges has added to the profile and status of their listed companies.

But the arena has changed dramatically in recent years. NASDAQ's National Market System, in which market-makers are linked electronically in a national multispecialist system, has earned increasing respect from many quarters. Hundreds of larger companies have opted not to move from NASDAQ to one of the traditional exchanges.

Meanwhile, the smaller regional exchanges have carved out a niche by listing lesser-known companies, in some cases, and by offering lower-cost trading markets in companies listed on both the traditional exchanges and with NASDAQ. More recently, a number of independent trading organizations have begun paying brokerage firms to direct order flow to them so they can make a market in specific stocks outside of both the NASDAQ and exchange systems.

The whole issue of payment for order flow has raised concerns in many quarters, particularly as the additional profit earned by brokerage houses and the private market-makers comes out of someone else's pocket. To the extent that it represents a new slicing of the brokerage house or exchange share, such payment can be seen as a relatively benign restructuring of the trading business. If, however, the shifting of orders comes at the expense of investors, the process is not quite so harmless. Each side, predictably, claims to be improving the efficiency and, consequently, pricing and liquidity of stock trading.

At present, exchange listing can offer superior trading liquidity and lower bid/ask spreads than NASDAQ's market-maker system. A combination of NASDAQ's system with listing on a regional exchange can yield even stronger liquidity for some firms. The New York Stock Exchange still has higher prestige and a certain cache for foreign investors, relative to other exchanges and NASDAQ, but that edge is thinning as well. The American Stock Exchange, meanwhile, is undertaking a series of marketing initiatives to regain some lost stature and capture specific niches of the listing market.

At the same time, more states will automatically clear stocks for trading under provisions of their "Blue Sky" laws simply based on an exchange listing than will based on NASDAQ affiliation, including stocks on the National Market System. However, the NASDAQ clearance rate has been increasing, reducing the NYSE and AMEX edge.

(Blue Sky laws regulate the trading of securities within a state, ostensibly preventing unscrupulous individuals from selling unwary investors pieces of the sky. This author's opinion is that for modern IR practice and most public companies, state Blue Sky statutes are a cumbersome anachronism that should be replaced by a uniform national registration system.)

Listing with the New York Stock Exchange tends to entail much higher costs than staying with NASDAQ or the American Stock Exchange. Thus, the perceived benefits of a listing must be weighed against costs. And since delisting from the NYSE requires a supermajority vote of shareholders, it is easier to get on this exchange than off it.

Another negative comes from the support that can be lost with market-maker firms when a company lists on an exchange. Quite often, firms that make a market in a specific NASDAQ company will also provide research coverage of that company. The added volume and profitability of making a market can help justify the investment in research, which in turn can add more trading volume for the market-maker.

Furthermore, the commissions on Over-the-Counter (OTC) stocks generally are higher, or spreads wider, leading to lost profitability for brokerage firms when a company moves to an exchange. In many instances, the decision to list on an exchange will lead a market-maker firm to drop its research coverage of the listing company. (This is a double-edged sword for the IR director. While greater brokerage-house profitability can lead to more active marketing of a company's stock, the higher spreads on OTC shares also can reduce the stock's appeal to many investors.)

As a rule, decisions to list on the New York Stock Exchange are driven as much by ego as by any trading fundamentals. Many chief executives and boards simply believe that one of the rites of passage for a growing company is to move onto the NYSE.

The IR executive should keep an open mind regarding each trading arena and stay alert to changes in the relative merits of each. It is important to remember that an exchange listing is considered permanent and should not be undertaken with any temporary perspective.

CORPORATE GOVERNANCE

Issues of corporate governance are increasingly moving into the investor relations sphere as activist institutions lobby for greater control over corporate management. Although executive compensation has been one of the catalysts for change, it appears that the growing level of shareholder unrest will continue for an extended period and that concerns will include an increasing number of governance aspects.

Because corporate governance issues are a growing concern among high-profile investors, the IR executive must assert a role in the debate. Even if participation is limited to surveying existing holders and potential investors, and reporting their views to the board, the IR executive must be perceived as a key expert and adviser. Governance issues that should be of particular concern to the IR executive include:

Board Structure   Many major investors have become increasingly restive over the incestuous nature of board membership. Too frequently, they argue, the board consists of the chief executive, who also serves as chairman, four of his top executives, and a handful of nominally independent directors who hail from the company's law firm, its investment banker, and the chairman's country club. Too often, this complaint is valid. Many top investors balk at taking a position in companies that have limited numbers of outside directors or boards that exhibit significant cronyism. For the IR executive, it's a delicate but essential challenge to keep the chairman and other directors up to date on investor concerns and board trends, and to recommend changes to improve the company's marketability to major potential investors.

Compensation   Compensation of top officers, once an afterthought among investors, has become a major public policy issue and the battle is expected to rage indefinitely. In 1993, all companies were required for the first time to include graphs comparing their stock market performance with peers and with broad market indices. In addition, the compensation committee of the board is now required to explain its philosophy for setting compensation and the correlation between the chief executive's compensation and the company's stock market performance. The general push is clearly toward pay-for-performance and aligning executive compensation more closely with the interests of shareholders. How far the trend will move is anyone's guess, but the IR executive is involved whether a role is sought or not. As major investors seek an active voice in compensation issues, and as politicians seize on this seemingly populist cause, the job of marketing company shares will only get more complicated.

Takeover Defense

While the best takeover defense is a high stock price, adoption of legal defenses of various sorts became the rule in the late 1980s. Multiple classes of stock (voting/nonvoting), poison pills and other defensive maneuvers have been less an issue since the takeover surge subsided, but these measures still cause some chafing among investors who resent any limitation on their ability to profit on a tender offer.

CORPORATE RESTRUCTURING

At times, the obstacles to effective investor marketing are so substantial that only a restructuring of the corporate body will open the way for increased valuation. The urge to restructure can result from a sea change in investor sentiment, such as the shift from a 1970s love of conglomerates to a 1990s interest in pure play investments, or from fundamental changes in tax or other laws that make certain structures more desirable than others.

In some cases, a corporation will own two businesses, with one perceived as high-growth and one in an out-of-favor segment of the market. Quite frequently, the valuation of the two segments combined is less than the valuation that the more popular business would receive on its own. In such an instance, a spinoff of one segment to shareholders or to the general public through a stock offering is the best way to maximize shareholder value. (See 12-2, *The Value of a Spinoff.*)

In the late 1980s, we worked with one company that was dividing into three and, ultimately with a second spinoff, four publicly traded entities. With businesses in several industries, the company had lacked for coverage from analysts who focused on only one of the markets addressed by the conglomerate. As the spinoffs approached, and we worked to create a clear identity and investment message for each of the successor companies, total market capitalization rose rapidly. As a pure play, each successor company in a restructuring can establish its own identity and following, achieving a valuation on its own merits.

Likewise, restructuring can flow from changes in tax laws, as occurred following the Tax Reform of 1986. As various tax shelter investments lost value under the new rules, especially in the energy business, many firms rolled up their shelter partnerships into corporate shells to assume new identities as stock investments.

Restructuring offers a major opportunity to build long-term value for a company with limited or confusing investment messages. The investor relations executive, as the primary officer responsible for maximizing market valuation, should be continually focused on whether the company's structure is itself the largest impediment to raising shareholder wealth.

CAPITAL FORMATION

The main benefit of a high stock price is the currency it provides for the issuing company. That currency can be used, without benefit of a public offering:

- when an acquisition is made via a stock-for-stock transaction,
- to raise funds through an employee stock ownership program, and

163

12-2   The Value of a Spinoff

Although the partial spinoff of subsidiaries can seem to be a sure-fire winner in terms of market capitalization, looks can be deceiving. Let's consider both the opportunity and the risks.

Smith, Jones & Johnson manufactures printing presses and owns a chain of retail wallpaper stores—a long-ago diversification of the printing business. Stores yield a high return on utilized capital and cash flow, while presses are more cyclical and offer lower return on investment. SJ&J sells at a p/e ratio of 8, the average assigned to cyclical manufacturing companies, while other wallpaper chains sell at an average p/e of 26.

SJ&J spins off 40 percent of the wallpaper chain to shareholders, expecting a higher combined value of both operations. At a p/e of 26, the value of SJ&J's continuing 60-percent investment in the wallpaper stores should add 25 percent to SJ&J's share price.

Does this plan succeed? Maybe. SJ&J might benefit from the market's valuation of the subsidiary. However, consider the following possibilities.

1. The wallpaper stores remain captive, and everyone knows it. Investors are unlikely to give the stores a 26 p/e when they know SJ&J can grab excess cash (special dividends) and controls the board. In addition, with 60 percent of shares locked up by the parent, the wallpaper stores probably will have trading liquidity problems, and there's scant potential for a takeover premium in the share price.

2. Investors who didn't give SJ&J added value based on 100-percent ownership of the wallpaper stores might see even less value when the stores are 60-percent-owned.

3. Costs rise with two managements and boards, two IR programs, two annual reports, etc., giving the two entities a lower combined earnings level than when they were one.

A partial spinoff might be the right choice. Equally likely, the best returns to existing shareholders might result from a 100-percent distribution or a sale of the subsidiary and special distribution of cash to SJ&J holders. As in all of investors relations, the answer isn't obvious.

- to increase the attractiveness of stock options in attracting top executive talent.

But the primary benefit of strong market support comes when the company seeks to raise capital by selling new shares of its well-regarded stock. For any publicly held company, the IR executive is a critical conduit to investors who might prefer one type of stock over another or desire a convertible debt offering instead of preferred shares. While investment bankers and financial officers work on the specific structure of an offering, it is the IR executive who is best positioned to provide advance insights into investor appetites.

Consider, for example, a company whose industry peers sold convertible debt during a specific time window a few years earlier. While convertible debt-offerings have become less popular since then, the investors indicate that they were happy with the offering and wish there were more such vehicles to purchase. That insight, relayed to the executive committee, might lead to a convertible-debt offering the next time the firm seeks public funds. Conversely, investors disappointed in the performance of preferred shares sold by peers might lead the IR executive to recommend that his own company bypass the preferred stock route for the next fundraising venture.

Capital formation also can be furthered by simplifying the existing capital structure of a company. Some firms include multiple classes or types of stock, debentures, bonds, warrants and other securities—the result of several offerings over a long period. Cleaning up the books through a buyout or swap of securities can lead to a cleaner capital structure and greater trading liquidity for the securities that remain.

CORPORATE NAME CHANGES

Finally, the corporation can be changed, at least cosmetically, by adoption of a new identity achieved through changes in communications materials, corporate graphics, marketing programs and, in extreme cases, the name.

The need and value assigned to a corporate identity program is highly subjective, especially when it includes a new name. Frequently, it seems, the pursuit of a new name develops a life of its own in which the benefits of change are heavily inflated and the value of the existing identity is dismissed.

Existing names have history and tradition behind them. They offer recognition and value. New names, on the other hand, offer a fresh start and, with ample investment in advertising and other promotion, substantial opportunity to build support. However, it is certainly arguable that such support could be built by investing the same dollars to promote the existing identity, rather than advertising a new one.

Name changes should occur no more frequently than once in three decades. Valid reasons include:

- major acquisitions, mergers, restructuring/spinoffs;
- long-term shifts in operations or markets served, making the existing name misleading; or
- development of a brand identity so strong its value can add substantial market capitalization to the parent company.

In any event, any new name should have a clearly defined meaning and indicate what the company does. Alphabet-soup names are not quite as easy to market as names with clear meanings.

For the IR executive, corporate identity programs can provide a major marketing challenge and opportunity, leading to improved market capitalization and investor support. However, corporate identity efforts don't necessarily require a name change. Newly designed logos and other icons, combined with increased marketing budgets, can provide ample returns on invested cash without altering the company's historic identity.

13

PACKAGING THE MESSAGE

The IR executive has examined the company's financials, culture, peers and audience; determined the financial resources that can be allocated to the marketing program; and considered or implemented steps to change the company's structure. It is now time to package the message for delivery to the outside world.

(Okay, maybe the process is this neat once in a million times. The order of these steps will vary for each company and, in fact, the continuous nature of IR program adjustments will require that each step be repeated over a course of years. For simplicity of structure, however, we'll consider all of the preceding as preliminary steps in the process.)

The investment message must be clearly defined and it must answer only one eternal question: "Why Should I Buy This Stock?" The answers to this question, beginning with "To Make Money!" create a chain of arguments that range from the value-oriented to the conceptual. The best investment theses have these common strengths.

1. **Brevity.** The investor focuses first on an idea and then on the evidence supporting the idea. A good message will assert, in relatively clear and thrifty terms, the reasons for an

investment. While supporting information can be volumi-
nous, the core message or investment appeals should fit on
the back of a business card.

2. **Options.** While some companies clearly have just one
investment message, others can be viewed in more than one
light. A firm with proprietary products and a recovery from
prior management errors can be positioned as a growth stock
or a turnaround story, or both. The IR executive will identify
the option with the greatest potential and lead with that, following up quickly with the second message or kicker.

3. **Data.** A good investment message must be supported by
numbers that prove the case. These include the company's
own historical numbers and projections, industry factors and
economic or cultural trends. As mentioned earlier, the factors closest to the company are the most important and convincing, while megatrends and other externals are the least
credible.

(There are, of course, exceptions to this rule, but they
tend to be short-lived. Investors in the early 1980s believed
that energy prices would increase indefinitely and favored
the energy sector for that reason. In the early 1990s, gaming
stocks were viewed as headed for an unending rise. But
even when such a fervor takes hold of the market, each
company must seek to distinguish itself on its own merits
and, in fact, to separate itself from the market frenzy. Otherwise, when the buying charge turns to a rout, the individual
company will have no friends to maintain support.)

4. **Consistency.** Consistency comes in many forms. It includes
consistency between the message and the corporate culture,
or a pattern of activity and strategies that extends over time.
Consistency is compelling because it links the company's
success to strategies that have been implemented effectively
and which have stood the test of time. Consistency also covers projections that mesh with one another, as opposed to
those that seem impossible to realize simultaneously. For

example, a company that is seeking to grow at a 30-percent compound rate for sales is unlikely also to target a major debt-reduction program as a simultaneous goal.

Here are a few examples of well-crafted investment messages.

Books Near Us Corporation, the leading (35-percent market share) retailer of sports-related books, trading cards and collectibles in its 12-state market, plans to expand into six adjacent states in the coming year. The company, which recently introduced its own line of sports insignia collectibles, had achieved compound sales growth of 25 percent—including same-store gains of 9 percent—and earnings growth of 43 percent over the past five years, partly by choosing store locations within one block of suburban elementary schools.

We now know that the company is adding approximately 50 percent (six new states) to its base of stores, which should add a similar amount to its sales base. We also know that the company has gained a leading share in its markets, that the expansion is into adjacent states, that the firm is expanding the products sold through each store, and that the stores are successful in part because of their locations near schools.

Thane's Pie Company, which closed its unprofitable frozen foods group in 1994, is anticipating strong growth in the fresh desserts market during the coming year, based on new distribution agreements that add 12 percent to its customer network and major dessert promotion programs at its top five restaurant customers.

This is both a turnaround story and a growth story. We expect to learn that this company has an inherently more profitable business going forward, simply because the unprofitable part was jettisoned, and that this profitability will be extended as the improved marketability of the product yields its impact. The investor, of course, will want more information on long-term impacts of the frozen-foods closing, the ability of the remaining businesses to absorb overhead expense and so on, but the message about company potential is still clear.

In each of the cases cited, the message is brief and intriguing, but unconvincing. Certainly, any investor would demand more answers than these simple premises provide. That's acceptable because the investment message is more than a single phrase or paragraph.

It is, as the chapter heading suggests, an entire package. While the core message may fit on the back of a business card, the package must be larger. The package needs to be large enough to contain all the essential messages and proofs, without being so cumbersome that the potential investor is distracted by ancillary factors or minor business strategies that do not truly have significant potential for the firm.

It is not uncommon, for example, for the sexiest part of a company's investment story to be the smallest part of the business. However, focus on that component must be limited to prevent investors from assigning an overly large and unattainable impact in their projections. *An example: A client with a large share of the contract furniture market began generating strong orders from many of the new casinos being built in the early 1990s. The company had served many of the traditional, larger gaming companies in the past and the incremental business accounted for no more than 5 percent of total sales. We added the casino angle to our investment message as a hook to draw interest, but quickly focused investors on the strength of the underlying business.*

Packaging the message is as much a process of disposal as selection. The question to be asked is not whether a particular factor about a firm makes it a better company, but whether it makes the company a better investment. In this winnowing process, many historical and static elements of the company will be eliminated. The fact that the company's headquarters has been in the same building for 50 years may be a point in favor of good corporate citizenship, but its value as an investment merit can be zero. The fact that a company has the leading share of its market has significance only if that success can be extended. A company with the leading share in a no-growth market can emphasize its market position without success among investors,

13-1 Boiling It Down

Creating the core message begins with a list of all investment merits and leads through a process of elimination to a handful of key images to drive investor interest. Guidelines to follow in selecting the top five or six messages are these:

1. Can cause and effect be shown in terms of financial performance?
2. Is the strength one that distinguishes the company from its competitors or does it simply match peer levels?
3. Does the favorable trend have a direct impact on performance or is it a megatrend with longer-term, unspecified benefits?
4. Does the success flow directly from management's strategy or is serendipity at work?
5. Does the strength suggest opportunity or risk? (A firm with 100-percent market share has downside risk, not upside potential.)
6. Is there evidence the success can be duplicated?
7. Is there any predictability regarding profitability?
8. Does success depend on a major hurdle—such as refinancing or regulatory clearance—that has yet to be achieved?
9. What is the likelihood the company will reverse direction in the coming year regarding this strategy?
10. Will investors see the strength as a compelling reason to buy the stock now?

because this leading share suggests that growth prospects are limited. (See 13-1, *Boiling It Down.*)

Similarly, the data used to back up the message must actually show some cause/effect or other evidentiary value. If Books Near Us plans to open near suburban schools, the company should tell us whether the number of schools or the student enrollment is growing or shrinking. Is the site selection based on any other factors, such as neighborhood wealth, neighboring store types or professional teams in the vicinity? How much does the average customer buy and how many years will a student continue investing in basketball cards? Is there any barrier to entry in this market or can anyone with $15,000 compete head-to-head with Books Near Us?

The questions and answers must flow in a relatively straight line so that the investment message is packaged in an almost conversational format. Although the format of documents won't necessarily follow question-and-answer style, preparation should anticipate use of that approach. Let's go back to our pie company and put the discussion into question-and-answer format.

Why should I invest in Thane's Pie Company?

The company has expanded its customer base with new distribution agreements and earnings won't be dragged down by the frozen pie operation, which they dumped in 1994.

What does that mean for margins going forward?

Gross margins in the fresh pie business have traditionally run in the 45-percent range, but the frozen pie margins were closer to 32 percent due to the extra costs of refrigeration and the fact that the pies were shipped to volume buyers who demanded more of a discount. If all of 1993's sales had been fresh instead of frozen, the company would have recognized an extra $8.3 million in gross margin and about 4 cents per share more in net earnings.

Without the frozen food sales, how much excess capacity does the company have?

Frozen pies were about 25 percent of sales, so the bakery section now is running at roughly 65 percent of capacity. That means the company can absorb significant added demand without requiring plant expansion. The refrigeration equipment and other expenses related strictly to the frozen-foods component were written off completely in 1994 and the company is looking for a buyer for the equipment.

Until the facility is fully utilized again, how much cash is being generated to cover debt?

There's essentially no difference here. The frozen pies generated only a small amount of positive cash flow. Meanwhile, it's worth noting that payment terms in the fresh pie market are net-10-days versus the more generous net-30-days that had been negotiated by many of the high-volume grocery chains that bought the frozen pies.

How much impact will these restaurant pie promotions have and is this a long-term impact?

Restaurants traditionally emphasize fruit pies in the late summer and early fall, and the company is usually called upon to meet heavy demand at this time. The current promotions are expected to add to sales in a generally slow period and the company has ample capacity to handle the demand. The impact will be near term, but if the promotions at these chains are successful, we expect them to be duplicated at other customer establishments and to be repeated more often by all of our restaurant clients.

And so on. By focusing on the questions raised by each statement, the question-and-answer approach helps focus the packaging and avoid irrelevant tangents. For instance, a company's advertising might emphasize that Thane served as the cook for the first governor of Virginia, adding a nostalgic or historical image to the product. But *Who is Thane?* would likely be the 512th question the average investor would ask and the basic investment package being created wouldn't hold that many answers.

The questions being asked wouldn't be limited to the company. An investor would also want to know about the market, the investment environment, performance of competitors and other matters. Certainly, the price of the stock relative to peers and its trend versus the market would be relevant issues.

That requires some focus on the stock itself. Although the investor relations executive won't be telling investors that the stock should or will be trading at higher levels, the point certainly should be made that a discount exists, if it does, and the cause of the discount explained.

Where's the stock price?

Thane's is selling at $15, which is an adjusted price/earnings ratio of 9 if you back out the frozen pies group. The three other publicly traded pie companies are selling at multiples of 13, 13 and 16. Before Thane's entered the frozen pies market, it had been selling at a price/earnings premium to its peers.

How much risk is there from a competitive standpoint?

The bakery business continues to be largely regional, particularly in the fresh pies segment, and Thane's is the largest and best known brand in its markets. Two of its publicly traded competitors have relatively high debt service, so they aren't expected to undertake major expansion programs or try to buy market share by cutting prices. But the third competitor does have the funds to enter Thane's market if that choice is made.

As this Socratic dialogue continues, it becomes clear that even the briefest of core messages can generate reams of text in support of the message. That makes the need to limit core messages, and otherwise focus the story, all the more pressing.

Boiling the core messages down to their basics leads, in some cases, to a very clear "earnings model" approach. Here, the discussion that ensues creates an understanding of the way earnings will be created.

1. Books Near Us Corporation is expanding its sales base by 50 percent, which would lead to a 62-percent increase in earnings if the new stores match sales levels of existing stores and the gross margin on new sales tracks with historical levels.

2. The sales per store could increase an added 12 percent as the private label line of collectibles is introduced, and these incremental sales at existing facilities would yield higher than average margins.

3. The store locations are in areas with combined student populations of 2,000 to 5,000 in grades 5 to 8, the primary buying group for trading cards. But the populations of grades 1 to 4 in these same districts is 15 percent higher, indicating a likely 15-percent increase in the size of the customer base within the next four years.

4. Combining the expanded stores, the increase in sales from the new private-label line and the expected growth of the customer population, the anticipated sales level of Books Near Us would be 93% higher in 1999 than it is today. And net earnings would be 105 to 110 percent higher if current trends and market dynamics continue.

Of course, current trends won't continue and market dynamics will change. That's one of the few guaranteed bets in the investing world. However, the earnings model doesn't have to focus on all possibilities. It merely has to quantify how the various components of the investment message contribute to growth in corporate performance and, by inference, in share value.

Note as well that the investment messages presented here focus on both near-term and long-term opportunities. In the case of Thane's Pies, the message includes future benefits from temporary restaurant promotions and relatively permanent potential increases in the sales base due to new distribution agreements. For our card retailer, the message covers several years of growth in the customer base.

Consistency of messages becomes all the more important because of the long-term nature of investment. Certainly, it would be difficult to make a case a year from now that frozen pies are the best investment Thane's Pies can make, or that sports collectibles stores quite distant from suburban schools are as good as those near the students. Once chosen, an investment message must be maintained for a respectable period—usually several years.

The packaging of messages is an investment in credibility. By presenting the package to investors today, the investor relations executive is promising that these appeals will continue to be relevant for some time to come.

If the company's fundamentals change, or if market shifts lead to substantial adjustments in the core strengths of the company, the IR executive will need not only to explain the new investment story, but also to discuss how the old story became obsolete. While the focus of investors is always on the future, how the company adjusted in the past creates or kills confidence in how well management can handle future obstacles.

A bad example: A client company invested substantial time focusing investors on its expansion into one geographic market, highlighting the potential benefits of such an investment. Even as the expansion provided disappointing returns, management sought to assure the world that this market was a long-term investment arena. (Partly, management was concerned about sending negative messages to customers, leading them to bail out and doom the project.) Ultimately, the expanded operations folded and the company had no good explanation for what seemed to outsiders as an abrupt departure from plan.

It's relatively rare that market changes are so abrupt the investment story changes overnight. More frequently, management seeks to play its cards close to the vest, portraying its subsidiaries as having great potential even as a sale or write-off is considered. Too much of this puffery is the stuff on which shareholder derivative suits are based. At the least, the IR executive should lobby for a reduced amount of discussion and emphasis on the operations that are underperforming or in jeopardy, so that less backtracking will be needed, and less legal risk created, if and when the unit is jettisoned.

In summary, packaging the message consists of figuratively putting the company into a box. The box contains the most compelling reasons for investing in the company, with carefully selected supporting information. The package is small, with little or no room for extraneous material. Lastly, the message has a long shelf life, so that the contents of this box will still be fresh even if the package is opened a year from now.

It is widely accepted that the fundamentals of a specific company create only a small percentage of its valuation in the investment market. The overall trend of the stock market is believed to rank first in establishing the value of all corporations, in keeping with the concept that a rising tide lifts all boats. Next, industry trends or fundamentals determine whether a company is in favor or not. Finally, the characteristics of the company itself are considered.

The general insight provided here is undoubtedly valid. On average, the investor relations executive works at the margin. The last 20 to 30 percent of pricing, rather than the first 70 to 80 percent, is the average area influenced by the investor relations program.

But this common wisdom, like actuarial tables, is valid only in the broadest sense. It fails to take into account the level of proactive effort devoted to marketing each company. If most companies have only limited investor marketing efforts, does their valuation essentially get set in a vacuum? Without an aggressive IR program, do general market and industry trends serve as a disproportionately critical proxy for the company's characteristics?

One could readily argue that this is so. If a corporation makes no effort to distinguish itself from peers or from all other stocks, and if management is content to allow investment assumptions to be based on general market models, then the result is a stock price driven almost exclusively by external factors.

This isn't to say any specific stock can be immune to overall market pressures, but rather that the investor relations program can influence far more than the 20 to 30 percent cited above.

Intuitively, this should not be surprising. In any product category, it is the value added, the last incremental addition to quality or marketing that makes the major difference. A buyer of gasoline, for example, buys regular gasoline for 1.4 cents per octane rating; however, the last four points of octane that make the gasoline "premium" are priced at 2.5 cents each. A cup of coffee at the diner costs 85 cents, while a premium blend at a gourmet coffee shop goes for $2. The producer's cost of the added value is irrelevant in these examples. The perceived difference in value to the buyer is what makes the higher price acceptable. Value-added marketing works the same way in investor relations.

Creating that added value—or more accurately, identifying it—requires an intense analysis of the corporation. From the financials to the corporate culture to the product pipeline to how well the CEO and CFO get along, every facet of the company has the potential to influence investors. The best of efforts will identify those features that make the investment a "premium product" in the minds of investors, justifying a relatively higher valuation than something that is almost, but not quite, as good.

In this analysis, the IR professional is looking for the edge. It's not simply a search for the right numbers or facts. This search is directed toward the few key ideas that separate this investment from all others in a positive way.

Before we start looking for these advantages, it's important to consider some fundamental notions.

1. **Risk/Reward.** Everyone knows that, all other things being equal, the investor who takes a riskier position demands a greater potential reward than one who assumes a more conservative position. But risk and reward are constantly changing and *the perception of risk and reward can be influenced through IR efforts.* Interestingly, it is the perception of risk, rather than reward, that is most readily influenced by investor relations work. Perceived risk can be reduced through more consistent communications. Investor confidence can be increased and perceived risk reduced by assuring consistent access to top management. Early and frequent insights and updates regarding problems or opportunities, properly disclosed, can make performance more predictable and add a premium to stock valuation. This means that a proactive, credible IR effort, by itself, can add to relative stock valuation. In addition, IR efforts can build value by demonstrating why risks are less than might be obvious or potential rewards greater than might be assumed.

2. **Weakness Is Strength.** While this Orwellian concept is not obvious to most people at first blush, the idea has tremendous value when marketing the investment return potential of a company. A firm with 100-percent market share and 99-percent gross margin has only one direction to go—down. But a company that is underperforming its peers has higher upside potential if it can improve performance. *An example: A banking client makes the point that, despite rapid progress in building return on assets, the ROA level still is well behind*

industry averages. Simply bringing that number up to industry norms would create a dramatic improvement in earnings. By showing how the bank will achieve that improvement, we increase investor confidence that this is a high-potential investment.

2a. **Strength Is Strength.** While too much strength can suggest downside risk, as would be the case for our company with 100-percent market share, it is often easier to explain how a company will maintain its position than to convince people a weakness can be overcome. In trying to influence investor perceptions of reward, past successes give rise to confidence that future ventures will succeed as well.

3. **Memories Are Long.** For better or worse, actions taken by a company a decade or more earlier can influence valuations today. Historical context must always be considered in developing any internal analysis. The challenge is always to explain why the present is or isn't similar to the past. Even if the explanation is kept in abeyance as a response to inquiries, not offered as a proactive discussion point, that perspective is important.

4. **Moderation in All Things.** Investors may love it when their stocks suddenly begin to soar, but high-fliers also have a tendency to crash and burn. When a company's shares are enjoying spectacular growth, the credibility-minded IR expert will seek to temper enthusiasm just a bit. *One of this author's best investments was a high-tech darling of Wall Street that lost about two-thirds of its value after announcing earnings wouldn't rise as fast as the analysts expected. As the stock price rose, analysts needed to ratchet up their expectations to justify holding the stock. When those expectations weren't met for just one quarter, everyone headed for the door, creating a buying opportunity for new investors—and a nightmare for the IR department.* Distancing the company from Wall Street's excesses is a good defensive practice and a long-term credibility builder.

CHOOSE YOUR WEAPONS: MARKETING MATERIALS

While packaging a message is a figurative process, presentation of the investment story relies on physical constructs. The message is delivered directly or indirectly through marketing materials, or directly via personal contact.

In this chapter, we review marketing materials, which range from documents filed with the SEC to annual reports and database entries. For the IR exec, the choice of vehicles and forms should focus on the best medium for demonstrating the investment story. While written materials can serve quite well for simple stories, for example, an IR executive might choose videotape for stories that must be seen to be understood. Similarly, photographs might be worth a thousand words in treating retail operations, but an illustration could be essential for explaining biotech research.

As the array of options is examined, one question must be first in mind: *Why should I buy this stock?* A brief review of marketing materials follows.

SHAREHOLDER REPORTS

Shareholder reports make up the first group of marketing materials and fall into the *entitlements* category for most companies.

14-1   The Annual Report Is a Strategic Planning Tool

The annual report is one of few IR documents subject to deadlines. The set date of the annual meeting guarantees that management will focus, eventually, on the report and its messages. For the IR executive, this certainty creates the opportunity to use the annual report process as a strategic-planning exercise—if not for the corporation, certainly for the IR program itself.

Annual report planning begins well ahead of year-end, as does the budgeting process. Both efforts should be guided by the company's outlook and financial needs. The IR executive should use the access and focus provided by the annual report to:

1. Determine how the IR effort can facilitate corporate goals. If, for example, the company plans to expand facilities over the next five years, the IR executive should study the timetable and learn whether public markets will be accessed to fund the expansion. If the goal is to build a small unit until it can be spun off or sold, the IR director should begin looking at potential buyers and forms of spinoff.

2. Incorporate these insights into the strategic planning of IR marketing efforts. If long-term spinoff is planned, the IR executive might recommend a near-term higher profile—more pages in the annual and segment breakouts—for the subsidiary. A visit of analysts to the subsidiary facility, rather than corporate headquarters, might also become part of the marketing mix.

3. Demonstrate linkage between messages to be sent and long-term business goals in the annual report plan. For some companies it might be appropriate to offer a multiyear plan for the annual reports, just as a multiyear plan for IR marketing might be in order.

For many companies, strategic planning efforts are postponed by the crush of daily business, and there are few reality checks for management's view of the future. The IR executive, leveraging off the annual report process, is uniquely positioned to force management to take a hard look at its own assumptions and goals. Often, management views and statements will be recast as the annual report process continues.

Although the size and form of the annual report can vary widely from company to company, some form of annual report is required for all public companies.

Shareholder documents offer high leverage potential as marketing materials, simply because some of their cost is already covered in an *entitlements* budget. In addition, because these documents will automatically be requested and reviewed by any significant potential investors, the information they contain—for better or worse—will constitute much of the message *received*.

Annual Reports. The annual report is widely maligned as the only book read by more people prior to printing than afterward. Surveys suggest that few individual investors and relatively few brokers read it cover to cover, and that leads many corporate chiefs to consider it a necessary and expensive evil.

Such executives will often choose to send shareholders nothing more than their annual report on Form 10-K, a report required by the SEC and, as such, the minimum acceptable standard for annual reporting to shareholders. The 10-K covers key points about the company's operations, facilities, financial performance and other matters in a strictly defined format, and using it as a marketing tool is about as effective as selling cruises with schematic drawings of the engine room.

Too bad. The annual report is singularly the best opportunity and vehicle the investor relations executive can use to define and deliver the investment message. Because the report must be written, and must be delivered prior to the proxy and the annual meeting, the need to focus on investor marketing issues cannot be postponed indefinitely by other priorities within the company. If the investor relations executive leads the charge for making the annual report a true marketing tool, the development and production process will focus management's attention on these messages more certainly than any other ongoing effort. (See 14-1, *The Annual Report Is a Strategic Planning Tool.*)

The first challenge is to gain control of the report. The annual report has many expert contributors, including: attorneys who will worry about potential lawsuits if the company talks too much about its plans; marketing vice presidents who believe anything but the most positive descriptions will send customers into a panic; auditors who decide they are also professional writers; and designers who view text as a constraint on their artistic freedom.

For the investor relations executive, the result can be a series of firefights over seemingly minor issues and the ultimate homogenization of the report into a document that could serve for 50 other companies, if only the names and a few numbers were changed. Ultimately, such reports detail activities that occurred three to 15 months earlier, while lauding employees and management for whatever terrific—or rotten—results were achieved.

In many companies, changing this process is an uphill fight, but the results are worth it. The investor relations executive must seek to create a conspiracy—a conspiracy of thought. Through lobbying or persuasion, the IR exec must convince each internal constituency that the annual report:

- is the company's primary investor marketing tool and therefore must focus primarily on the need to convince (a) current shareholders not to sell their stock and (b) potential shareholders to buy it.

- must show consistency in projections, strategies and achievements from the front of the book to the back. (Too often, the issues covered in the financial review are remarkably different from those in the letter to shareholders, and neither bears much resemblance to the text about operations.)

- creates the perfect opportunity for all members of management to focus on the company's investment message, plans and obstacles, and on marketing of the firm in the investment community.

That last point is absolutely critical. The process of creating an annual report involves many departments over a long period of time. Through repeated contacts, interviews and editing cycles, the IR executive can act as the chief negotiator in both hammering out the updated investor marketing plan and convincing the various executives to sign on to the program.

This is not to suggest this is always a Herculean task or that the IR executive will change each manager's views or practices. However, this exercise does create the opportunity to explain and re-explain how various messages or gaps in presentation will influence the value of the company's stock—along with executives' stock options.

One of the best ways to gather ammunition is to survey current opinion leaders and conduct a competitor analysis. Current opinion leaders include analysts following the company or its peers, individual shareholders and financial news writers. Such surveys should be relatively brief and should focus more on messages and questions than on the annual report. (See 14-2, *Annual Report Checklist*.)

First, the IR exec should send the opinion leader a copy of the prior year's report, with a request that the recipient review the document. Then, the IR exec should ask essentially two questions:

1. Did last year's annual report answer the questions and concerns you had about the company? How do you think it did or didn't do this?

2. What are the most important questions or issues that will determine whether you increase or decrease your investment in (or rating of) the company in the coming year?

Note that these questions are not focused on what the person wants to see in this year's report. The person being queried is not an annual report writer and the purpose of the survey is to identify issues, not photo selections. At the same time, comments on the prior year's report will provide insights into technical issues (small type, odd color choices) that made the report harder to read or understand.

Prior annual reports also are a good starting point for message selection. Because major potential investors will ask for several years' worth of annual reports as part of their due diligence, consistency of messages or approach from year to year can make

185

14-2   Annual Report Checklist

Once work begins on an annual report, the project takes on a life of its own. Equally significant, schedules for the report become compressed as daily life intervenes. Effective planning is the key to successful implementation. Before the first interview and before the report outline is written, the IR executive should cover the following ground.

Review

___ Prior company annuals and all other documents.

___ Competitors' annuals and published documents.

___ Research reports on company and competitors.

___ Professional articles on trends in investor thought.

___ Changes in reporting requirements.

___ News articles and critiques on annual report practice.

___ Corporate strategic plan and IR marketing plan.

Consult

___ Analysts, reporters, other opinion leaders.

___ CEO, CFO and several other top corporate executives.

___ Designers, auditors, attorneys.

Establish

___ Small group session on goals of company, IR and annual.

___ Rough timing for annual report plan and review process.

___ Responsibilities for coordination, writing, review.

Decisions made under fire, during the rush to complete the annual, often interfere with the message the company intends to transmit. If the IR executive completes the previous steps, decision-making will be more effective because each factor can be judged against standards already established, standards that have been communicated to all on the annual report team.

---

a major difference among investor targets. Each year's annual report should revisit issues raised in the prior year's document and review progress made, new developments, etc.

Next, a study of competitors' annuals is important. While the investor relations executive doesn't look to copy approaches taken by others, it is important to know the industry standard of performance. For example, do competitors break out lines of business in great detail in both the operations review and the financial tables? Do competitors review the legislative or environmental issues that influence the market? Do competitors disclose only the minimum information required?

Just as the IR executive looks for the incremental edge in other areas, the focus on competitors' annuals is geared toward gaining some advantage in marketing materials. Whether the goal is to meet or exceed industry disclosure standards, or to find out what claims made by competitors contradict claims made by the IR exec's company, knowing the enemy is essential.

As with anything else, creating the annual report is a process of elimination. While all sorts of good ideas for sidebar text, photos, graphs and other bells and whistles might be recommended, the primary screening question is always the same: *Does it help us sell the stock?* Obviously, that doesn't mean every sentence has to focus on the company's shares. But it does mean that budget dollars should be used where they will do the most good. (See 14-3, *Types of Annual Reports.*)

Thus, a photo of products on display in a retail store might be of minimal value, unless the caption can explain that the use of the new display format has increased sales per foot by X percent. Likewise, a photo of employees meeting with management will add little to the report, unless the company can cite management's regular schedule of meetings with production-line workers in quality circles or other joint efforts. Pictures that look forced or artificial can detract from the strength of the IR message, even as they add to the cost of the report.

Here's a shorthand way to begin the annual report process:

1. All the shareholders of the company are about to sell their shares.
2. What can I say to change their minds?

Quarterly Reports. Everything that applies to the annual report applies to the quarterlies. Surprisingly few companies,

14-3   Types of Annual Reports

Each spring, financial reporters check the first few annual reports received and tell us how this year's batch differs from the past. In fact, annual report practice is fairly stable. Most firms are consistent in content and format of the annuals they produce. The types can include:

10-K Report. Some companies simply file the required report with the SEC and mail copies to shareholders.

10-K Wrap Report. Many companies send a 10-K report with a shareholder letter or other supporting information wrapped around it. Some are quite effective, using the wraparound pages to send the investment message convincingly, while others betray a lack of interest on the part of management.

Glossy Annual. The standard annual report includes a letter to shareholders, operations review, insights into strategy, financial tables and analysis of performance. Glossy annuals can sell the investment message convincingly, although many reports end up too slick in style and bland in content to be effective.

Summary Annual. The summary report is simply a glossy annual with limited financial numbers because much required disclosure is moved to the proxy statement. Summary annuals have cost advantages for very large or highly regulated entities, but they offer no advantage for most firms and run counter to the trend toward greater disclosure in annual reports.

Special Formats. Annual reports on videotape, on computer disk, in the form of notebooks and other special approaches can present information in novel and effective ways. Few companies will attempt these special formats without also preparing some form of standard annual.

Whatever the form, it's important to maintain focus on the investor message. Frequently, pretty pictures are selected solely for artistic merit, even though they fail to tell the investment story, or type sizes are adjusted to maximize "negative space" (air) in the report. As always, form should follow function.

14-4   Quarterly Report Checklist

The quarterly report should continue the communications role begun in the annual. Among the features to be considered for each quarterly report are these:

__ Design continuity with the annual, including pickup of design elements, icons, theme statements or photos.

__ Continuation of discussions from the annual report, with reference back to the annual, whether these continuations appear in a "Strategic Update" section or in the shareholder letter.

__ A company description that restates the investment message covered in the annual and other documents.

__ Feedback mechanism, including a contact name, address and phone number for individuals seeking more information.

__ Financial tables including at least an income statement and balance sheet, but also including cash flow statements for companies whose cash flow is a subject of investor attention.

__ Shareholder letters that look back to promises and strategies made earlier, as well as toward plans currently being implemented.

As with the annual, the investor message should be the predominant focus of the quarterly report to shareholders.

---

including many large ones, take advantage of the opportunity to make their case with interim reports to shareholders. Instead, the quarterly reports consist of little more than a bland shareholder letter that simply recites the numbers in the accompanying tables. (See 14-4, *Quarterly Report Checklist.*)

As long as the company is going to invest the money in some kind of report, it pays to focus on interim benchmarks and progress since the start of the year. A very simple and effective approach is to put a series of bulleted highlights on the cover or to have a news panel inside to review recent developments in a context different from the letter to shareholders.

In addition, very few quarterlies include a recitation of the company's investment merits. While many include some description of the company, very few direct that text toward investors. Compare:

"One of the nation's largest buggy-whip manufacturers, Oxtails International Corporation, is expanding its distribution into four new nations in 1994, bringing its total potential market population to 357 million. . . ."

versus . . .

"Founded in 1827, Oxtails International Corporation designs, manufactures, distributes and sells products related to horse drawn conveyances, including buggy whips...."

From the company description to the shareholder letter, news panel and financial tables, the quarterly report must be approached as an opportunity to reinforce the investment message.

Proxy Statements. Proxy statements are to marketing as:

a) warning labels are to snowmobiles,
b) instruction manuals are to children's toys,
c) menu listings of calories and cholesterol are to dining, or
d) worse than a, b and c combined.

The correct answer, of course, is "d" because proxy statements combine the worst of legalistic prose with the most detailed disclosure of costly details about company operations. These include the disclosure of top executive compensation levels, employee retirement and other benefit plans, and the review of the company's stock-price performance in comparison to both peers and a broad-based index of other stocks.

Because the proxy statement is the format in which shareholders are asked to exercise their ownership rights—by voting their shares at the annual meeting—the format and language of the proxy are dictated almost exclusively by lawyers seeking to avoid potential problems.

Prior to 1993, few investor relations executives would have looked at proxy statements as a marketing document of any kind. After all, the issues presented to the shareholders at annual meetings tend to be relatively noncontroversial matters such as ratifying the auditor selection, affirming management's choice of directors, or approving changes in employee stock ownership or option plans. In the takeover binge of the 1980s, poison pills and other antitakeover issues also might have appeared as proxy issues, but these, too, presented little opportunity or cause to promote investment in the company.

The personality of the proxy changed in 1993, however, when the Securities and Exchange Commission began requiring three new forms of disclosure, all resulting from the ongoing debate over the level of executive compensation at public companies.

First, the SEC required a simplified and more standardized disclosure of compensation among top executives. Next, the compensation committee of the board was required to report on the standards applied in setting compensation levels. Finally, the SEC required a graphic display of stock price trends, comparing the company's price performance against a peer group and a broad-based market index.

A survey conducted by our firm indicated that most professional investors would appreciate having the extra number crunching done for them, but didn't expect to see many surprises or to change their investments as a result of that disclosure. The point they stressed was that most of the information already was available in proxy statements and from other sources, so the new rules simply made it easier to get the same information and, in some cases, more precise numbers.

In the first year these rules were in effect, most companies adopted a wait-and-see attitude. They complied with the letter of the law, but were careful not to stray far beyond that bright line.

But some companies did take the opportunity to explain their cases more forcefully in the proxy statement and to add extra detail and insight into executive compensation and price trends. After all, the SEC rules set only the minimum standard of disclosure, not a maximum.

Before the new rules took effect, most of the articles published on the subject focused on how to comply with the rules. Which broad-based indexes were acceptable? How should the compensation committee's report be written? Lost in the shuffle was the more important question for the IR executive: *How do you turn this regulatory exercise into a marketing message?* (See 14-5, *Making the Proxy Statement Work for You.*)

Granted, rapid increases in executive compensation at the same time share prices are plunging, both nominally and relatively, creates a rather negative form of disclosure. But companies with moderate compensation or relatively strong market performance have an opportunity to use the proxy statement to explain the *whys* and *hows* of the trends. Companies that don't believe the required disclosure covers all the relevant points are certainly free to offer an explanation of added issues, as long as the information is presented in a circumspect manner and the required documentation also is provided.

In coming years, this disclosure is likely to be expanded voluntarily by companies that have more positive stories to tell, and ultimately the information will begin creeping into annual reports as part of the discussion expected, although not required, by investors.

Until then, even the simplest of proxy improvements has yet to be adopted by most companies, such as a letter inviting shareholders to the annual meeting and describing the issues to be covered. Most proxy statements greet shareholders as warmly as a draft notice, but again, there is no law requiring that this be the case. Will a friendlier welcome letter on the proxy statement add a few price/earnings points? No way. But it's one more minor adjustment that can be made to an expenditure that's already an entitlement, while adding just a bit to the company's favorable image among its owners.

Statement-Stuffers. For companies paying dividends, a statement-stuffer or other message can be sent along with the dividend checks mailed to those shareholders who hold their stock in their own names. (Those whose shares are held by brokers simply have dividends credited to their accounts.) Many

14-5 Making the Proxy Statement Work for You

The proxy statement is written by lawyers for regulators, making it an unlikely source of IR marketing opportunity. However, the required disclosures of executive compensation and share-price performance now included in these documents make them a must-read for investors. The IR executive might propose:

1. **Changing the language to a more user-friendly style.** This requires delicate negotiation with attorneys who will likely consider the proxy off-limits to others, but it's worth a try. Proxies can be written in clear language and the investor would be better off if they were.

2. **More disclosure in the compensation and stock performance sections.** The SEC's rules for filed documents allow for little variation when a company is merely meeting the minimum requirements. But this *one-size-fits-all* approach might not tell the story for any specific firm. A company could add tables and charts showing compensation and other data in forms that make the investment case or explain a compensation issue. Phrased properly, such a presentation approach should add no risk of successful litigation, and it can help in marketing the company.

3. **Including proxy information in the annual report.** If the attorneys won't permit much change in the proxy itself, there's no reason the same kinds of discussions and commentary cannot also appear in the annual. Management can discuss the proxy data in the context of other events, programs, strategies and issues not covered in the proxy. (These separate discussions cannot contradict one another, of course, and it would be a mistake to add substantially more detail to one as opposed to another.)

Most companies will miss the opportunity to achieve any benefits from the required disclosure. This failure gives other IR executives a chance to separate their firms from the crowd and get added attention for their message.

firms simply send the quarterly report and dividend check together, but some will print a message on an enlarged check stub, insert an attractive reprint or otherwise ensure that this welcome correspondence includes an investment message.

Shareholder Welcome Kits. It's an adage on Wall Street that stocks are sold, not bought, which means that many investors purchase shares without having conducted a full-scale research effort on the company. This is the case for both individual and institutional investors.

The investor relations executive who wants to retain the shareholder's long-term commitment will send a welcome kit to new investors. Whether for all investors or those buying some minimum number of shares, the kits can include a letter about the company, the latest annual and other corporate reports, and a reply card. The reply card can be used to identify the investment merits that led to the purchase, the broker or other opinion leader who brought the company to the holder's attention, and so on.

For institutional investors, the kit can certainly be more thorough than for individuals. It might include several years' reports, the home number of the investor relations executive, a key chain or other small gift with the company's name on it and other extras.

A corollary is the shareholder farewell letter. Here, the investor relations executive sends a letter to those who sell their shares. The mailing briefly expresses concern about the sale of stock, encourages the former holder to keep the company in mind for repurchase later, and includes a reply mechanism such as a postage-paid card to identify any trends in the reasons people sell the stock.

PROSPECTING MATERIALS

In addition to materials that must be sent to shareholders, the corporation should provide a number of documents intended to solicit new support for the company. While these prospecting materials can be sent to current shareholders and other audiences, their primary purpose is to attract new followers.

News Releases. Many companies send news releases directly to shareholders, while others send them only to the news media.

News releases are considered materials because they are printed documents sent to the contacts on the fax list and the mailing list of followers, and sometimes are distributed to investor prospects as well. News releases might just as accurately be considered indirect selling tools, which are covered later, because their immediate objective is to lead third parties like reporters, analysts, newsletter writers, etc., to update, translate, and redeliver the message.

Although the recipient of a news release is expected to call management for comment prior to writing an update report, the release itself must be prepared so it can stand on its own and answer any questions that arise. It must be believable and thorough, addressing both the negatives and the positives in clear and convincing language.

Frequently, managements will seek to gloss over negative points in a news release, hoping to emphasize the positives alone. Such releases usually end up getting no redistribution or, worse, stirring up the more cynical reporters and analysts who then write reports that highlight the negatives. (See 14-6, *Ensuring Success, Guaranteeing Failure.*) Because the news release is management's proxy, making a presentation of results in lieu of personal calls from the chief executive, the release must be put together to achieve three goals:

1. *Explain recent developments* within the context of corporate strategies, previously announced events and industry trends. Absent this context, the person who is preparing a report based on the release might jump to the wrong conclusion about its meaning or about how the results fit into the big picture.

2. *Increase support for the company* by displaying the kind of credibility and commitment to the investor that leads

14-6   Ensuring Success, Guaranteeing Failure

Ideally, a press release will appear exactly as written on the financial wires. More commonly, releases are drafted in ways that guarantee they will be misinterpreted, rewritten with errors or simply tossed in the garbage. Here are some ways to ensure successful pickup.

1. **Write It Like a News Article.** No one has seen a news article that began, "Joe Dokes, Chairman and Chief Executive Officer of Dokes Company (NASDAQ:JOEDOKE) today announced results for the third quarter ended September 30, 1994." Amazingly, some people still write releases this way.

2. **Tell the Story.** The reporter wants the first paragraph to include the news and some explanation (reasons or future impact). If the reporter would likely write, "Thane's Pie Company plans to acquire its largest competitor, furthering its strategy to have operations in all 50 states by 1997," write the release that way. Don't bury the 50-state goal on page three and hope the reporter will see the connection.

3. **Include Comparative Data.** Many companies will leave numbers out of a release, forcing the reporter to call to get the information. This creates potential for errors, as discussion of numbers is translated to paper.

4. **Be There.** Reporters often complain that contacts listed on the release are unavailable when they call, leading to incomplete articles.

5. **Give Them Time.** A release sent during the busiest time of day or the busiest week of the quarter will receive less attention and care than one sent when the reporter is less busy. Use this knowledge.

Unlike other printed documents, press releases are translated and retransmitted by a third party before reaching the intended audience. A no-fault system should be pursued to assure accurate translation.

reporters and analysts to give management the benefit of the doubt on judgment calls. Sometimes that requires some pain, as when negative developments are described in detail, but that pain can be alleviated if management also explains what is being done, or has been done, to eliminate the problems.

3. *Gain ample coverage.* Whether the news is good or bad, the purpose of the news release is to get third parties to pay attention to the company. While it would be foolish to suggest that any coverage at all is a positive (as long as the name is spelled right), the fact is that regular coverage and updates from the investment community and journalists let investors know that the company is important enough for these third parties to pay attention to developments.

The news release must be crafted with great care and intensive focus on the audience. Even if the recipient is expected to absorb or report only a limited amount of what is in the release, the company is, in effect, making its record and its public plea for support. Consequently, this indirect mechanism of reaching investors is a more complicated and influential animal than many firms realize.

Fact Sheets and Books. The fact book or fact sheet is the most flexible and effective approach to direct prospecting among potential investors. While the annual report and other shareholder documents have several constituents and participants, both internally and externally, the investor fact book falls solely within the domain of the investor relations professional. That makes it a relatively simple matter to craft the message and develop the document with minimal conflict, although the non-required nature of the document also makes its timely publication less certain. Fact sheets or books tend to be indefinitely postponable, unlike annual reports, so getting them to print requires strong commitment on the part of the IR director.

The fact book gives the company a chance to present its investment message in its purest form—as a straight sales document prepared by the company for the express purpose of gaining investors. In addition to providing the most compelling case for the company, these documents offer a critical advantage to investors: time. Because the investment message is unadulterated by text directed at employees, vendors and other corporate constituencies, the potential investor needs to spend less time studying the story.

Many companies prepare both a fact book and a fact sheet, but it is more common for a firm to prepare one or the other. Each has its own advantages.

The fact sheet affords the lowest cost of production, the least time input and the greatest ease of update. It is effective with both retail audiences and institutional investors and it makes for a good brief backgrounder for reporters preparing for interviews.

The fact book tends to be more costly and detailed, so it is done on a longer timetable and is less likely to be updated on a regular basis. On the other hand, the level of depth it can provide makes it a solid research document for investors, financial reporters and others.

The best fact sheets/books will resemble research reports in style and content. They will present an investment thesis, following up with ample documentation. The reason for this similarity is simple. The company is speaking the same language as the audience, which is essential to effective communications.

Books containing extensive visual effects, whether glossy photos or bold graphics, might look too slick and more like marketing materials than investor reports, which can actually cost some credibility among investors. The more "packaged" a document appears, the more likely it is to raise the defenses of the reader.

At times, financial writers at major publications have become exercised over fact books that look too much (in their view) like research reports. Investors, they suggest, will become confused and see these documents as coming from independent third parties, as opposed to being funded by the company. In several instances, their concern has been justified. A number of outside sources provide fact sheets/books on a fee basis and dress them up to look as if the provider was an outside brokerage house or research boutique.

However, a fact book/sheet that is identified as coming from the corporation and includes attribution to the company is morally and ethically beyond reproach, no matter who writes or distributes it. Such documents should not include price targets or recommendations (buy, accumulate, etc.), as these fall strictly in the domain of independent investment advisers.

Videotapes/Audiotapes. Videotapes and audiotapes are an extension of the corporate fact book/sheet. Utilizing a different technology, these nonpublished materials can offer a level of insight unavailable through the printed page. Certainly, a videotape can take the investor inside a facility and enable the prospect to see the surgery or examine the interior of the store. An audiotape can literally speak in several voices, giving added impact to comments from employees, customers or others who provide various testimonials and comments.

Several years ago, our firm conducted a survey that pointed to videotapes as an effective marketing tool for investors. Although penetration levels for videorecorders were lower than at present, a majority of the brokers who had viewed videotaped presentations indicated they had ended up recommending at least one of the companies introduced to them via videotape.

While both videotapes and audiotapes require equipment for playback, unlike printed pages, they also offer added sound/image dimensions. It's also quite safe to listen to an audiotape in a moving car, but reading and driving simultaneously are not recommended activities.

In addition to developing corporate videos or audiotapes to explain the company story, many firms will put together tapes of the annual meeting or of an analyst meeting. Such tapes broadcast the messages delivered at these events and give the viewer/listener a sense of being at the scene.

But every message loses something in translation, and a direct transfer from a live presentation to a videotape format represents less than an optimal choice. The presentation provided at the analyst meeting might reflect the best approach to telling the company's story to a live audience of many people. However, this approach probably isn't the best for the lone videotape view-

199

er. The media are different and the dynamics of the relationship between individual and audience are different, so the effectiveness of one format may be reduced when the same presentation is transferred unchanged to a different medium. (However, the cost/benefit advantages of a simple transfer might be too compelling to ignore.)

Speech/Slide Presentations. The investor presentation that includes speech and/or slides represents a compromise of approaches. The large-scale meeting between corporate executives and potential or current investors requires a human-level communication effort. It simply doesn't do to have the CEO turn on a videotape and watch along with the audience. While a brief video, audiotape or other format might be utilized effectively to present added detail (new advertisements, views of operations, etc.) within the speech, it is specifically the live presentation and Q&A session that the investor presentation audience seeks.

In the ideal case, the corporate spokesman will have a conversation with each member of the audience, reviewing key points of the investment message and then taking questions. With a larger audience, the conversation becomes a speech and the give-and-take that follows is just a bit more formal. (See 14-7, *How to Write a Speech.*)

Printed documents can be somewhat less repetitive than verbal presentations. With the printed page, the reader can refer back to an earlier point, but the same cannot be done in the case of a speech. Therefore, the classic format of effective speaking applies to most investor presentations:

1. Tell them what you're going to tell them.
2. Tell them.
3. Tell them what you've told them.

Speech content will vary by company, but the fundamentals never change. The speaker's opening comments must serve only one purpose: to convince the listener to pay close attention to the rest of the speech. Just as the single purpose of an annual report cover is to get the prospect or shareholder to open the book, so the speech must be designed to spark enough interest to maintain attention as the talk continues.

14-7   How To Write a Speech

Analyst presentations are relatively simple, yet few companies execute well in telling their stories to large groups. Reasons are many, including a tendency toward excessive detail and historic focus. Good speech writing depends on several elements.

1. **Structure.** Structure is based more on the mechanics of auditory learning than on the company itself. The first minute or two of the speech must be devoted to getting the audience's attention; the speaker should tell why investors should be interested in the company. In the several minutes that follow, the speaker should build the case one appeal at a time, showing how the pieces fit to form the whole. In the final few minutes, the speaker should recount the original points and tell how the details prove the case.

2. **Cadence.** The words and flow should match the speaker's vocal patterns. For example, a forceful speaker often uses shorter sentences than a passive person. Failure to match speech to speaker can lead to a presentation that sounds unnatural.

3. **Visual Support.** While slides and other visual aids must support the speech, they should not duplicate all points in the text. Slides should reinforce the highlights, but cramming in too much detail tends to bury the key points.

4. **Know the Audience.** Write the speech based on what the audience needs to know. If the audience needs a hook to sell the stock to retail investors, or a detailed explanation of debt to calm institutions, cover these points clearly. Invariably, the audience needs to know about company plans and outlook because all investment is future-oriented. History offers less value.

Repetition is key to effective speeches because it is how auditory messages are internalized. By repeating key points and linking them repeatedly to other matters in the speech, the speaker can force the core message into the listener's memory.

The length and level of detail in each speech will vary according to time, audience sophistication and size, meeting type and so on. Comments made during a conference call tied to quarterly earnings will differ in structure and scope from those offered at an annual meeting or investor conference.

201

Reprints. The company's own documents can be customized to tell the investment story exactly as the investor relations executive intends, but the best of these materials may lack one critical element—the credibility that comes from endorsement by an independent third party.

Reprints of third-party documents, including news articles or brokerage reports, can provide compelling support to any investor relations program. While the third party will never say exactly what management would like, or do so as management would, the credibility of an independent observer can more than compensate for this gap.

Recommendations and write-ups can be reprinted and sent to investors and prospects as part of an overall marketing program, adding credence to the statements of management. However, a number of caveats apply.

1. *Reprint permission is essential.* Many financial publications and brokerage houses have become extremely protective of their copyrights and some have placed substantial restrictions on the types of mailings that can be conducted with the documents. Even though an article appeared in a publication reaching a million readers, the publisher might balk at a mailing of the piece to potential investors. The reason: the publisher doesn't want to appear to be endorsing the company, regardless of the words in the text.

2. *Disclaimers are important.* Not every statement made in the report will match management's view, although the decision to mail the report to followers can imply that management endorses it all. In the case of research reports, a mailing to followers might be taken as management's confirmation of the earnings estimates contained in the report. In any case, distribution should include a disclaimer that indicates the company doesn't necessarily agree or disagree with each point in the document and that the mailing is for informational purposes. (Check language with your legal counsel.)

Reprints can include documents that don't mention the company at all. A firm developing casinos in Oklahoma might send out a series of reports on how the growth of casinos changed the economy of Texas. Or a company developing a cure for the flu might distribute an article on the number of people who get the flu each year, emphasizing the cost of lost work days, doctors' appointments, etc.

Computer Disks. The computer disk is yet another format for telling the corporate story. Such disks often are interactive, enabling the prospect to select various options to review or to manipulate numbers on the screen.

These disks tend to be less forceful than videotape and less flexible than printed documents, limiting their effectiveness as an investment marketing tool for many companies. However, the use of these disks is likely to continue and could become more effective. Increasingly powerful personal computers, including systems with CD-ROM drives, can accommodate higher sophistication levels and features in the disks sent to investors.

Gifts. Gifts, mementos and freebies of all sorts can be effective marketing tools for investors, as they are for commercial prospects. However, the cost of the gifts and the impact on share purchases make this avenue one of limited economic value to most companies. While major shareholders or other supporters might qualify for a paperweight with the company's logo, relatively few people will fit the criteria for receiving the item. Small tokens often are distributed at analyst meetings or annual shareholder meetings, but broad distribution is relatively rare.

The best gifts are those that highlight the company and its products. It helps, of course, to be in the market with a product that your investors can use. For example, a company that makes pocket calculators can distribute its own product as a freebie.

Gifts should also lend themselves to recipient use, rather than passoff to the recipient's children or spouse, and repeated exposure keeping the company's name before the investor. Calendars, if used by recipients, are ideal because they are used—and the company's name viewed—for a full year.

15

CHOOSE YOUR WEAPONS: SALES AND DISTRIBUTION

The dividing line between the last chapter and this one is arbitrary. Materials, sales platforms and distribution mechanisms form a continuum of sorts. While the speech for analysts counts as marketing material, the analyst meeting itself is a sales platform. Mailing the videotape (materials) of the meeting to investor prospects would be classified as distribution.

At some point, it becomes essentially impossible to draw a bright line between the messages conveyed, the media used to convey them and the delivery mechanism. For purposes of this discussion, sales formats include delivery mechanisms rather than the materials delivered. The three forms of delivery for the investment message are:

- Direct personal contact
- Direct distribution
- Indirect distribution

Each has its values in the IR marketing mix, and each combines a specific weighting of investment of management's time and dollars, and effort on the part of the audience.

205

DIRECT PERSONAL CONTACT

Direct personal contact is the most expensive type of IR marketing because it requires investment of management's time in addition to dollars. Personal contact should be reserved for the opportunities with highest leverage in terms of potential support.

Management Presentations. Presentations by management, which usually involve the CEO and/or CFO, can be conducted in a variety of formats, the only common link being that the format permits an interchange between management and investors. Such presentations can be arranged by the company, using its own resources and lists, or under the auspices of an outside enterprise, which can include a sponsoring brokerage firm, a stock exchange club or brokers' club, or industry organizations.

The self-sponsored meeting has a number of major advantages. All details are within the control of the company, from the time and location to the food served and the list of invitees. Especially for firms with a large following of investors, the self-sponsored meeting provides the best opportunity to speak to a highly pre-qualified group of supporters. (See 15-1, *Selecting an Audience.*)

Self-sponsored meetings can and should include both existing followers and high-potential prospects, so that management can attract new support at the same time existing support is maintained. In any case, the self-sponsored program offers the company the maximum potential to customize the presentation, location, logistics and audience.

Meetings sponsored by outside organizations offer less room for customizing and more volume, in most cases. Quite often, the company picks up the tab for the meeting, including lunches, without any control over the program or the attendance list. On the other hand, some forums require that attendees or the sponsoring organization pick up the cost.

A firm that opts to present to a local brokers' club or analyst society, for example, will usually be required to cover the cost of

15-1   Selecting an Audience

Audience selection is always a daunting challenge. No matter how carefully the IR executive screens a group of prospects, the ultimate group of attendees for any large meeting will include some clinkers. Continual pre-screening and weeding of the prospect lists is essential. Audience selection should follow a few simple rules:

1. **Consider Existing Holders First.** People who already have an investment should be the first to receive an invitation.

2. **Match Interest/Influence to Meeting Size.** The closest followers or the most influential prospects should receive invitations to smaller meetings or one-on-one sessions so they can receive more personal attention from management.

3. **Focus on Group Dynamics.** Sometimes contrary to rule 2, top followers and prospects should be invited to larger meetings. People in attendance will look around to see who else is interested, and the presence of a well-regarded expert can lead to greater interest from others.

4. **Look for Linkage.** Encourage your prospects to identify and invite other top prospects. Although this kind of open invitation will sometimes bring free-lunchers through the door, selective use of secondary invitations can also extend the network to otherwise hidden investors.

5. **Leverage Management's Time.** Once the commitment is made to hold a meeting, it's a calculated risk to include a few marginal prospects in the audience. It takes no more of management's time to set a few extra places at the tables and the last few invitees could turn out to be solid supporters over the long term. Of course, this approach applies only to large-scale meetings, not to one-on-ones or other intimate arrangements.

Audience selection is both art and science. While screening should be proactive, excessive hurdle levels can close out potentially favorable contacts. The right balance can be found, but only after time and trial.

the room and refreshments, including lunch or dinner, but will not have the opportunity to pre-screen the audience to determine how good a match the listeners will be to the company's investment story. At the same time, members of broker clubs can attend meetings to network, see old friends and (Yes, it's true!) take advantage of a free lunch. In broker club meetings, management has no opportunity to block out the plate-lickers. On the other hand, in a city where the company has few followers or one in which the company's management will be traveling for other business, a meeting of this sort might be worthwhile. As always, the key issue is the availability of time and budget.

A second type of program sponsored by outside organizations is the investor forum, often put together by a brokerage house, publication or a few independent seminar groups. While these usually require some payment by the company making an appearance, many do not. Some of the most attractive of these events are the themed programs put together by brokerage firms for their institutional clients. Companies invited to present at such conferences are related to the sponsoring organization in some way, usually through research or an investment-banking relationship. A conference on biotechnology companies or a seminar on the revival of the Rust Belt might be an ideal setting for a specific company to present its case. Certainly, the audience that attends such a conference is pre-qualified in two critical ways: interest in the company's industry and status as an important customer of the sponsoring brokerage firm. The size of the audience at each speech will vary, and management will be presenting its case in direct competition with others in the same or related industries, but the matchup is potentially very attractive.

Somewhat less attractive, but still appealing, are the small meetings arranged by a sponsoring brokerage house. These are sessions that include the company and some institutional customers or brokers in a given city. Depending on the firm's connections in that city, the size and quality of the audience will vary, and those invited to attend will be limited to investors within the broker's universe. When preparing to attend a meeting of this type, management should organize its calendar to make time, in the same city, for a self-sponsored presentation to other investors who will not be included at the brokerage firm's private session.

Meetings of the type just discussed usually fall into the large, formal category. At such meetings, management is expected to present a slide show and formal speech on the company's outlook and performance. Large-scale meetings are the best format for prospecting for new support or for updating existing followers in cities where substantial support already has been generated.

Over the years, large-scale meetings have become less popular among many corporate executives, due to the belief that only retail brokers attend such sessions and that the only investors worth targeting are the major institutional buyers. This is a fallacy. In fact, for most companies, major new support can be generated and existing supporters can be served quite well with this kind of presentation.

At the same time, large-scale meetings have become a tougher sell for a number of legitimate reasons. One is that retail investors have shifted much of their buying from individual stocks to mutual funds, and brokers have shifted away from single stocks—selling more proprietary products, including their brokerage firms' own mutual funds, commodity pools, Real Estate Investment Trusts (REITs) and so on. Among brokerage houses, cutbacks in research staffs have limited the number of analysts available to follow any one company. Thus, it has become more difficult in any given city to identify a large number of individuals who should be interested in a specific company.

As a result, large-scale meetings for many companies have declined from the 35–50 level to the 20–30 level. Such a meeting today is likely to include a number of the independent money managers and research boutiques that have proliferated as cutbacks in brokerage-house research staffs led individual advisers to open their own research and management businesses.

Smaller meetings, including 8–15 people, are usually much less formal than the larger sessions. A brief set of talking points replaces the speech and slide presentation, and the session takes place around a lunch table in a quiet restaurant or club. Such sessions have the advantage of offering excellent prospecting impact and updating potential because the environment is much more intimate and the discussion often more direct. Since the size of the group is much smaller, the meeting arranger must be more focused on the quality and potential of any prospects invited. (A dud at such a meeting is much more obvious than at a presentation for 40 people.) At the same time, the time required to arrange such a meeting and the cost of the presentation are far lower than for the full-scale meeting. In fact, without the cost of the slide presentation, equipment rental and other charges, the meeting of 8–15 people can offer the best combination of costs per attendee and quality/quantity of contact.

One-on-one sessions, the smallest of the meeting formats, must be reserved for the closest followers or most important prospects. In a session of this type, management is focused on one person (or two or three) who requires a great deal of information and insight, and who can influence the stock price greatly.

Finally, the last form of face-to-face session is the headquarters/plant visit. Although an individual target can be invited to headquarters, this is more commonly a large-scale meeting in which analysts, fund managers and others are brought to the company's facilities for a full day (or two) of presentations and tours.

Attendance is a self-selecting process. Only those investors with the largest budgets and the greatest commitment to the company will invest the time and dollars to travel to headquarters and sit through a day of presentations. As a result, this meeting format is an excellent investment for most firms. One caveat: there must be something to see once they get there. For some companies, headquarters is just a corporate office. A visit to a major plant or distribution facility may be superior in such a case because it gives the audience a chance to get hands-on exposure to the company's operations. In any event, the visit provides an opportunity to showcase management depth and quality.

(Warning: Analysts will often call people they meet on such visits for follow-up information, bypassing the CEO/CFO/IR exec and increasing the risk of subsequent leaks. Staff members must be alerted to disclosure policies in advance of any headquarters visit.)

The last type of management conference is personal, but not in person. It's the conference-call briefing, which can be conducted via video-link or telephone. Telephone conference calls are more common and less expensive. The telephone conference call, especially one tied to release of quarterly earnings, is one of the few investor relations techniques for which one size fits all. The conference call enables management to bring together all key followers of the company for a review of recent performance, to answer questions and, most important, to demonstrate management's commitment to maintaining contact with its followers. One common complaint among investors is that companies court their interest when times are good or stock is being sold, but disappear when numbers are poor or the investment banker has delivered the check. Conference calls eliminate that concern.

Conference calls can be arranged on a call-in basis, in which a toll-free number is announced and anyone can sign on, or on a call-out basis, in which only pre-selected individuals are contacted. The audience can include followers and prospects, but followers are the most important target. While the call-in approach saves the company some time and cost that would be eaten up getting people on line, it also enables competitors and others to participate when their attention is not wanted.

Note: All the rules about disclosure apply on conference calls. Management may let its guard down because all the company's key followers are on the phone, but the fact is that any statements of a material nature made during the call must be limited to previously disclosed subjects. For some clients, we invite reporters from Reuters, Dow Jones, Bloomberg or other financial reporting services to sit in on the call.

Shareholder Calling Programs. Phone calls to shareholders by key managers can be arranged as an ongoing program for

211

the company. Such calls would be random, from the investor's view, although a schedule and list of targets should be maintained. Shareholder calls help management spot potential problems or misperceptions in the IR marketing program. As a rule, the IR executive should conduct most of the shareholder calls, leaving the CEO or CFO to handle a relative handful of these contacts.

Media Contact. News media contact, which will be covered in greater detail in Chapter 19, is a special type of direct personal contact. Whether the session is an outlook interview on upcoming results or an interview intended to generate a full profile on the company, contact with reporters and editors is one of the more attractive and risky forms of personal contact. Such sessions can lead to valuable third-party endorsements that rival any research recommendation, but they also can lead to negative coverage that damages a firm's reputation.

Prospecting. Prospecting sessions, which differ from formal or informal meetings, usually include personal or telephone contact by someone other than the chief executive or chief financial officer. These meetings can be arranged by an investor relations executive with various potential supporters. Usually, prospecting sessions should be conducted face-to-face, following some initial pre-qualifying efforts. Targets can be identified through reply card mailings, phone inquiries, lists of holders of the company or its competitors and other means.

DIRECT DISTRIBUTION

Because time is the original scarce resource, no investor relations program will be built on personal contact alone. Instead, various means will be pursued to spread the word without leaving the office. Direct distribution includes various mailing, facsimile and other approaches to getting information into the right hands.

Investor Hotlines. Investor hotlines often include toll-free numbers, giving investors a chance to call the hotline number and hear a taped message on recent developments at the company. Those seeking more information might be encouraged to leave their name and number, so that a return call can be made. Less frequently, dedicated staff will be assigned to handle inquiries.

Facsimile Transmission. Facsimile transmission, which has become inescapable in the past few years, offers nearly instantaneous distribution of news releases and other documents at a cost that rivals direct mail in many instances. Facsimile lists, or hot lists, include both news media and the top followers of a company.

Many vendors offer fax response systems that enable interested investors to call in on a toll-free number to obtain faxes of information, using their touch-tone phones and a series of recorded instructions.

Direct Mail. Direct mail to followers and prospects rounds out the direct distribution options. Included are lists of shareholders, both those who hold the stock in their own names and those whose shares are held in the names of their brokers; lists of investment community followers who might or might not currently hold a position in the stock; opinion leaders such as financial newsletter writers, reporters and editors, regulators and others; prospects who hold a position in related companies or whose investment parameters match those of the investor relations executive's company; local libraries, database services and other resources that investors might access in their research; and directors, officers, employees, vendors, customers and others.

INDIRECT DISTRIBUTION

Indirect distribution includes the use of a third party to reach followers and prospects. Essentially, the indirect method relies on a translator or other third party to deliver the message to an ultimately unspecified audience.

Indirect methods highlight the overlap of classifications among communication approaches. Conference calls with analysts could be classified as indirect, rather than direct, if one focused solely on the expectation that analysts would retransmit the information to investors. News releases could also be placed in this category if the focus was on reporters who rewrite the information for the mass audience.

Advertising. Advertising is a classic form of indirect distribution, even though it also could be classified as a marketing material. After all, management determines specifically which text will appear in print, unlike the news release, and the timing of the announcement is within management's control.

Advertising is indirect, however, in that management has only a rough sense of who will receive the message. While mailing lists and personal meetings bring management in contact with known persons, the use of mass media to distribute a message directs the company story to an unknown audience.

Because the audience is not known and because advertising is one of the less effective mechanisms for generating share purchases, the use of this mass medium approach should be limited to special situations. For example, advertisements are important during takeover contests and other proxy fights because the owners of the company are changing rapidly and lists can be out of date before any direct mailings go out. Advertising also can help raise or reinforce a company's image, leading to greater shareholder confidence, although the expenditures required for a corporate image program place this option outside the reach of most mid-size firms.

In addition, advertising can be used to distribute company news in management's own words. While a news release might or might not be picked up by a particular publication, and might or might not be reported in a way that reflects management's intent, an advertisement that includes the text of a news release can ensure that the full story reaches large numbers of investors.

Paid News Services. Paid news services, including news wires that transmit news releases for a fee, represent an indirect distribution mechanism because the individual recipient isn't known, much as is the case in advertising. Of course, the list of organizations subscribing to the news service is available to users, so some added insight is available.

The major publicity news services, such as PRNewswire and Business Wire, reach both news media and brokerage houses and offer both local and national distribution options. As such, these organizations provide rapid dissemination potential that can be an attractive complement to the company's own facsimile list. For companies with a high concentration of news outlets and sponsoring brokerage firms in a specific region, paid news services offer significant efficiency.

Databases. Database networks offer easy retrieval of historic information by investors, making databases a significant distribution point for information. Unfortunately, the connection of one database to another often leads to a seemingly endless duplication of any error that creeps into any single system. For the IR executive, servicing databases with information is only one tenth of the challenge. Tracking database reports and continually proofreading the information is the larger and usually more frustrating part of the job.

16

LISTS, LISTS, LISTS

In the plodding course of turning unknown prospects into supportive investors, the development and maintenance of contact lists is one of the least glamorous, most frustrating, and most essential challenges around. A thorough IR effort will entail at least a half-dozen lists. Each list will need continual updating and adjustment as individuals move from one rank to another and others are added or deleted from the universe.

To simplify the process, view the entire priority system like a funnel. At one point, the number of potential contacts is extremely large, but further screening and communication leads to the elimination of most prospects. Ultimately, the company has a series of top followers, primary prospects, and others who make the A List, the B List, and so on. (See 16-1, *The Prospect Funnel.*)

PROSPECT TARGETING

Working from the top, prospects are identified. Prospects, as mentioned earlier, can include people who invest in competitor companies, people who invest in firms with similar investment

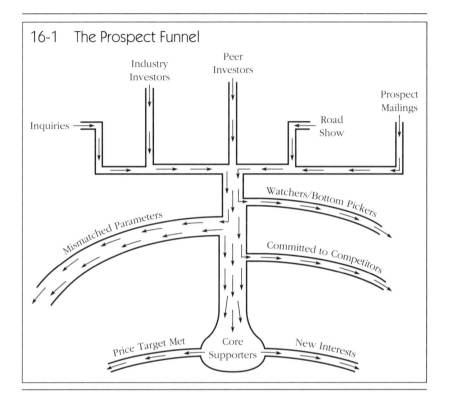

16-1   The Prospect Funnel

parameters, people who subscribe to publications that tend to focus on similar companies and, at some point, every other investor in the universe.

Of course, no company begins with the entire universe of investors. Instead, some initial screening is done to identify those lists of prospects that have some measurable likelihood of generating a reasonable return on any investment in contacting and cultivating them.

At first, some of these assumptions are arbitrary. The investor relations executive begins with a check of analysts, brokers and institutions that invest in direct competitors or investment peers and then seeks to identify the gatekeepers who determine whether those investments get made. Then, the IR exec might decide to look at investors who favor stocks with similar price/book ratios and earnings growth rates, or similar corporate cultures and proprietary product lines.

Effective prospecting is always a search for some incremental edge. The IR executive examines all variables and tries to create a superior combination. Variables can include the materials sent, the investment parameters of the audience, time of year, earnings trend of the company at the time the mailings are sent, whether the prospects are institutions or retail-oriented, their leanings toward other companies in the industry or companies with similar trading characteristics, and so on.

In the beginning, the best funneling approach is an educated guess. Certainly, the number of variables is high enough that dozens of combinations can be considered and tested before the optimum few are identified.

Sources of lists abound. Many publications and associations will provide lists for a fee, as will some analyst societies and all types of mailing-list companies. Lists can also be generated based on the 13F reports filed by large institutions, naming the stocks that they hold.

One of the best sources to tap is sponsoring brokerage houses. Most managements assume that a research report written by a brokerage house analyst will be distributed to all of the firm's brokers. For most companies, however, this is not the case. A sharp investor relations director might arrange to have multiple copies of a research report sent to all of the brokerage firm's offices for distribution to the sales force, or send some other prospecting materials with a notation that the company is followed by the brokers' own firm.

Prospect mailings are cold calls. The prospect is assumed to have no prior knowledge of the company and is encouraged to provide a response indicating presence or lack of interest. The feedback mechanism in this and all cases is critical. Reply cards serve quite well here as a means of harvesting names of interested individuals, but management should take the time to ask more than the basic, *Are you interested?* As long as the card is

16-2   A List of Lists

Lists can be organized according to a number of standards and most IR executives will have multiple screens for each list. A sample follows.

- Shareholders
- Shareholders who receive information directly from the company
- Shareholders who hold more than 1,000 shares
- Professional (institutions, brokers, etc.) shareholders
- Investment club members
- Analysts whose firms have provided support for the company
- Newsletter editors
- Financial reporters whose beats include the company
- Financial reporters who have written on the company
- Trade publication writers who can influence investor views
- Reporters in cities where the firm has facilities
- Reporters who cover competitor companies
- Brokers who have placed customers in the stock
- Gatekeepers, such as fund advisers and trust officers
- General media whose coverage includes the company's industry
- All persons who have asked for information on the company
- Libraries and databases that track the company
- Employees, vendors, suppliers and other commercial interests
- Directors, investment bankers, rating agencies
- Prospects who follow/invest in industry competitors
- Prospects who follow/invest in investment peers
- Opinion leaders whose purchases will influence others to buy
- Former owners and followers
- Persons who should have immediate access to the CEO
- Persons who should be invited to large-scale meetings
- Persons who should be included on conference calls
- Persons who should be included in one-on-one meetings
- Persons who can arrange contacts with other prospects
- Prospects who should be contacted monthly, quarterly, yearly
- People who should receive all materials on the company by mail
- People who should receive a selected number of mailings
- People who should get alerts by facsimile or personal calls

The list of lists goes on and on. Keeping the lists up to date and figuring out how to classify each individual can be a full-time job. At some point, distinctions lose their meaning, so one of the necessary challenges is to trim the number of lists to a workable and sensible level.

being sent and returned, additional insights should be sought. For example, what similar companies does the investor own? What investment parameters are important? Does the person own the stock at present? Has the person heard of the company prior to this mailing?

ESTABLISHING PRIORITIES

Once prospects are identified and they indicate interest in the company, they should be added to a mailing list for regular updates on the firm. In some cases, the IR professional might decide to send a welcome letter or background kit as well. The basic updates the prospects receive should include, at a minimum, the annual report and four quarterly earnings announcements. For more aggressive companies, fact sheets, news reprints and other materials might also be used.

This list might be the same one that includes existing followers of the company, such as brokers who have placed stock with clients or fund managers who have attended management presentations. For simplicity's sake, the IR executive might opt to maintain just one master mailing list of prospects and followers in the investment community. (See 16-2, *A List of Lists.*)

Meanwhile, followers who turn out to have significant influence on the stock, such as major fund managers or research analysts, might also appear on additional mailing lists. These could include lists of people to receive the 10-K and 10-Q reports, to receive quarterlies or to be invited to participate in management presentations and conference calls.

Yet another list can include those people whose opinions are important enough to warrant sending them materials by facsimile rather than by mail. These might include the top 10 or 20 or 75 persons influencing the company's marketability.

Needless to say, these lists must be worked and updated regularly. It is difficult enough to keep track of all the job changes, title changes and new addresses for key followers. Add to that the ebb and flow of support for the company's stock, and the relative importance or interest of each individual over time, and the task becomes even more complex.

PURGING THE SYSTEM

At least once every two years, and more frequently if the situation warrants, each company should conduct a thorough purge mailing of its prospect/followers lists. For most companies, a list that rises above 2,000 names is due for a purge.

Purge mailings are one of the clearly profitable ventures in investor relations. Usually, the incremental cost of the mailing is more than covered by postage saved as names are deleted. An effective purge will eliminate 35 to 65 percent of the names on a mailing list, including former supporters who lost interest, people who expressed initial interest but never made a commitment, and those who have moved, died, lost their jobs, etc.

The purge should be conducted along with a mailing of regular materials, such as releases, annuals, fact books or whatever. If a purge is going to be done in any event, it's best to do it around the third quarter. That enables the company to complete the purge in time to save enormous expenses linked to annual report printing and mailing.

The mailing should include a reply card that asks more than simply, *Do you want to stay on the list?* The reply card should seek to identify changes in investment parameters, title and duties of people on the list, whether the person has purchased stock or convinced clients to do so, and so on.

While it is certainly appropriate to give a person a couple of chances to stay on the list, the purge mailing should require a response from anyone wishing to receive the mailings. If a person isn't willing to move a reply card from the "in" basket to the "out" basket as a prerequisite for staying on a list, the individual cannot be terribly interested in the company. (See 16-3, *The Favour of a Reply . . .*)

Purge mailings can lead to major reductions in the size of lists, and that's for the good. Most people who express initial interest in a company will not end up becoming supporters, and

16-3   The Favour of a Reply . . .

Purge mailings represent a substantial opportunity to gain incremental feedback from holders and followers, and to identify new prospects for investor targeting. Besides *Do you want to stay on the mailing list?*, questions that could be added to a prospect- or purge-mailing reply card include these.

1. Do you own the stock? How many shares?
2. Have you increased or decreased your holdings in the past year? Why?
3. How did you hear about the company? What made you decide to buy the stock?
4. Who is your stockbroker?
5. What investor-oriented publications do you read?
6. Do you belong to an investment club, American Association of Individual Investors or similar group?
7. Do you buy our company's products? Which ones? What do you think of them?
8. Other than our mailings, where else do you look for information on the company?
9. Do you own shares of any similar companies?
10. If you were considering another investment in our company, what would lead you to make that investment today? What would keep you from making it?

Mailings with significant numbers of questions should have a sweetener of some sort to increase response rates. This could come in the form of a specific gift ($1, coupon for product, memento) or the promise of some further action *(We'll share the results with you, We'll send you a coupon after we get your response, We'll add you to our shareholder council,* etc.) that will follow receipt of the response.

most supporters ultimately will lose interest and move on to other investments. As a result, mailing lists become stale quickly and need continual refinement.

Purge mailings also can help identify major holders who have escaped notice previously, but should be moved up in priority to the meeting-invitation or conference-call list as well.

Helpful Hint: When doing a purge mailing, order three copies of the list, on labels, simultaneously. One set of labels will go with the first mailing. Names of those who respond to the first mailing are removed from the remaining two lists. Then the labels from one of the remaining lists are mailed with a second request card. Responses to that mailing are pulled from the third list, and any names that remain after that are purged. Using this method of pulling multiple sets of labels, a company reduces to nearly zero the risk of removing a name that had been added between the time of the first and second mailings, as well as other sources of confusion.

COST-EFFECTIVE SELECTION

Although the cost of mailing a single document is relatively small, mailing lists are large enough to make up in volume what they save in unit costs. That means investor relations executives should be cautious regarding the names that are kept and the names that go on the list in the first place.

Simply asking for information about a company doesn't qualify an individual to be added to the mailing list. Commercial lending officers, libraries, competitors, local government officials, individual investors and others who cannot be classified as *investment professionals* are questionable additions to any list. Management might decide to add these people, but the cost can be high.

The average cost of keeping a name on a mailing list for a year, including materials, labels, postage, handling and other expenses, is at least $8. That's a pittance to keep in touch with a major analyst, but too much if the recipient is a commercial banker looking for sales leads.

To limit the number of unqualified recipients, addition to a mailing list should be a two-step process. Persons who request information should receive a package and a reply card. Only after the reply card is returned and the answers reviewed should the person be added to the mailing list. Too many companies simply add people to the list as soon as materials are requested. If the person receives the information and has no subsequent interest, he or she still is on the list.

FACSIMILE LISTS

In addition to prospect lists and mailing lists, no company can do without a fax list these days. For major news media and key followers, faxing of releases and other updates is now the norm. Putting people on fax lists is a balancing act. Many investment professionals and reporters will complain about receiving too many unsolicited facsimiles and ask that the number be reduced. At the same time, these same people often will complain that someone else received a copy of a press release before they did. Suffice it to say that facsimile lists should include only those influential individuals who have either asked to receive fax copies or who are so important the company cannot allow them to be the second or third to know about developments.

Keeping the fax list up to date is a massive undertaking. Because of the explosive growth in the use of telecopier technology in recent years, a single broker might have three or four different fax numbers during the course of a year. As new fax machines are added to the office, the machine and phone number assigned to an individual or department may change rapidly. Fortunately, updating the numbers is a relatively easy process because the people on the fax list are the same ones management will be speaking with most often, so occasional check-ups can be completed during regular contacts.

Should people on fax lists also be on mailing lists? Almost invariably, the answer is yes. Because the fax list will be used only for very time-sensitive information, a person on the fax list will be penalized if omitted from the regular mailing list for annual report distribution, fact books and so on. Certainly, no follower wants a fax machine tied up while a fact book is being sent, and the company doesn't want an important supporter holding a faxed copy of a four-color annual.

225

MEDIA LISTS

As a rule, media names should be kept on separate lists. The needs and timetables of reporters are different from those of shareholders, and their temperaments are different as well.

While investment professionals often insist that materials be faxed as a matter of instant gratification, many financial reporters complain of being inundated with "junk faxes" and insist that faxing be done by request only. (Of course, the reporter doesn't run your company, so you might opt to use a different method of communication than the individual prefers from time to time. However, since the reporter or editor is a customer of sorts, acquiescing is usually the best idea.) *An example: One small company needed to issue releases on several developments that were material to its operations, even though the financial wires were unlikely to pick up the stories. After a few releases, we received a complaint from Dow Jones regarding our issuance of too many releases. Since the reporter didn't run the IR department, and certainly wouldn't indemnify us if the SEC claimed information was being hidden, those complaints were ignored.*

As with investors, media are divided into several categories.

- Disclosure media
- National news media
- National feature media
- Broadcast outlets
- Headquarters city financial pages
- Branch/division headquarters city financial pages
- Key customer/regulator locations
- Industry trade press
- Functional professional press

Disclosure media represent the most time-sensitive communications requirement and should therefore be on a facsimile system. Disclosure media include such financial outlets as Bloomberg, Dow Jones, Reuters, Standard & Poor's and so on. These are the media generally accepted as providing prompt, broad dissemination of information throughout the investment community.

Of course, because disclosure begins with the financial news wires, these outlets should be on a separate list from the top investors who receive facsimile transmissions of announcements.

Usually, newspapers and radio stations in a home town, whether the headquarters city or a major plant location, and trade publications that include financial tables or reports on industry competitors will also be on a fax list. These recipients have an immediate need for fresh information and, in the case of daily publications or radio outlets, fresh can turn stale within a day.

Other publications that pay attention to the company on a more infrequent basis, or those that have less frequent publication schedules, can be added to the mailing list. Feature outlets and professional publications shouldn't be on the mailing list at all, except for the largest or most influential of companies, because placement with these outlets requires a customized approach.

As a rule, media lists should be relatively small. While any given company might have a target market of 25,000 or 50,000 brokers, fund managers and other professional investors, the list of potential media followers is more likely to be in the 200–800 range, and that includes everyone who might conceivably write anything about the company—ever.

In reality, an investor list will seldom rise above 2,000 names before a purge mailing is vastly overdue, and media lists with more than 100 names are questionable. Exceptions to the rule usually apply for companies with dozens of large facilities around the country or around the world, and household names that command attention from the entire universe.

THE VALUE OF A NAME

Whatever the list being maintained, every entry should include a specific person's name. Mailings that go to libraries, trading desks, news desks and other locations tend to get lost. Worse, they defy effective follow-up and feedback.

Names present challenges, of course. Although names will seldom change, individuals do move to new departments, cities and companies. Reporters change beats, analysts change industries, and so on. Keeping the mailing list up to date is more complicated when specific names must be assigned to each address.

However, the payoff is valuable. When a person leaves a firm, someone will probably ask that the name be removed from your mailing list or that mailings cease. That alert system, which wouldn't exist if the materials were being sent generally to the firm, can lead the IR professional to remove the name or inquire further about the person's whereabouts. If a significant supporter leaves her company, the IR exec will probably want to track the contact to her new office and seek to establish a connection in the new location. Her replacement at the old firm should also be identified and courted.

Granted, the significant follower may eventually contact the company to be added to the mailing list at the new location. But not everyone will bother to do this, and a change in jobs can lead a person to be distracted from prior interests and investments.

Like names, firm identifications are critical. Many brokers will ask that materials be sent to their homes so they can be sure to receive the items they need where they have the time to review them. It's always fine to comply, but the mailing list should include the company identification along with the name and home address.

If a research report is going to be distributed to all Merrill Lynch brokers on a company's mailing list, for example, a sort of the mailing list won't pick up brokers receiving their mailings at home, unless the company name is included in the listing.

This higher level of detail will invariably lead to more mistakes, because there are more pieces of information to coordinate. However, the improved control and measurement potential of the list compensate for the added complexity.

17

FEEDBACK MECHANISMS

Investor relations is a continual process of fine tuning. Whether it's the message itself, the corporate structure, the list of targets or the site of the annual meeting, the IR executive is running as fast as possible to adapt to constant change.

That makes the collection and understanding of feedback indispensable to any IR effort. Feedback includes both views and data, aligning this effort most closely with the industry and peer research that any firm must do in packaging its message.

Feedback can come from both formal surveys with statistical accuracy and from informal checks that provide insights and ideas. Mechanisms can include major studies using prepared questions and shareholder hotlines that simply record the (statistically invalid) views of those who choose to call.

THE AUDIT

The most thorough form of view collection is the audit, which covers multiple audiences and multiple activities. A full audit will cover the following groups.

- Shareholders.
- Professional investors who have made the decision to buy or convinced others to invest in the company.

- Professionals and individual investors who follow the company but haven't invested.

- Professional and individual investors who follow other firms in the same industry and/or firms with similar investment merits.

- Financial writers who follow the company regularly.

- Financial writers who have followed peers or are believed otherwise to have some knowledge of the company or its industry.

- Trade/industry publication editors who follow the company's industry.

- Investment newsletter editors who have covered or might be convinced to write up the company.

- Internal management, directors or employees who have reason to be involved in corporate issues.

Needless to say, an audit covering this large an array of individuals is a massive undertaking. Most firms that conduct audits will trim back on the project to balance insights against costs (dollars *and* time).

The purpose of this survey is to measure the system in its entirety. The audit reviews the materials being produced by the company, the frequency and effectiveness of mailings, the impact of messages and missteps, the cost-effectiveness of distribution systems, the accuracy of targeting efforts and so on. (See 17-1, *Scripting the Audit.*)

The audit is one of those projects best undertaken by an outside organization. Analysts who are interviewed by the CFO or assistant treasurer are unlikely to be as forthright as they might be to outsiders. Outside resources will tend to have less ego and personal investment tied up in the answers. Finally, the number of hours required for an audit would be far beyond the internal capacity of most companies.

In an ideal case, the audit will indicate that the right messages are being transmitted clearly, received willingly and acted upon aggressively. More important, the answers received would

17-1 Scripting the Audit

The number of possible questions to be included in an audit is limited only by imagination, time and dollars. Following are a few of the basics.

For current stockholders

- Why did they decide to make the investment?
- Do those investment reasons still apply?
- Are they the same merits the company had been stressing?
- Do those appeals help identify other likely targets?
- Do answers vary by group, i.e., individuals vs. institutions?

For those sitting on the fence or who don't plan to invest

- What obstacles do they see?
- What must the company do or prove to obtain sponsorship?
- What competitors do they see as better investments and why?
- Would they buy the stock without selling competitors or are they limited to one company in an industry?

For readers of company reports

- Did they read the document?
- What messages did they get out of it?
- What information were they looking for, but couldn't find?
- How does our disclosure compare with competitors?

For reporters who follow the company

- How do they see the company's situation and challenges?
- Do they think the company is suitably responsive or proactive regarding problems, developments and inquiries?
- How does disclosure, availability, etc., compare with peers?
- Do they see management as industry experts?

As a rule, reporters want their responses off the record or not for attribution and will be loath to state opinions. The image of objectivity they seek to project makes opinions a sensitive issue. However, insights can be gleaned from careful listening.

be clear and accurate, with no false signals or misleading conclusions. However, such ideals seldom, if ever, materialize.

Most frequently, responses simply don't show a clear pattern. The investigator learns that some investors want the dividend to be higher and some are willing to do without the dividend entirely. Reporters simply indicate that things are fine, but don't give any real insight that can help the company do a better communications job. Readers of materials shrug and say everything is fine, and then resist further questions. Whether to recast the survey and try again, or simply decide to leave things alone, is a judgment call.

But investor relations executives should be wary of the traps that can be laid in any audit or other survey. Sometimes, the misdirection from an audit, if it develops, comes from some common sources.

A FEW WARNINGS

Beware of Negative Responses. It's easier to get insights from the reasons people invested than from their decisions not to invest. That's because investing is a decision point and it is reached after consideration of numerous inputs. Not investing can result from inertia, laziness or simple disinterest, but few people will tell an interviewer, *"I just never got around to it,"* or *"I don't want to take the time to study the situation."*

Beware of Bottom-Pickers. Some people who don't invest will invariably say they are looking for a lower price. But call them up when the price declines and they will say they are looking for an even lower price. Some people really do focus on price targets, but most bottom-pickers will never invest. They'll never be convinced the price can't go lower.

Beware of Circular Responses. Some responses are self-selecting, and a negative influence can be seen as a positive. *After tallying a shareholder survey for one client, we were pleased to note that shareholders weren't interested in high dividend payout ratios. Then we realized that people interested in current* *income wouldn't have bought the stock of this growth company in the first place. What seemed at first to be reaffirmation of our dividend policy turned out to be valueless. On the other hand, if many respondents said they were income investors, it would have indicated some crossover appeal that might have been worth exploring further.* Try to anticipate the self-selecting questions and add more inquiries to dig deeper than the initial question would allow.

Beware the Missing Guest. Companies will seldom ask about investment appeals they don't have or materials they don't produce, but questions about such items can be insightful. If a company has very little institutional ownership, but believes institutions should be interested, the audit might rightly go well beyond the existing arena of holders and interested individuals to focus on the missing investors. *In one instance, we were auditing a company that had no fact book—but should have. If we had limited our inquiries to the documents that actually existed, we would have missed an important marketing opportunity.*

Beware of Sloppy Reading. In some instances, a respondent will suggest that a document would be greatly improved if it contained certain information. Then, the interviewer discovers that this information was, in fact, in the report (or speech or conference call) and the respondent simply missed it. The right follow-up here is to simply send the document back with a note highlighting the discussion and/or asking the respondent to examine whether the language used and design emphasis were adequate to give the topic proper prominence.

Beware of Sloppy Weighting. The best people in any business usually are also the busiest and, consequently, have less time to spend on an interview. Their insights might be the most valuable, but the effort required to get their thoughts and the care that must be used in phrasing questions create a barrier. The person whose views are less important might also be one with more time to spare and a greater willingness to explain views in detail. At the end of the research, the sheer volume of responses from the less important targets can lead to an overweighting of conclusions *based on the least qualified responses.*

EVENT FEEDBACK

While the audit is an all-inclusive approach that can be undertaken once a year, at most, the investor relation program will incorporate dozens of events that can call for response. Some examples might include:

- Analyst presentations
- Conference calls
- Interviews with reporters
- Publication of articles
- Annual meetings

Events are defined by the singularity of their occurrence and their relative importance to corporate IR goals. Any time management meets with investment professionals, it's important to contact the audience later to identify red flags raised in the presentation, comfort levels increased or decreased, actions (buy, sell, etc.) undertaken as a result of the meeting, and so on.

When an interview is conducted for a profile article, it's important to get back to the writer after the interview, but before publication, to identify pending issues or questions, sources of confusion or concern, needs for added information or testimonials, etc. Once the article is published, feedback must be sought from key followers regarding their reactions to the story. A favorable reaction by the investor audience might encourage the company to reprint and distribute the article, while a negative reaction may kill that plan, regardless of whether management thought the story was good or bad.

Such event feedback is best obtained quickly after the event and in most instances through a phone call. Face-to-face interviews are a costly follow-up method; they also imply greater weighting than is usually appropriate. A company that sends a messenger to interview each audience member personally after a meeting is indicating an excessive level of concern regarding opinions.

Some event feedback can be arranged by mail, with a reply card, especially if the audience was large or the follow-up is not time-sensitive. Annual meeting follow-up can be done by mail, and many companies will want to follow up with analysts who attended meetings more than once: first by phone shortly after the meeting and then by mail a few weeks later.

ISSUES MANAGEMENT

Feedback on events is naturally targeted toward people who attended events, but response on corporate issues can be targeted selectively and obtained through a variety of mechanisms.

Usually, corporate governance opinions are sought only from a select group of investors, investment bankers, directors or other advisors. But a company might conduct a more broad-based shareholder survey on issues like charitable giving as an appropriate use of corporate dollars.

Issues-management feedback is more commonly collected after the fact than before. A company that announces a staggered board or one that opts to create two classes of stock (voting/ nonvoting) might encourage its IR exec to gauge reactions from key investors immediately following the announcement.

This is usually too late, of course. Negative feedback is unlikely to convince a company to backtrack on a decision already announced, and the very fact of asking can lead to a negative reaction. "If they wanted my opinion, why didn't they ask before they made the decision?" a respondent might ask, and quite rightly.

Certainly, feedback on issues should be obtained on an informal basis during discussions on other matters, so that the key issue isn't flagged or overemphasized, and the feedback should be obtained before the fact, rather than after.

The Shareholder Advisory Council. Some companies will establish advisory councils of shareholders to create a permanent feedback mechanism. Spot surveys can provide substantial insight, but the advisory council can create various timeline measurements. In addition, the advisory council approach gives management the opportunity to involve major institutional holders on a non-adversarial basis.

The Shareholder Advisory Council can be established according to various criteria. The company can choose only major holders, only long-term holders, a representative sample, only retail or institutional holders, etc. Likewise, the council can be structured to eliminate former employees or to block out the reporters and analysts who might feel compelled to write up the council's activities.

DATA GATHERING

Some of the best feedback available is informational. How many shares of stock were purchased by people who attended the last analyst meeting? How many shareholders also own company products? What percentage of investors hold the stock in retirement (tax-deferred) accounts rather than regular accounts of various types?

One of the best kinds of data that surveys seek to identify is opinion leaders who might otherwise be hidden. Immediately after any public offering, shareholders should receive a reply card they can use to identify the broker or other adviser who sold them the stock. Such information is valuable in identifying supporters who should be added to the mailing list and invited to analyst meetings, etc.

Data gathering is best done by mail, as it tends to be higher volume research and focuses on information rather than opinion.

INTERNAL RESPONSE

No investor relations executive should ignore internal feedback. Messages sent outside the firm are responded to in many ways, including informal contact with company management and employees. The most thorough and precise survey might end up carrying less weight than a comment made to the chairman on the seventh tee or at a charity dinner.

However, internal feedback isn't simply a defensive mechanism. Messages sent by the company might strike a discordant note among members of operating management—a possible signal that the investor message is beginning to veer away from reality.

This reality check can pay off substantially when reporters, analysts or other interested parties discuss the company with competitors, operating managers, vendors, customers or other informed sources. A divergence of views within the company, or among close business partners, can be taken as a danger signal.

18

INVESTOR TARGETING

Without a doubt, the megatrend shift in investing is toward the institutional investor, and the focus on global investing—marketing a company to institutions around the world—has taken hold among many large companies, and small ones as well. The reason for this shift is simple: that's where the money is.

Equally important, that's where the money continues to go. The rise of pension plans as a corporate benefit and reductions in the number of years required to vest in various plans has created a steady stream—or torrent—of funds flowing into the institutional management arena. Even 401(k) plans, unless self-directed by employees, represent funds taken out of paychecks before taxes and placed with mutual funds or other institutional managers.

At the same time, individual and other retail investors have shifted an increasing share of their investment dollars into mutual funds, rather than individual stocks. Stock brokers, likewise, have gravitated to the higher-margin, proprietary products offered by their own brokerage firms, spending less time researching and selling individual companies' shares.

As a result of these trends, institutions now hold more than half of all outstanding shares of U.S. traded corporations, up from about 15 percent in 1965. Based on these trends, many companies accept as gospel the need to focus on institutional investors as the repository for their shares. That emphasis can create opportunities for firms that countermarket toward the retail buyer.

Clients frequently ask whether the individual investor is dead, whether the retail market can absorb enough stock to make a difference. They always receive the same answer. *Retail investors cannot buy up every share of stock on Wall Street, but they can comfortably buy up every share in any single company.*

For a company with 10 million shares outstanding, it's irrelevant how many billion shares of stock are held by institutions and how many billion shares by individuals. The firm's 10 million shares are such a small percentage of the total that the megatrend is meaningless.

The savvy investor relations executive will focus on the best approach for the company, rather than the drift of market accumulation. And the best approach is to achieve a balance of retail and institutional ownership. (See 18-1, *Selecting the Investor Mix.*)

The balance points will vary by firm, of course. A company with 50 million shares outstanding will naturally be able to seek more institutional support than one with 5 million shares. A company with local appeal might attract far more interest among individuals.

Each company should target a rough ratio of institutional ownership that is desirable, and the type of institutions and retail investors who will be pursued. Keep in mind the pros and cons of each type of investor:

- Institutions can buy large volumes of shares, sopping up a high percentage of the firm's float. When institutions are actively supporting a company, the purchases of shares can send prices soaring. However, too much institutional ownership can lead to *institutional gridlock,* a condition in which the float available for trading shrinks to too low a level to support the kind of transaction volumes institutions prefer. Institutions might begin buying when float supports trading volumes of 50,000 shares per day, but the accumulation of shares leads to relatively lower volumes, such as 10,000 shares per day. Soon, an institution that wants to buy or sell a block of 10,000

18-1   Selecting the Investor Mix

The right mix of institutional and retail investors is important for firms seeking efficient markets. While institutional interest can add to trading volume and pricing, the large average-order level can also sop up essential liquidity. Here are some ways to identify an appropriate mix.

1. **Begin with Investment Peers.** Because the mix is based on trading fundamentals, industry peers are not necessarily the most comparable group. Instead, look at other firms with similar shares outstanding, float, sales levels, research coverage and so on. Try to determine whether some combination of institutional/retail ownership can be linked to narrow bid-ask spreads, consistent trading levels and low price volatility.

2. **Move to Industry Peers.** The industry might be one with particular appeal to retail buyers, or to institutions, beyond what the market averages would suggest. Assume some industry impact in your own ownership mix.

3. **Set Targets in a Range.** Focus investor contact efforts on the area where building is desired, but also recognize that mix adjustment is a long-term process.

When building institutional support, remember that institutional buying tends to gather momentum over time. Thus, an effort should be targeted to build institutional ownership to a point somewhat below the optimum level, with inertia carrying the company past the finish line.

shares will need to do so in a special transaction, lest its order have an undesired impact on share price. In addition, the same stock-price improvement that results from heavy institutional buying can turn to a rout when it's time to sell. A firm that focuses solely on institutional owners might have no backup support for shares when these large owners head for the exit.

- Individual investors tend to be more loyal and less reactive to investment community psychology than institutional managers. Individual investors tend to be less active as traders, holding their shares significantly longer, on aver-

241

age, than institutions. However, they also tend to be very costly to service on a per-share basis. When a company is issuing shares, a heavy retail buying contingent can help provide stronger pricing. Institutions, as volume buyers, tend to buy wholesale, while individuals pay retail. Although everyone pays the same price at a public offering, strong retail interest can give the investment banker and the issuing company greater pricing leverage.

It's also important to keep the spectrum of investor buying power in mind. A multi-billion-dollar institution might be outside the target mix of a small company, based simply on the company's float and the minimum purchase commitments of that institution. A large stock club might be in a position to buy as many shares as a small fund manager. A single retail investor, in fact, might accumulate enough shares to rank among a company's top 20 owners.

Generalizations are helpful, but the exceptions are always an important aspect of IR mix strategy.

INSTITUTIONAL OWNERS

The largest concentration of investment dollars and the sharpest growth rate make institutional investors an enormous, and enormously attractive, investor audience. Although institutions are generally perceived to be multi-billion-dollar funds, the fact is that they come in all sizes.

Independent pension funds that manage $50 million in assets are institutional investors in the same way as the California Public Employees Retirement System (Calpers), which controlled more than $19 billion of equity investments at the end of 1992.

Institutions also have all types of investment approaches. Many, including Calpers and other megafunds, are index funds. These funds apply complex quantitative formulas to create an investment portfolio that mirrors some broad-based market index. Stocks are added or deleted from their portfolios based on their values as components of the index model. As a result, standard marketing efforts are not effective with such groups.

The same is true of many institutions that apply other types of quantitative investment approaches to their operations. Certain funds will set a screen of parameters for sales and earnings growth rates or other measures of financial condition or performance, and then essentially buy any stock that passes through the screen. The concept here is to apply strict investment rules, without exception, to the market.

In any type of formula investing, a fundamental premise is that human intervention is a source of error. A model with a 55-percent success rate will at least match and possibly exceed gains in the overall market. But if humans get involved in adjusting the selection process, the reasoning goes, they will merely add to uncertainty and increase the likelihood of failure.

For the investor relations executive, the search for institutional support leads to those fund managers who focus on fundamentals and specific companies, the so-called qualitative investors. Motivated by as many theories and trends as any individual investor, these institutional buyers simply offer the opportunity to place more stock for each buying decision.

Getting to an institutional buyer can be a challenge for an IR executive. The ultimate decision maker at a fund might have several gatekeepers and advisers who must stand as intermediate targets for the IR effort. *In targeting one institutional buyer, we learned that he placed orders through several brokerage firms and played off one brokerage house analyst against another. Based on information received and the level of service gained from each, he shifted his business around frequently, and kept everyone on their toes. The challenge for us and our client was to gain unanimous support from the analysts he used as opinion leaders, rather than targeting him directly.*

Not surprisingly, any large organization has a number of layers of management, operations people and other decision makers. Institutions are no different. A pension fund trustee is most likely to assign investment decisions and fund management to one or more—usually more—investment managers. These might include people employed by brokerage houses or independent money managers of various sorts. Each of these investment managers will receive advice from various sources, including broker-age house analysts or independent analysts, or might choose to hire in-house analysts to advise on investment decisions.

Each investment manager might have a different responsibility. One might be assigned to focus on equity investments, another on bonds and so on. A committee or single adviser will help to coordinate the activities of these fund managers and determine the proper allocation of funds among them.

The IR professional searches for the key contact, the person in charge of the type of investments that his company represents. Seldom is that person the pension-fund trustee or someone at the pension fund. Most often, the target is a fund manager or investment adviser in the employ of one or more funds.

The examples given so far are for pension funds, but the same rule applies with mutual funds—pools of stocks, bonds or other investment vehicles. Although mutual funds are generally thought of as investment vehicles for individuals who don't want to select single stocks, the fact is that institutions often will invest in funds, especially funds created specifically for institutions and other large investors.

These funds might include real-estate investment packages, stocks, preferred stocks, managed futures or other securities that can be sold in 50 parts to institutions, instead of 5,000 parts to individuals.

Institutions are generally referred to as the *buy side* of the investment market because these investment professionals are in the business of buying for their own funds. Analysts who serve institutions are referred to as buy-side analysts.

As with any kind of selling, the search for institutional support must lead to the person who can place an order. Identifying these people is a multistep process that begins with a review of 13F reports.

Each institution that manages more than $100 million in assets must file a quarterly report with the Securities and Exchange Commission, detailing its holdings and any change in holdings since the prior quarter. These 13F reports are available through a number of databases and can be ordered for any pub-lic company whose shares are held by such institutions.

Because the IR executive wants to identify institutions that are likely to buy her stock, the first step is to identify those funds that hold shares of competitors or of investment peers. People who have been willing to invest in the same industry or in simi-lar types of companies (growth, turnaround, asset play, technolo-gy, cyclical, etc.) are the most likely suspects.

Then, the IR executive contacts the institution to learn which adviser (internal or external) is responsible for the fund that includes the competitor's or peer's shares. In the 13F report, for example, ABC Corporation might be identified as owning 100,000 shares of a competitor. But ABC manages five funds and it isn't clear which fund contains the ABC shares. Tracking down the decision-maker is the critical first step in gaining placement of new shares. (See 18-2, *Finding Mr. Right.*)

Institutional salesmen, brokers who sell stock to institutions, also are good targets for an IR effort. Some salesmen will identify themselves by contacting the company with an offer to place large blocks of stock that become available. Others will ask to attend an analyst meeting.

Because institutional salesmen trade in large blocks of stock—often blocks too large to move in normal daily trading—they have a business need to gain access to both sides of the block transaction. As a result, they often will want to gain the favor of both the institutional buyer and the issuing company. The chief financial officer or the IR exec might be a key contact for the institutional broker who is looking for the opposite side (buyer or seller) of whatever transaction she seeks.

Cultivating the institutional salesman is advantageous because the broker can rely on cooperation from a publicly traded compa-ny will tend to work harder at arranging transactions. Such con-tacts also are helpful when a company needs to acquire a large number of shares for various needs and wishes to obtain the shares with minimal transaction costs.

Whenever a new institution buys shares in the company, as indicated by the 13F report or transfer-agent update, the IR execu-

---

18-2   Finding Mr. Right

The search for investors is a networking nightmare. Especially for large institutions, the decision maker might be different from the adviser, who is different from the holder, who might be different from three other holders at the same firm. For the IR executive, finding Mr. Right depends on continued questioning and hard-nosed detective work.

The search begins with leads. The names of current holders are an excellent starting point, as are the names of firms or individuals holding shares of competitors or investment peers. Phone calls can bring the IR executive through the labyrinth to identify the person at an institution who is responsible for the position. That person might have bought the shares or inherited them from the last person in that slot.

The IR executive will then ask for the names of advisers who work with the responsible individual. One of those advisers, or more than one, might have recommended the stock originally, and the right questions can identify that adviser.

But the search doesn't stop there. That adviser also advises other fund managers, and might have received insights on the company from yet another adviser such as an independent research boutique.

By following one trail after another, the IR executive can establish a prospect/supporter list including dozens of analysts, fund managers and other investment professionals, all linked to one ownership position at one institution.

---

tive should identify the decision maker and contact that person directly. Making the person-to-person contact immediately can make the difference between a decision to hold and one to sell during a subsequent crisis. The new owner should also receive a complete welcome kit, including financial reports for the past two years, reprints of articles, appropriate marketing or other materials, and a calendar of corporate events (dividend-announcement months, earnings-announcement months, annual meeting date, analyst meeting schedule) if available.

INDEPENDENT MONEY MANAGERS

A special segment of the institutional market is the independent money manager. These individuals often manage under $100 million in assets and, therefore, fly under the 13F radar screen. Many of these independent managers previously worked with insurance companies, brokerages or other institutions before deciding to strike out on their own with a few clients. Staff reductions within the Wall Street community in the late 1980s and early 1990s have added dramatically to their number.

Because of their size, independent money managers can be difficult to identify, and even more difficult to classify according to investment philosophy. A major surveying effort could be undertaken, beginning with directories and moving through personal calls, but one of the best ways to begin cultivating this link is through the news media.

Frequently, reporters will interview independent money managers for insights into particular stocks or industries. Mention of an independent manager who tracks competitors or investment peers should lead the IR executive to the telephone for a quick background call to the manager's office. A few minutes on the phone will indicate whether there might be a fit and, if not, whether the manager being called might know of other independents who invest in similar equities.

ANALYSTS

Analysts are the most obvious advisers in the chain of investment decision-making. Although some analysts serve both the institutional (buy side) and retail (sell side) sectors of the market, many are hired specifically to focus on the institutional market.

In addition, the same staff reductions that led to the expansion of independent money manager ranks in the past several years have led many analysts into the private research market. Many small money management firms, and large ones as well, will leverage their investment in analyst salaries by selling research to other money managers and brokerage firms.

Thus, cultivating an analyst at a small boutique operation can lead to de facto coverage at larger institutions and brokerage houses. Frequently, the research boutique will also become an independent money manager on its own, pulling investment dollars from established investment community contacts.

Analysts can be identified in a number of ways, the most cost-effective being a review of directories that list the research reports issued on specific companies. Here, again, a search organized according to competitors and investment peers can lead to a highly customized and profitable analyst target list. (See 18-3, *Achieving Closure.*)

Analyst coverage is generally a promise obtained from an investment banker prior to the time of a public offering, and the IR director should pursue the matter following any offering to make sure the promise is fulfilled. While some investment banking houses will remain quite attentive after an offering, many will pay lip service to support issues, including research coverage, but fail to deliver consistently.

Even if the last public offering was many years earlier, the IR executive who sees an offering within the following one to five years can hold out investment banking business as a carrot to lure a brokerage house into research coverage.

Because analysts are compensated both with salary and various bonuses—tied to trading in the shares they recommend or investment banking deals they bring in—these advisers tend to focus on those companies that offer additional returns to the brokerage house. These returns could be measured in sales commissions on stocks bought or sold as a result of their research, trading volume in shares they cover for which their firm makes a market, or investment banking business that comes in as a result of their relationship with the issuing company.

Knowing this, the IR professional can begin to assemble a strategy for drawing analyst attention. While the initial pursuit will be of an analyst who fits the mold in terms of other companies or industries covered, cooperative efforts to make the relationship more profitable are an added benefit. *We find it advantageous to identify institutional customers or others linked to the brokerage firm who already own client stock, or the firm's brokers who have placed client stock with their customers, prior to approaching an analyst. This provides an immediate connection*

18-3 Achieving Closure

As with selling any other product, the goal of the IR marketing effort is a buying decision. After all the targets are identified and all the meetings, materials and updates are provided, the time comes to close the sale. Closure can be achieved in several ways.

1. **Bringing in the CEO.** Frequently, it is a final conversation with the chief executive that yields the buying decision. The extra attention the buyer receives, together with the assurances only the CEO can provide, can be used effectively if timed properly.

2. **Provide the Added Value.** Whether it's a visit to a store opening or an assurance to be on call 24 hours a day, offer the added value the investor seeks in terms of support, access or responsiveness.

3. **Ask for the Order.** At some point, every stockbroker must pause and ask the customer, *"Can I put you down for XXXXX shares?"* The IR executive must do the same. Even though the IR exec won't be brokering the trade, it is essential to ask the buyer or analyst for some action that leads to share purchase. "When can I have you meet the chairman," or "I'll be in town next week and can work with you on your due diligence then," or "Should I have our CFO work with you to find blocks of shares or would you prefer to work independently?"

Closure comes in different forms for each investor or each type of target. In each case, it flows from defining the obstacles between thought and action, overcoming those obstacles and then asking for the action.

---

between the analyst, the analyst's firm, the opportunity for a profitable relationship, and the client's company. For some small companies, the best way to draw an analyst's attention is to marshal the voices of the brokers at the firm.

It goes without saying that a heavy-handed approach will backfire. Analysts might welcome an opportunity to increase their own value to their firms through a well-developed relationship with an issuing company, but most will resist a suggestion of a quid pro quo. *One client, however, experienced an unex-*

pectedly hostile response from one analyst when another broker-age firm was chosen to undertake a series of overseas institution-al meetings. Although the analyst had never mentioned a desire to arrange such a trip through his firm, he argued after the fact that he thought his own research was the quid-pro-quo contribu-tion for future business.

Analysts require more attention than institutions because their views are so highly leveraged across all investment arenas. An influential analyst in a particular industry will be called upon for comment from the media, encouraged to take part in analyst roundtables at industry conferences or in investment publica-tions, and asked for views by retail and institutional brokers and investors alike. That makes the analyst the most potent of invest-ment professionals.

Any analyst following a company should be invited to par-ticipate in quarterly conference calls tied to earnings releases, in annual meetings and analyst meetings, and other corporate finan-cial events. In addition, while each analyst wants to gain special insights from management, the IR professional must make sure to keep the playing field level. An analyst can live with not getting special attention or insights, but will absolutely detest the idea that someone else is getting such attention instead. Playing favorites can backfire in many ways.

FYI: Disclosure rules apply to analysts and major institutional shareholders in the same way that they do to the rest of the uni-verse. Managements must be careful to keep close counsel with these advisers, without stepping over the line on material inside information. Some analysts and other investors will seek to obtain whatever information they can, as is their role, so it's management's job to hold the line on the depth of disclosure.

BROKERS

Brokers, both retail and institutional, are vastly undervalued by many IR professionals. Taking a lead from the common wisdom on Wall Street, some IR execs will dismiss brokers and focus instead on fund managers and analysts exclusively. Why go to the broker, they reason, when they can go to the original opinion leader (analyst) or the ultimate buyer (fund manager) directly?

Contrary to that reasoning, the universal truth is that stocks are sold, not bought. The number of investment options always exceeds the number of investment decisions any buyer will make. Motivating the salesman can help shift those investment decisions more to the IR executive's advantage.

Of course, brokers come in all shapes and sizes, and finding the right ones to support is another of those multistep efforts that IR executives undertake continually. One good place to start is with brokers who have already placed the company's stock with their customers.

These brokers can be identified through a reply-card mailing to the company's financial mailing list or by sending a *Who's Your Broker?* reply card to shareholders, large and small. They can also be identified simply by asking institutional holders which brokers they deal with, promising in turn to put those brokers on various update lists.

As with analysts, the news media are a good source of leads for influential brokers. Articles in financial publications will often cite opinions of leading brokers as well as analysts or fund managers who specialize in a particular type of company. These brokers merit a call if the fit seems right.

Brokers can be motivated to sell more stock simply by getting more timely updates on the company or an occasional update call from management. Because so many firms focus solely on the analyst or other gatekeeper, the broker can be left in the cold. For example, a research report written by a brokerage firm's analyst will be sent to institutional clients, but not necessarily all institutional brokers, and definitely not more than a handful of retail brokers. Sometimes, an investor relations exec can break new ground by arranging to have a firm's research report distributed to that firm's own brokers. The analyst who wrote the report must be consulted first, of course, but even a note to brokers reminding them that the report exists can provide some benefit.

Here, it should be noted that some brokers focus strictly on institutional clients and others on retail investors. Many overlap

251

18-4   Building Broker Support

Brokers like stocks they can sell. Compensated through a commission system, brokers can be recruited as allies by companies offering the opportunity to build commissions and keep clients happy. The IR marketing program should include the following.

1. *Broker participation* in regular conference calls tied to quarterly results or in after-the-market presentations by management.

2. *Regular updates,* including fact sheets that give them a simple story to sell and the details needed to answer customer questions and close the sale.

3. *Access,* especially to blocks of stock they can sell to major customers. Cooperative companies can keep large blocks from having a depressing effect on stock price by cultivating the brokers who can place those shares. The brokers, in turn, appreciate the opportunity to generate attractive commissions on such sales.

Any good marketing effort seeks to energize the salesmen to do their job better. When it comes to investor relations, the marketing department and the salesman work for separate organizations, but the fundamental relationship doesn't change.

---

between the two investor categories. In any case, the driving force for any broker is the sales commission, and companies that give the broker more of a selling advantage will win loyalty and continued support. (See 18-4, *Building Broker Support.*)

The selling advantage could come from inclusion on conference calls or in meetings, special update reports or corporate fact books. Whatever the case, the broker is an underserved player in the market, creating an opportunity for IR marketers.

TRADERS/SPECIALISTS

In the over-the-counter market, the person who makes a market in a company's shares is called a market maker. On an exchange, the market maker is called a specialist. Behind all of the exchange rules and NASDAQ regulations, these are essentially the same animal.

Of course, the company can have more leverage with market-maker firms, because many market makers also have investment banking relationships with the companies whose shares they trade, and because each market maker must compete for order flow while the specialist has a monopoly. Traders, like analysts and brokers, are compensated in part for their contribution to the profitability of their firms. To the extent that the IR executive can offer a carrot, added cooperation and insights can be obtained.

Because these key traders set the prices paid for shares bought and sold, and the spread or difference between asking and selling price that creates their profit, the trader is an important factor in market liquidity. Traders tend to respond to the market and not to the fundamentals of a company. If the order imbalance favors purchases of stock, the trader will move up the price, regardless of the reasons for the imbalance, and vice versa.

But how fast that price moves and how wide the spread becomes depend to a great extent on the trader's perception of risk. Wide spreads denote stocks that trade infrequently, trade in low numbers relative to the number of market makers, or experience significant price changes in response to relatively low levels of trading activity.

On a second-by-second basis, the trader responds only to the direction of order flow. But discussions with traders can provide enough perspective to give the trader a more comfortable sense of risk regarding a stock, or give the IR executive ideas on ways to change the company or its reporting to improve trading liquidity.

Traders can be tapped for information when unusual patterns of activity develop in a stock. Although many will decline the opportunity to tell the IR executive which of their own customers was buying or selling, they will often provide insight regarding the customers of other firms or rumors that led to or accompanied the trading activity.

Whether the trader is an over-the-counter market-maker or an exchange specialist, the IR professional should arrange to meet with each of these individuals at least once per year.

253

INVESTMENT CLUBS

Investment clubs are most aligned with independent money managers as a target investor group. Investment clubs invest on behalf of several investors and decisions are made by the group on the basis of pre-set parameters or other club guidelines. The size of investments will generally be lower than for large institutions, but the investment club is usually a much more substantial investor than any individual.

According to the National Association of Investors Corporation, the parent of the National Association of Investment Clubs (NAIC), the nearly 200,000 members of that organization in 1993 managed a combined $25 billion in assets, most of it in equities. NAIC's members, including clubs and individuals, held more than $165 million in Wal-Mart shares alone in 1993.

Because they meet on an infrequent basis and must reach consensus on any buying or selling decision, investment clubs tend to be long-term oriented. The combination of that orientation and their ability to invest in numbers that rival many small institutions makes these clubs an attractive target.

They also represent an underserved market. As with individual investors and brokers, the common wisdom regarding the importance of institutions often leads companies to bypass investment clubs as a marketing target.

Investment clubs can be targeted through advertisements in NAIC publications or mailing list/marketing programs offered by NAIC.

INDIVIDUALS

At the bottom of the food chain for most companies, and hence an underserved market, is the individual investor. Individual investors historically were the kings and queens of Wall Street, holding the vast majority of American corporate shares. But the growth of institutions has finally shoved individual holdings below the 50-percent level.

Still, interest in individuals is cyclical. Every few years, investor relations experts will rediscover the retail investor and proclaim the common man to be the future focus of IR practice. Hyperbole reigns. The retail investor is dead. Long live the retail investor.

Reached largely through the news media and brokers, individual investors tend to buy small quantities of shares while requiring large servicing costs for mailings and other efforts. But individuals tend to be less activist in nature than many institutions. They don't require much of management's direct time investment, tend not to trade shares as frequently as larger investors and provide excellent word-of-mouth recommendations.

Individual investors also offer an opportunity for cross-marketing programs, especially for companies that sell consumer products. Many companies offer special benefits to shareholders who buy their products or use their services. Similarly, satisfied customers can become long-term shareholders as well. Some companies will add to their product packaging the information that their shares are publicly traded.

Even without the promise of special discounts, many firms will offer catalogs and other marketing materials to readers of financial documents. The incremental cost of this marketing support is extremely low and the potential payoff can be significant in terms of long-term relationships with shareholder/customers.

Individual investors can be targeted through lists provided by the National Association of Investment Clubs, the American Association of Individual Investors and publications that reach individuals as their primary market.

LEAD-STEER MARKETING

Clearly, a quick reading of this chapter suggests that the number of potential investment contacts is, for all practical purposes, unlimited. To make the marketing effort as cost-effective as possible, IR professionals should adopt a *lead-steer marketing* approach.

In classic marketing, this approach requires the initial targeting of opinion leaders or early adopters, people who are most likely to make a commitment of some sort and, even better, most likely to influence others to make the same commitment.

Analysts and brokers are lead steers, of course, as are certain newsletter writers who have a wide following or are quoted in the general financial media.

Within these classes of investment advisers, certain individuals have a tendency to jump in and bring others along. Their purchases have a multiplier effect as they let others in on their new find. Frequently, the lead steer is a single broker who can recruit others to favored stocks. This broker might be more experienced than peers or simply have a hot hand in stock picking over the past few months.

Lead steers will sometimes announce themselves by offering to bring the issuing company in contact with major buyers. In such a situation, the lead steer wants to flaunt access to investors in order to impress the company and access to corporate management so as to impress customers.

In many cases, the lead steers won't give themselves away, but a careful review of buying patterns can identify them for the sharp IR executive. *An example: We began getting a flurry of calls for information from the East Coast a couple of days after conducting client analyst meetings in New York and Texas. Follow-up calls to these new investors told us they had been alerted to the company's prospects by a lead-steer type in Texas who also had purchased shares.*

The lead steer deserves special attention beyond his own holdings or position because he represents a network that responds to particular views on the company's stock. That special consideration can include invitations to one-on-one sessions with management, participation in conference calls and other hand-holding.

19

MEDIA RELATIONS

The most potent and most elusive of the third-party endorsements in this business is an unabashedly favorable article in a top financial publication. Advertisements and corporate fact books are written by the company. Analysts and other investment opinion leaders often own the stock of the company they are writing about, so they have a vested interest in the stock's appreciation.

However, two essential factors make the published article special. First, the press is perceived as having nothing to gain—no ownership role or consulting arrangements—from a positive article. Second, the press is generally believed to be antibusiness, and this includes many writers for major business publications, so any wholehearted endorsement is seen as an anomaly.

(Antibusiness means just that. Even at some of the nation's top financial publications, some writers simply don't believe business serves a useful societal function. Many writers object to specific practices of businesses or industries, making them critical but not antibusiness. Others see business as an evil institution that abuses workers and destroys the ozone layer in the interest of enriching the few and enslaving the many. This is antibusiness, and it shows up in their writing.)

257

Media relations efforts are a special challenge for the investor relations executive for some of these reasons:

1. The rules of public ownership require disclosure of specific information in regulated formats at times that are beyond the control of the company.

2. Rumors that would never reach the media or receive coverage if they involved a company's products are broadcast by individuals or groups (such as short-sellers) who stand to gain from a falling stock price. These rumors are picked up and redistributed by members of the financial media who report that the market is responding to the rumor—and then encourage further credence by rebroadcasting it.

3. Despite the fact that they are backed up by giant printing presses or broadcast towers, reporters often believe they are the overwhelmed line of defense against a corporate juggernaut. In short, the power is with the corporation and not with them. This tends to create a desire to counterbalance corporate views with opposition opinion.

4. The entire post-Watergate mentality of the media and the country is that any institution is, by its nature, wrong and that any nonprofit group, civic watchdog or self-proclaimed reformer is right.

This assessment is somewhat harsh, but it is necessary for readers to understand the field on which the game is played. The corporation is surrounded by people who will view positive news as puffery and negative news as truth, who will view favorable opinions as self-serving and negative views as independent analysis. The goal of the investor relations professional is to maneuver to a draw, over time, with occasional victories along the way.

That means half the challenge of media relations is risk avoidance. An analyst invited to visit a company to research it might decide not to write up the firm, but is very unlikely to write a sell recommendation as a first offering. A reporter who interviews management and comes up with a negative opinion will, most likely, generate a critical article. Not liking a company is a reason for an analyst to lose interest. But a reporter who is unfavorably impressed will believe it is his job to call it as he sees it—in print.

Enough about the negatives. Suffice it to say that the challenges of media relations are greater and the target universe substantially smaller than for investor contact. While the rewards are potentially worth the risk, careful planning and implementation are necessary.

Any effective media relations program has four primary goals.

1. To build a credible, long-term relationship with the reporters who are most likely to influence views on the company.

2. To maximize the amount of favorable profile coverage of the company.

3. To maximize the number of times the company is cited favorably in industry roundup articles.

4. To minimize the damage from negative developments or rumors.

The first item is the most critical for media relations, just as it is for investor contact, because it makes the other points achievable over time. As previously noted, the IR executive is the company's chief credibility officer and as such must ensure that dealings with reporters are forthright and kept in perspective. (See 19-1, *Building Credibility*.)

That means self-defeating efforts must be avoided. The IR exec doesn't work for the media and must often keep certain information confidential, even when it would make a good story better or a bad story less damaging. At the same time, the IR exec must readily admit to problems—considered "challenges" or "opportunities" by some—in the context of describing potential solutions.

19-1   Building Credibility

Credibility is based on consistency, access and honesty. It is the essential ingredient in any long-term business association, and a company's relationship with the press is no different. IR executives interested in building trust should do as follows:

1. **Avoid Lying.** This is so basic, it's often missed. The IR executive doesn't have to discuss everything, but whatever is said must be the truth. It's far better to say nothing than to mislead.

2. **Respond Quickly.** Be sensitive to the reporter's needs and deadlines, and respond quickly to requests. If answers won't be available in time for the reporter's deadline, call to let the person know. Reporters have less faith in people, however honest, who leave them hanging.

3. **Stop Selling.** If every conversation with a reporter relates to a story pitch, no relationship of trust will develop. Credibility comes, in part, from learning what makes the IR executive tick, and that insight doesn't come in repeated sales calls.

4. **Keep Quiet.** It's a small world, and people never know the identity of the person at the next table, on the bus, or behind them in the checkout line. Telling tales, voicing negative views regarding specific reporters and otherwise talking too much can lead to damaged relationships, often without the IR executive being aware that a rift was created.

Credibility is built with a long-term focus, as is all of investor relations marketing. Common sense applies absolutely in this all-too-human sector of personal communication.

KNOWING THE AUDIENCES

As with investors, media are divided into several categories.

Disclosure media, including the financial news wires, are those outlets that must receive news announcements in order for the company to achieve prompt, broad dissemination of material information throughout the investment community. These wire services, which include Reuters, Dow Jones, Bloomberg, Standard & Poor's and others, are primarily spot-news oriented, although they are willing to interview management on financial issues and corporate outlook stories in addition to carrying financial results.

National news media encompass both the general news wire services, which include the Associated Press and such syndicate services as those maintained by Knight-Ridder, the *Chicago Tribune, Los Angeles Times* and so on, and publications of national significance like *The Wall Street Journal, Investor's Business Daily, The New York Times, Business Week, USA Today,* network news outlets and others. While these are sometimes targets for spot news announcements, they generally respond to spot news only from local or very large companies, or to developments of national importance.

National feature media include all of the national news media listed above, along with such national business and general interest publications as *Forbes, Fortune, Time, Newsweek, Inc. Magazine, 20/20, 60 Minutes, Nightly Business Report,* and others. These outlets should seldom receive news releases, unless truly unusual information of major interest is involved. Feature outlets are just that: targets for profile and other feature placement only.

Local presence media include the newspapers and radio stations in cities where the company is headquartered or has major facilities. Local presence media can also include locations where the company has a major supplier or customer. For example, news about plans for aircraft purchases by a major airline might be of substantial interest in cities where aircraft are built. Local presence cities are primary targets for ongoing media effort because the company has a clear local impact and the audience will be interested in the stories.

Industry/trade press outlets are generally read by beat reporters at major publications, so favorable coverage in these outlets can lead to stories in more general media. Such outlets usually have a positive focus on the industry being covered. Puff pieces might be no more common here, but hatchet jobs are definitely less likely. In addition, many industry-focused publications have added financial sections in recent years, creating one more avenue for telling the financial story.

Functional professional press, almost exclusively composed of periodicals rather than broadcast outlets, includes such vehicles as the *Harvard Business Review, Management Review, Chief Executive, Journal of Business Strategy, CFO* and a host of others. These outlets give management the opportunity to showcase expertise in a given area, which can bolster a company's claim that its team is well equipped to counteract problems within a certain part of the business.

Investment newsletters, which could also be classified as analyst publications, include a broad range of publications focusing on specific industries, investment styles or other specializations. Investment newsletters generally are boosters of the stocks they cover, although some are directed toward short-sellers.

Each type of media offers a different mix of coverage opportunities, reprint potential, endorsement value, timing, space availability and other variables. Each specific publication and reporter also offers a different combination of risk/reward ratio, depth of knowledge, initial distribution impact, etc.

DEVELOPING THE PLAN

Whether the investor relations executive is going to handle financial media personally or hand off all press contact to another department, a thorough understanding of the process is critical. If the best IR placement today is an opinion piece in a trade publication, it's up to the IR executive to recognize that need and either place the story or motivate the media department to do so.

Without a doubt, the most appropriate comparison for media relations programming is with an iceberg. At least nine-tenths of an effective media program is hidden. The interview and the published article are available for all to see, but the strategy development, preparation, coordination and reassessment are, by their nature, done behind the scenes.

The first issues to be covered are whether the firm wants coverage and what type is desired. Every company has a media relations profile, just as each has an investor image. The question is whether such images are determined by plan or by default.

Assuming the media relations effort is going to move by plan, the first step is to develop that plan. And while it might seem contradictory to ask whether coverage is desirable at all, companies can have many reasons for seeking to avoid coverage at any given time.

1. A company that has been favorably profiled several times in a short period might wish to avoid overkill. Being profiled everywhere means there will be no one left to profile the firm again next year. Worse, the next reporter to come along might decide to take the contrarian view, building a case that negates all the stories written by the reporter's competitors.

2. Conflicts among constituent groups might make the timing of a story problematic. An article on earnings growth and the company's status as the industry's low-cost producer might not be the best idea when union negotiations are underway. Articles published when sensitive regulatory issues are being resolved are more likely to lead to a stiffening of resistance among regulators than any concession from regulators in response to media pressure. *One client served many competitors in the same industry, and each competitor was paranoid about information slipping into enemy hands. For this company, the risk of media spotlights turned out to outweigh potential rewards.*

3. Recent problems are too fresh to be relegated to the end of the story, so even the favorable articles will begin, "Financially troubled just a year ago, ABCD Company is trying to brighten its outlook with a series of new products announced Tuesday. . . ." Sometimes it's better to wait until all of that "financially troubled" commentary moves down to paragraph 20.

263

4. The story isn't finished yet. Sometimes the corporate plan is in flux, so an article on today's company will be obsolete in a few months. Three months from now, the reporter might not be interested in a follow-up feature, so it's best to wait until the changes are in place.

Each of these negatives can be overcome in most instances, either by targeting less risky outlets or by seeking to place articles that focus on issues other than the most troublesome ones. Note here that avoiding a sensitive subject is not the same as refusing to discuss problems. Just as each reporter can decide whether to write a story or not, each company can decide which aspects of its business to promote.

Certainly, investor media relations should seek to achieve the goals of the overall investor relations effort. Those can include articles that lead to investment and a higher price, articles that display management's expertise so as to reduce the perceived risk among existing and potential investors, and articles that strengthen relationships with customers or vendors, or highlight existing strengths, so that investors will see the firm as a solid competitor.

Goals can also be defensive. A company that has been undervalued due to misimpressions in the marketplace can seek coverage that sets the record straight, or the IR executive can arrange background sessions with reporters and editors to provide the facts in advance of any future stories. A background session that never leads to its own story, but prevents the misimpression from being repeated, can be a very valuable, and very hidden, component of media relations.

PUBLICIZING THE STRATEGY INTERNALLY

Whatever the strategy and goals selected, don't keep them a secret. The media relations strategy must be implemented by a large number of people, including those who will be called on to comment and those who, it is hoped, will refrain from making the wrong comments.

The strategy must be imbued in the hearts and minds of all who will be called upon to implement it, beginning with the CEO.

Most chief executive officers don't understand media relations, and that includes those who do a good job in interviews. The IR executive must review, repeatedly, the goals of the media effort, how they fit into the overall IR effort, the timetable for achievement, the types of stories envisioned and how they fit the timetable, interim benchmarks, budgets, potential rewards and other participants.

Explaining the need for other participants is important. Consider a company whose founder is chairman and suffers in valuation because no one knows who will manage the company, or how well they'll manage it, if the chairman dies or retires. Media placements that include interviews with subsidiary presidents, the CFO and other managers can demonstrate depth of management talent and allay those fears. But the effort will be in jeopardy if the CEO isn't clued in early.

Two Warnings: Let the CEO know there will be mistakes in the story, any story, and that outside experts or critics are likely to be quoted. Emphasize also that no single article will determine the success of the media effort, just as no single product determines the fate of the company. When an article appears, and it includes criticism from a competitor or an error about last year's results or some other glitch, many chief executives are surprised—and angered. A little bit of preparation can limit this negative reaction.

CHOOSING THE STORIES AND STORYTELLERS

Once the strategy is explained, agreed to, and re-explained, the IR executive begins to focus on the specific story angles that will be presented to specific targets. Story ideas and targets can be spaced out across a grid of sorts, with stories matched to specific outlets.

In each case, the IR executive must identify the reason that a particular story will appeal to a specific reporter at a predetermined publication. Why this story? Why now? Why this set of readers or listeners or viewers?

Using a multiple story/multiple outlet approach enables the IR executive to place several articles at the same time, without having the same story appear simultaneously in two competing publications. Such a result can damage relationships with the affected reporters. While an IR executive shouldn't be directing the same story idea to all targeted writers at the same time, different story ideas can be presented simultaneously. This approach helps limit the ideas that get rejected.

If the same story is sent to five financial publications at the same time, and rejected by all five, the next idea submitted to these publications starts at a disadvantage: "Here's another wild idea from those guys we turned down last month." But if the story idea is rejected by one publication and then another, it gives the IR exec a chance to rethink the proposal before submitting it to publications three through five.

It isn't enough, of course, to target a publication. Reporters, too, must be identified and targeted. Although a company sometimes must deal with a specific beat reporter at an individual publication, most feature placements offer the company some latitude regarding the reporter approached.

Sometimes a general assignment reporter or a free-lance writer is the right avenue of access to a publication. In all cases, avoid proposing stories to killers.

A killer is a reporter who is often antibusiness and who seems almost invariably to write hatchet jobs. One might get assigned to write on your company, and you might end up dealing with one if it's the only option available, but there is no reason to be so foolish as to invite one into your office.

Avoiding killers is easy, at least in the story proposal stage. Every reporter creates his or her own record in the stories written. All that is necessary is that the IR exec read those stories before proposing another.

Note: There's a big difference between a hatchet job and fair comment. A reporter might write a negative story based on negative developments or include quotes critical of management in the story. That is fair comment. If the reporter tends to sprinkle stories with references to a chairman's toupee, his second wife, or his third cousin's drunk driving arrest, it's a hatchet job.

PREPARATION IS EVERYTHING

Having decided to contact a specific reporter, the IR executive preps like crazy. Before picking up the phone or writing a brief letter, the IR executive reviews all of the pertinent details that could be asked about in the initial phone conversation. The reporter will be more amenable to future contacts, and rely on the IR executive as a source more often, if the executive proves knowledge of the story immediately.

Just as important as knowing the story is knowing the reporter's needs. The strengths of a story can be far different from the strengths of the company and the reporter is interested in the story. Matching the story to the reporter, and more importantly to the reporter's audience, is the critical connection that is missing from many proposals.

Effective, long-term media relations are built on mutual trust and credibility, which result from personal contact. Although letters and phone calls are helpful at times, there is no substitute for reviewing story ideas in person. Even if it's a five-minute discussion in the newspaper lobby, face time is essential in this effort. That's because the first thing the IR executive must sell to the reporter is the IR executive herself. A voice on the phone is one thing for story placements, but not much help when a crisis develops. Getting to know the reporter face to face, in a well-timed effort, can pay off dramatically when a crisis occurs.

Once an idea is accepted by the writer, follow-up is essential. A letter confirming the interview should restate the ideas originally presented. A follow-up call the day before the interview should enable the IR executive to spot any last minute needs or problems.

This follow-up is also important in the IR executive's efforts to prep the CEO and others who will be interviewed, including analysts or competitors who might be used as external sources by the reporter. Insights into the areas to be covered, the likely length of the article or reasons for it, can be very helpful in enabling outside sources to address the issues effectively and credibly.

The chief executive, or whoever is to be interviewed, should be prepared regarding the original proposal, the areas of interest cited by the reporter, the materials sent to the reporter, and the reporter's level of depth and preparation. *My Most Embarrassing Moment, Part 257: I set up an interview with a national newspaper reporter, sent him five tons of materials and called him three times, including the day before the meeting. I reviewed the materials and the story idea with the chief executive. When we sat down for the interview, the first question the reporter asked was, "What was it you do again?"*

The IR executive should invariably sit in on the interview, not as a participant but as an observer who can spot areas of miscommunication, track topics covered and missed, and note further information that should be forwarded to the reporter. The IR exec can discern when the CEO begins to seem evasive, possibly due to material, unannounced information, and can spot friction that results from bad chemistry rather than poor questions or answers. *(Some reporters balk at the presence of a third party, but I have never seen anyone object who wasn't also a likely hatchet-murderer.)* The IR executive's presence can avoid problems later, including errors that are embarrassing to the reporter. Once reporters get to know the IR executive's professionalism and benefit from error-avoidance, their concerns subside. (See 19-2, *Rules of Engagement.*)

Prepping is just as important after the interview. Reviewing points with the CEO and the reporter can identify unexpected turns in the article, gaps in discussion, further research or sources required, and so on.

19-2   Rules of Engagement

Preparation should include some of the standard practices of the news media and effective management of interview discussions. Even if a chief executive or other source has conducted interviews before, there's no harm in providing the extra assurance of reviewing some of these points.

1. Everything said should be considered on the record. Many reporters don't accept off-the-record comments and others will insist on not-for-attribution quotes. Executives being interviewed should play it safe by avoiding any comments they aren't ready to see in print.

2. Never guess at answers. Either the person being interviewed or the IR executive should offer to call back with the facts later.

3. No law says every question must be answered. If a particular subject is off-limits, the CEO should just say so, and then avoid getting caught in a game of 20 questions.

4. The CEO should try to be responsive to a reporter's need for information, and at the same time ensure that the story is getting across. If questions seem to be going in a dead-end direction, take the lead and bring the subject back to more substantive matters. Done properly, the reporter will appreciate this redirection. Handled improperly, of course, the CEO can come across as evasive. The best approach is for the CEO to simply state that while he or she would be happy to cover those questions in more detail, the issues being covered are relatively less significant to the company in comparison to X, Y and Z. Almost invariably, the reporter will move to X, Y and Z.

5. An interview is not a race, so the CEO should take some time in answering questions, avoid jargon, provide the appropriate background on industry trends, and otherwise give the reporter essential perspective. Many reporters cover large groups of industries and cannot become expert on each one, so they can benefit from these insights.

6. An article is part of the public record, just as much as a 10-K. In fact, with the ready availability of databases that track published articles, this part of the record is more easily obtained than many financial reports. That means the executives being interviewed must choose their words carefully and avoid explanations that might, in the light of subsequent developments, seem to be false.

ASSURING READERSHIP

Once an article appears, its value has just begun to be realized. Because even the most widely read publication will be seen by just a handful of a company's investors and potential investors, reprints are an essential part of any IR marketing arsenal.

Favorable articles should be included in kits, mailed to the regular list of investors, faxed if urgent, included in prospect mailings and, in many cases, mailed directly to shareholders. It's important for a company's followers to see how independent parties view the firm.

This is where prepping the CEO on the likelihood of errors or outside commentary pays off. Too frequently, a CEO who is surprised by any negative commentary will refuse to allow distribution of a generally favorable reprint. That loss of ammunition can be limiting to any cost-effective IR plan, especially when the article in question was one of several pieces that, in total, provide the full story of the company.

Getting that full story to the investors being targeted through initial readership, prospect mailings, supporter mailings or meeting/background kits is essential to program effectiveness. That makes proper CEO preparation and explanation of the media relations component absolutely indispensable for any IR executive.

20

IMPLEMENTING
THE PROGRAM

Program implementation is the unfinished symphony of investor relations. Clearly, there is a beginning, but there is no true conclusion to the effort. In part, that's what makes the investor relations challenge so enjoyable. The IR executive's task is never mastered, never simple, and never the same as before.

On the positive side of the challenge, the IR executive will find several hundred possible combinations of activities that will yield essentially similar success probabilities. Several thousand possibilities can be discarded immediately as inappropriate for a given company.

For example, a company with relatively low float might bypass marketing efforts to institutional investors or decide not to focus on investors outside the United States. A firm in the midst of litigation might opt to avoid the news media as a conduit for its investor messages.

Intuition is helpful in program implementation. At the beginning of each program, or when the program is reviewed prior to development of a new plan, it is impossible to predict which approaches absolutely will or will not work. A company with low float might find some favorable institutional interest, for example, or a company in a tough legal battle might, in fact, find a sympathetic writer.

But program implementation focuses on the optimum results based on time and dollars invested, so it is important to work with the percentages, rather than against them. If a company looks like a retail investment and walks like a retail investment and . . . well, you get the idea.

Implementation, which includes ongoing management of the program, is more a thought process than a series of actions. More akin to blazing a trail than reading a road map, the implementation effort should reflect the feel of the terrain, small changes that indicate likely problems and other midcourse obstacles.

STARTING FROM THIN AIR

Solid implementation always begins with reality, with the company as it exists today. As with any other form of marketing, there is no substitute for knowing the product.

The product defines the marketing opportunities, the possible buyers and the possible avenues of distribution. The product determines the messages that can and cannot be defended, and it provides the danger signals for fatal errors. The product also provides the first set of limits regarding the thousands of activity combinations that can become an IR program.

For the purposes of IR marketing, the product is defined as *investment appeal*—an intangible product, to say the least. Investment appeal has different meanings to different audiences, and is always measured on a relative basis, in comparison with other intangible products. The product marketed through the investor relations effort cannot be purchased, either. Securities are purchased and, in the case of stocks, represent an ownership interest in the company. But stock purchase is, of itself, only one of several goals for the investor relations effort.

At some point, this focus on the intangibles reaches a dead end. In translating investment appeals into stock purchases, the IR executive must move from the intangibles and concepts to the hard sciences of financial analysis and investment valuation.

20-1　The Moving Target

INVESTOR TARGETING

Still, the intangibles must always be the starting point for an IR program for a very basic reason. Once a plan is created, people responsible for implementing the program begin to focus on prescribed activities as the goal of the effort. After a series of meetings is scheduled, conducting the meetings becomes an end in itself. Once media targets are identified, the mission of obtaining coverage becomes sacred.

In other words, the trailblazing venture becomes an exercise in map-reading. It's a very human failing, and very common, but it also can destroy program effectiveness. No matter how vague the investment appeals concept may be, this vision of the IR effort must be reconsidered each time a specific action is undertaken. Does the action still make sense? Do the parameters still fit the company and market environment? Do the past month's activities or external influences change the product or alter the list of appropriate actions?

The IR executive must serve in the idealized vision of a chief executive: always focused on the long-term goals of the effort even as those goals are changing and near-term influences change the course settings. At any point, it might be necessary to change the specific plan in order to protect gains achieved, and the IR executive's focus on the intangibles—and on the feel of the situation—will be the key to success.

THE OTHER PRODUCTS

In moving from the conceptual to the concrete, the IR focus shifts to the product proxies, the tangible and measurable factors that make the company a good investment. Primary among these, of course, are the company itself, its commercial marketplace and its structure as a security.

The company is the source of long-term investment appeals, while the industry environment and the investment marketplace tend to provide more of the short-term appeals. This is intuitively obvious, based on the likelihood that physical facilities, management teams, corporate cultures, product lines and other company-specific factors have a longer life than most market cycles or industry sales trends.

The search for investment appeals begins with the company. Analysis of the company focuses on strengths or opportunities that will be valued, once known, by investors. These strengths can include operating efficiency, the management team's long-term working relationship, low debt levels, high cash flow, close customer ties, and so on.

The company's financial needs must also be reviewed. Will public markets be accessed in the foreseeable future? Will bonds be due or warrants repurchased? Will the company need to issue new shares for expansion or repurchase shares held by a joint-venture partner? Financing needs of the company are always on the horizon for investor relations marketing programs.

Next, the industry environment is covered. Still focused on the bedrock issues of competitive businesses, the IR executive looks for strengths that will be valued by investors. Strengths that investors won't care about, of course, are nice to know, but irrelevant from an IR marketing perspective.

Finally, the IR executive places the company's investment appeals into the competitive cauldron of all other potential investments. Here, the marketing effort begins to focus more precisely on audiences—and avenues for reaching them.

DEVELOPING THE PLAN

By the time this process is completed, the IR executive should have two or three marketing plans. With all of the possible approaches to IR marketing, it is difficult to imagine a company that cannot be presented to investors in several ways. A company that distributes computers, for example, can be positioned as a technology play or a distribution story, with a different mix of primary appeals for each type of investor.

In consumer markets, an example of this approach might include products marketed through mass media to a general audience and using a different message through neighborhood ethnic festivals or billboards. Similarly, a company might use different advertisements in a magazine directed at women than in one directed toward retirees.

The IR executive might decide to create different materials and marketing efforts for each audience, defining and describing the investment appeals differently and splitting the program into multiple channels. The IR executive might try to combine the investment appeals into a single unit and market this core message to different types of constituencies. Or the IR executive might choose to implement multiple marketing efforts sequentially, moving to one type of investor in year one and a second type in year two.

The ultimate decision rests on several factors.

1. **Budget.** With only so much time and money to invest, can the IR program support multiple marketing strategies?

2. **Audience.** Can the audiences be defined clearly enough, and are they both large and receptive enough, to justify separate marketing messages and approaches?

3. **Consistency.** Can the different marketing messages be delivered without seeming to contradict one another?

4. **Benefit.** Does the multiple marketing approach offer a true incremental benefit in terms of stock price appreciation and investor loyalty when compared with a single approach that encompasses all primary markets?

The internal analysis and marketing plan or plans are only half formed at this point. Early in the implementation stage, the thought process is one of elimination and refinement rather than accretion. Possible investment appeals are reduced to a handful of core messages that must be tested in light of existing market perceptions. Those perceptions cycle back to the appeals list, leading to changes in the mix and emphasis of key points.

Ultimately, the list of possible investment appeals is refined to include those that have the greatest impact on the targeted audience—and the target audience is defined as that group most likely to respond favorably and consistently to the company's investment appeals. The circle becomes smaller as the process continues, leading to a manageable set of core messages and a measurable, identifiable group of core investor targets.

Carried to its extreme, the IR executive would bring a single core message to a single investor who would pay an infinite amount for that investment appeal. This limit is never reached, of course, but the process of elimination leads toward that unattainable point. Along the way, the list of goals, messages and audiences becomes manageable enough to fit within the constraints of a budget.

TOOLS OF THE TRADE

As that process continues, options are considered and focus is narrowed with regard to the tools that will be brought to bear in the effort. These tools range from changing the corporate structure to listing on an exchange to preparing a videotape of complex operations.

Changes in the corporate structure or the structure/trading environment of securities tend to be one-time investments in the IR program and, as such, are seldom a prerequisite for IR marketing efforts. Very rarely, a company will be required to make a fundamental change (redeem warrants, implement a reverse split or pay deferred dividends) before launching an effective program. In most cases, the structural changes can be anticipated and need not be completed before the marketing begins.

Selection of marketing tools must flow from the selection of messages and audiences. Certain messages are communicated better in face-to-face meetings and others via videotape. Some audiences respond more directly to company documents and others to favorable news articles. The tools used must fit the audience and the message, and even the most standard marketing tools can be customized for a better fit.

Consider the annual report, in all its manifestations. The summary annual can be used to deliver a clearer marketing message to retail investors, while backup reports and other documents are utilized to fill the due diligence needs of major institutions and analysts. The 10-K wraparound can be used for firms that have limited financial history. The full-blown marketing annual can be used in a variety of approaches to reach a broad array of investors and other constituents. Annual reports on audiotape, videotape, compact disc or computer disk can demonstrate technical expertise of the company or display investment appeals that don't come across quite so well on the printed page.

Likewise, meeting formats can and should be adjusted to accommodate different types of programs. While complex technologies lend themselves well to headquarters visits or small group meetings, simpler, broad-based investment appeals can be

20-2 Who Does What

Early in the process, responsibilities must be divided among the people who will work the IR plan. The general rule is to limit CEO involvement to critical areas such as closing sales, making public appearances, clearing releases and shareholder reports, or conducting press interviews. The IR executive and CFO usually divide up the rest of the responsibilities.

Each company has its own staffing and management relationships. Some firms use agencies and others staff internally. Many companies assign IR efforts to the corporate communications director. While no rules are inviolate, the following guidelines should apply in most instances.

Chief Executive	Primary company spokesman, lead speaker at analyst meetings, annual meeting, press interviews; consulted on shareholder reports, planning and budgeting, policy issues.
Chief Financial Officer	Primary investor relations responsibility. Participates in analyst presentations with CEO and responds to inquiries from company's major followers, some media calls; primary responsibility for shareholder reports, planning and budgeting, policy issues.
Investor Relations	Primary responsibility for developing and implementing IR marketing plan, requesting and allocating budget, arranging and prioritizing program content. Handles day-to-day contact with investors and media, coordinates CEO and CFO time in IR effort, oversees mailing and fax lists, other essential activities.

Whatever the mix of duties, it is important to divide responsibilities early and review them annually, to avoid excessive overlaps or gaps in the program.

communicated quite effectively in a large-meeting format. Telephone conference calls are valuable when quarterly results are announced, but videoconferencing might be more appropriate for firms that need pictures to tell the story. (See 20-2, *Who Does What.*)

Just as the tools selected should reflect the needs of the investment story and the audiences selected, the tools themselves begin to limit the messages and audiences. A company that brings analysts to its facilities for a review of technology limits its audience to those who are willing to invest the time in such an excursion. A firm that puts all its messages on paper limits its impact to those investors who can glean the appeals from words alone.

THE INCESTUOUS TRAP

Continual refinement and limitation of the messages and audiences gives the IR executive a chance to focus more time and effort on the high priority, high potential opportunities. But it also creates an incestuous trap.

As the messages and audience—especially the audience—are limited, the size of the investor pool declines as well. A company can present the same story to the same target group over a period of months or years, refining and narrowing the scope of its key messages and audiences until gridlock is reached. Essentially all primary supporters know all the details and essentially none of the story is known by people who aren't already in the loop. Eventually, the company is preaching to the choir and the response reflects that meeting of minds.

In one extreme case, a client company refused to allow conference call participation to investors holding under 100,000 shares of stock. This seemed cost-effective in the near term because it limited the scope and cost of such calls, but it also limited our ability to attract new interest. Purchasing 100,000 shares of stock is, after all, a high price of admission to a conference call.

The IR executive who keeps the intangibles in mind and focuses on the long term is more likely to avoid this kind of trap. As the circle of supporters becomes more secure, the IR program must shift to include additional targets. These could be individuals who were added to the mailing list early, but didn't ask for invitations to meetings, or they could be investors considered as a third priority in the overall program mix.

279

TIMING, TIMING, TIMING

The element of time plays a major role in IR programming. Because the implementation extends over a period of months or years, the IR executive will have the luxury of weaving components of the program into a complete package. It isn't necessary to apply all tools immediately or even in the first few months. In fact, the best strategy might be to layer efforts on top of one another to build momentum, or to begin with a full-scale push that is succeeded by consolidation and follow-up.

A company with ample float, a strong track record and limited following outside its local market might begin with a broad-based series of meetings in new cities, duplicating the recognition and support already obtained at home. But a firm in the midst of a turnaround might build more slowly, with small meetings and conference calls, increasing credibility until a full road-show effort can provide the intended payoff.

Because the implementation effort reflects a continual process of inclusion and exclusion, the scope of messages, tools and audiences is never static. New investors are courted and the field is narrowed until solid supporters are brought into the fold. As the refinement reaches its midpoint, the search for new blood begins again, so completion of one recruitment exercise overlaps the beginning of another.

Consider, for example, a company that seeks to appeal to more individual investors. In beginning its efforts, the company cultivates interest from two financial reporters, leading to two favorable articles on the company. These reprinted articles are mailed with a company fact sheet and a reply card to 2,000 investment clubs.

Clubs that respond receive added materials and a follow-up mailing to identify those that have bought the stock. The clubs are put on a special mailing list to receive materials produced by the company for individual investors.

While the mailing is being sent to identify the clubs that bought shares, the company begins contacting its individual shareholders with a reply card to get the names of their brokers. These brokers then are contacted for participation in a conference call and are added to a list of receivers of the company's videotape, annual report and a fact book directed toward investment professionals.

As the investment club targeting effort is completed and moves into the maintenance phase, the broker contact effort is accelerating. The company continues the broker effort and simultaneously begins to prospect among newsletter editors whose audiences are primarily individuals.

Meanwhile, the IR executive is reviewing the entire premise of this retail emphasis. Has market capitalization moved upward enough, due to all of the retail purchases, to begin attracting fund managers? Have the individual investors soaked up enough of the float to justify the investment in courting them? Are the brokers identified through the survey now marketing the shares to other individuals or have they moved on to other investments?

Even if the retail emphasis has succeeded, the IR executive will want to examine whether it still represents the best investment. Has this focus reached the point of diminishing returns? Can the strongest return on IR investment now be found in a push for buy-side analyst support or independent money managers? Has the stock now moved enough to justify debt reduction via a new share offering that also generates investment banker research?

JUST SAY NO

Just as important as the choice of targets and activities is the decision on when to reduce efforts. IR marketing is a continuous process, but every building effort also must include some consolidation and review. Gains that are won must be reinforced and solidified, lest they slip away as the next target is sought.

Consider a firm that seeks to build support among sell-side analysts, leading to published research reports. The company invests heavily in a corporate fact book, meetings in cities where the targeted firms have strong broker networks, mailings to the

---

20-3 Capitalizing on Research

Just as a favorable news article offers substantial opportunity for subsequent distribution, research reports provide for multiple forms of marketing tactics.

1. Reprint and mailing of the report to brokers at the sponsoring firm.
2. Mailing of company fact sheet to brokers at sponsoring firm, with alert regarding recent research.
3. Mailing of research to publications that track and write up research reports.
4. Alerting of reporters who follow the company that new research recommendation is out.
5. Arrangement of meetings with brokers at analyst's firm.
6. Mention of research in annual/shareholder reports.
7. Arrangement of meetings with key institutional customers served by the analyst.
8. Use of research as lever to encourage coverage by other firms.

Written research reports are high-leverage endorsements, creating the opportunity to generate both further stock sales and added media and research coverage, if handled properly.

---

brokers of the targeted firms, and media relations efforts in the brokerage houses' key cities.

After several months, two research reports are generated. Now, what action is appropriate? For the insightful IR executive, the focus shifts from finding even more research writers to reinforcing the buying decision for the two analysts who have signed on with the company. That means arranging meetings with the analysts' institutional customers and participating in after-market meetings with brokers and clients at the sponsoring brokerage firms' key offices. It means working with the analysts to distribute research reports to the news media, leading to extra recognition for the analysts, and working with the analysts' trading departments for some transaction business. (See 20-3, *Capitalizing on Research*.)

In short, the IR executive will try to make sure the analyst's own fortunes rise as a result of the research coverage. That doesn't imply a specific tradeoff of services, but it does recognize the reality of the brokerage business.

Analysts are compensated in part for the commissions earned by their brokerage houses on stocks the analysts recommend. If the recommended stock produces limited commission business for the house, coverage is likely to wither over time. But if the coverage generates returns for the house, both the analyst and the issuing company benefit.

In the time following a new research write-up, the IR executive might pull back from new efforts so he can devote more time to consolidating the analyst's support. Once the reinforcement is provided, it will require less ongoing commitment of time to maintain the relationship. But the additional investment of time and dollars to support the new ally is one of the most profitable investments any IR executive can make.

UNLIMITED OPTIONS

Certainly, it is possible to imagine hundreds or thousands of ways to implement any program. Budget weightings and timing decisions are reasoned to a large extent, but also arbitrary. There is no special reason for making media relations 15 percent of a program budget instead of 10 or 20 percent, in most cases. The decision to target sell-side analysts might be objectively the same as a decision to focus on investment clubs. There is no single standard to indicate, in advance, the best approach to take.

Fortunately, such a standard isn't needed. Any good plan, conscientiously and consistently applied, will yield results over time. The search for the best plan is a waste of effort if it precludes the implementation process. With essentially no limit to the number of possible programs, the real indicator of success is the effectiveness of implementation efforts. Effective implementation of the third-best or tenth-best or hundredth-best plan is good enough to yield a strong result.

One of the most important balances that must be struck in any IR program is between planning and implementation. Excessive analysis leads to indecision and micromanagement. Inadequate planning leads to contradictory messages or unrelated program components.

Because so many factors are at work simultaneously, IR programming is extremely fault-tolerant. A single negative article doesn't kill a company's IR marketing plan any more than a single research report creates success. Some achievements or failings are more significant than others, of course, but there are few ways for any single error or obstacle to derail a program.

Still, a few general rules should be followed to make the IR effort even more resistant to external challenges.

1. **Don't Bet the Store.** Too narrow a focus on a single investment message or a single target audience can make the IR program vulnerable. *An example: One client, having received coverage from a few brokerage firms, was able to get a strong recommendation from one of the world's largest houses. Suddenly, no one else mattered but the single analyst who, in the client's view, put the company on the map. It was fun while it lasted, but when the analyst turned negative, there weren't many people waiting to take up the slack.*

2. **Let Time Work for You.** No law says every action requires a response, and the IR effort might be served best by relying on the greatest equalizer: time. Some obstacles cannot be overcome immediately, so the best strategy might be to allow them to recede into history. *An example: A client was beaten up in print by former directors who left in a dispute with the chairman. While good publicity is usually the best remedy for bad publicity, that general rule doesn't apply when the enemy is within. We counseled for a low profile until the pursuit of coverage could be done without the gratuitous swipes that had become the norm.*

3. **Expect the Unexpected.** The company that bills itself as the low-cost producer could suffer from a fire at the main plant. The firm that focuses its IR effort on a collegial corporate

284

20-4   Planning for a Crisis

Planning for crisis is essential in investor relations, as it is in public relations. A bear raid that cuts the stock price, a fire that threatens fourth-quarter production or illness of the chief executive can all lead to substantial negative results. The company can reduce liability exposure and mitigate negative effects through planning. Some things to consider:

1. **Lists.** Phone lists of key officers, attorneys, IR and public relations executives, and other internal team members are essential. Home phones, vacation-home phones and car phones should all be included.

2. **Spokesmanship Training.** In advance of any crisis, key members of management should receive training on dealing with crises as well as with the media, analysts, etc. Knowing the rules of engagement will make the executives more effective if called upon to represent the company.

3. **Information Flow.** In a crisis, information flow must be controlled, limited to facts, and released in a broad and fair manner. Guidelines must be established in advance regarding who will be allowed to speak for the firm and where calls should be directed.

4. **Making Friends.** If the company hasn't made any friends among its investment supporters and media followers before the crisis hits, it's too late. Proactive IR contact and credibility building efforts can create the good will that is essential when answers don't come as quickly as questions.

It's impossible to predict where the crisis will originate, or the direction it will take. All the IR executive can do is to prepare the players so that each is working from the same plan at the moment the disaster strikes.

culture could suddenly experience a series of sexual harassment suits. The IR executive who doesn't consider possible crises and responses is leaving the house unguarded. Crisis plans, like insurance, provide a return on investment whether utilized or not. (See 20-4, *Planning for a Crisis.*)

4. **Train the Team.** While the CEO and the CFO will be the front line in IR marketing, other key executives and directors

can add important insights—and warnings—if they know the plan. The IR program must be sold and resold internally, and not merely for budgeting approvals. Changes in market conditions or pending corporate governance decisions can spring up without warning, if the corporate leaders who see them first don't recognize their potential impact. The IR executive must encourage early warnings from multiple sources within the company and from such outside resources as investment bankers, agencies, lawyers and accountants.

MEASUREMENT AND REPORTING

Because the value of a publicly traded company is reassessed every day of the week, the effectiveness of any IR marketing effort can be measured in hard numbers. Selecting the numbers and divining their meaning can be a challenge, but the numbers are no less real for the effort.

Results, of course, complete the circle that begins with program goals. Goals lead to actions that should lead to measurable results that, in the best of cases, achieve the intended goals.

Because the terrain is always shifting, most statements of goals include enough qualifiers to permit an infinite number of supposedly successful outcomes. That failing is more a reflection of the market's complexity than a fault of the people setting the targets. A higher price/earnings ratio is a good goal, and if all other things remained equal, a specific number could be targeted easily.

But nothing stays equal. The p/e ratio moves with the company's own earnings momentum, with the company's earnings momentum as compared with industry and investment peers, with the quality of earnings perceived for the company and various peers, with market sentiment, broad-based market indices and the underlying economy. A two-point increase in price/earnings ratio can be a legitimate goal on Day 1 and either a major success or a major failure on Day 365.

To overcome the limitations of each goal, the IR executive should measure several components of performance. Although each of these components will suffer some limitations, the law of large numbers should begin to apply. A company that begins to see progress in most of its measured categories is, by inference, doing more right than wrong. It's more art than science, but the real world is sometimes very messy.

To simplify measurement, the IR executive should track interim achievements, measuring the effectiveness of each effort. Some of the interim measurements include:

1. **Shares Purchased Following Analyst Meetings.** Trading volume that spikes after an analyst meeting can lead to follow-up calls to attendees and identification of which people bought the stock. Further follow-up several weeks later might identify other purchasers.

2. **New Research Generated.** Both recommendations by buy-side analysts and written reports can be included in this calculation.

3. **Value/Number of Impressions from Published Articles.** The number of people who saw an article on the company, and the imputed advertising value of the space, are two measurements that indicate return on investment.

4. **Responses to Prospect Mailings.** Track both the number of qualified leads generated from a mailing and the number of those respondents who buy stock.

5. **Opinion Surveys.** Surveys can identify changes in perception among investors and potential investors, indicating how effectively core messages have been transmitted.

6. **Share Turnover.** The relative size of transactions or the average holding period of shares might change as a result of IR efforts. This indicator must always be considered in light of share price changes, of course. Accelerating share turnover can indicate either buying pressure or selling pressure, and only the share price tells which is the case.

7. **Market Makers.** For over-the-counter companies, the number of market makers might increase as broker interest and transaction volumes rise.

8. **Institutional/Retail Mix.** The number of institutional owners or the percentage of shares held by institutions will change as an IR marketing program brings in these key buyers. Of course, the underlying question is whether there is any cause-and-effect relationship between the IR program and institutional owners.

9. **Inquiries.** A growing profile leads to unsolicited calls, reflecting the successful communication of messages through the investment community.

10. **Followers.** Measured by fax lists or mailing lists, the number of people actively following a company will grow in response to an effective program. Of course, a mailing list purge will reduce the reported number of followers.

Each of these measurement opportunities gives the IR executive a chance to review program effectiveness in the near term. They also allow for comparison among program goals, activities and results. For each of these measurements, the underlying questions are two.

1. Is there a cause-and-effect relationship between actions taken and results measured?

2. Are these results consistent with the results that would occur in a program that achieves its stated goals?

The second question is the more telling. If the program goal, for example, is to generate added research coverage, does a larger mailing list indicate progress in achieving the goal? Does the institutional/retail mix have meaning relative to the goal of raising the price/earnings ratio relative to peers?

Goals and measurements must be chosen carefully. Although a group of measurements is needed to cover a broad range of IR marketing efforts, the choice of interim measurements must make sense in terms of ultimate targets.

Analysis of the measurements also requires great care. It is easy to overanalyze or stretch for conclusions based on near-term deviations. IR executives must always exercise restraint here, both to maintain their own credibility and to prevent others from reading too much into limited data.

Thus, it is not only the direction of the numbers that is important. It is the degree of change, consistency of change and predictability of result that provide true meaning. On some days and, indeed, in some months, the stock price moves simply because there are more buyers than sellers. Some prospect mailings are more effective than others because the post office delivers the materials in better condition—or worse—or because the mailing happened to show up on a record-volume day for the stock market.

The IR executive who seeks credit for every positive blip will be skewered for every decline as well. Perspective is critical, both for credibility and for career longevity.

A FINAL THOUGHT OR TWO

As this volume relates, investor relations continues to be more art than science. While rules of accounting and clear-cut cause-and-effect relationships form some of the basis for planning and action, the number of variables is far too large to allow for canned programs.

Even for basic IR marketing plans that emphasize the fundamentals, seemingly similar packaging can accommodate vast differences in execution. And it is the execution, not the sophistication of the plan, that is the deciding factor between success and failure.

Thus, it is the pursuit and process that excite the successful IR professional. Awards and p/e points are fleeting and the next day's market will invariably change the effectiveness of the program. The ability to incorporate the details into a master plan, to adjust the plan without overweighting the details, and to know when doing nothing is the best course of action are critical to effective practitioners.

Whenever I'm asked why I love investor relations, I answer that it's a discipline that cannot be mastered. An individual can become good at any or many functions and it is possible to become truly adept at most of the tasks required. But one never masters the art because the variables are far too numerous to permit such control.

This risk of failure is a constant companion. Each development provides new knowledge and highlights old errors. And each decision leaves several paths untrod. As a result, investor relations never grows old, never goes stale, and never becomes boring. Never mastered, the practice is always new, always a challenge.

INDEX